Applying Psychology
to Everyday Life

Applying Psychology to Everyday Life

A Beginner's Guide

Kenneth T. Strongman
University of Canterbury, Christchurch, New Zealand

John Wiley & Sons, Ltd

Other Wiley Editorial Offices

John Wiley & Sons Inc., 111 River Street, Hoboken, NJ 07030, USA

Jossey-Bass, 989 Market Street, San Francisco, CA 94103-1741, USA

Wiley-VCH Verlag GmbH, Boschstr. 12, D-69469 Weinheim, Germany

John Wiley & Sons Australia Ltd, 42 McDougall Street, Milton, Queensland 4064, Australia

John Wiley & Sons (Asia) Pte Ltd, 2 Clementi Loop #02-01, Jin Xing Distripark, Singapore 129809

John Wiley & Sons Canada Ltd, 22 Worcester Road, Etobicoke, Ontario, Canada M9W 1L1

Wiley also publishes its books in a variety of electronic formats. Some content that appears in print may not be
available in electronic books.

Library of Congress Cataloging-in-Publication Data

Strongman, K.T.
    Applying psychology to everyday life : a beginner's guide / K.T. Strongman.
        p.   cm.
    Includes index.
    ISBN-13: 978-0-470-86988-8
    ISBN-10: 0-470-86988-7
    1. Psychology, Applied.   I. Title.

BF636.S767 2006
158–dc22
                                                        2005026871

British Library Cataloguing in Publication Data

A catalogue record for this book is available from the British Library

ISBN-13 978-0-470-86988-8 (hbk) 978-0-470-86989-5 (pbk)
ISBN-10 0-470-86988-7 (hbk) 0-470-86989-5 (pbk)

Typeset in 10/13pt Scala and Scala Sans by SNP Best-set Typesetter Ltd., Hong Kong
Printed and bound in Great Britain by Antony Rowe Ltd, Chippenham, Wiltshire
This book is printed on acid-free paper responsibly manufactured from sustainable forestry
in which at least two trees are planted for each one used for paper production.

To Averil, again, and to Thomas, my grandson

Contents

About the author

Kenneth Strongman obtained his degrees at University College, London, and worked at the University of Exeter for several years. He has been Professor of Psychology at the University of Canterbury in New Zealand for 25 years. He is a Fellow of the Royal Society of New Zealand, Fellow of the British Psychological Society, and Fellow of the New Zealand Psychological Society. His current position is Pro-Vice-Chancellor (Arts) at the University of Canterbury. He is also Chair of the Humanities Council of New Zealand. He has published ten books.

Preface

I began by wanting to write a book entitled something like *Where Psychology Has Gone Wrong*. The reason for this desire came from thinking that psychology is a far more interesting and stimulating subject than it would appear to be from a glance at some academic texts and journal articles. Also, many students begin their psychological studies with enthusiasm and then rapidly have to come to terms with the subject not being quite as they thought that it might be. Somehow, it all seems rather remote from everyday issues and problems, in fact, not to put too fine a point on it, rather remote from people and what they do.

However, those close enough to me to receive my confidences about the proposed book gently suggested that it seemed a hint negative. So, instead I thought of writing something not only about where psychology had lost its way, but also about more positive and interesting directions it had taken and where it might go more positively in the future. This still seemed somewhat negative.

Finally, then, came the idea of picking the eyes out of psychology, of amassing in one place all of those aspects of psychology which *have* been developed in an interesting and practically useful way. When it came to looking for them, then there they were. There was also the further consideration of identifying the potential readership. This was an easier problem. The book is intended generally for any person who wishes to find out a little about psychology in a way that would be useful to them in their everyday world, be it at work or at home, when alone or in the company of others. The book is also intended specifically for any student who is required (or wishes) to study psychology for one year as part of some other training (teaching, medicine, paramedical services, police work, and so on). It will give them a reasonably thorough grounding in many (but not all) aspects of psychology, but will also ensure that this grounding occurs in the everyday world.

In the end, this is not a didactic book. It has a much more practical set of aims – to be useful and stimulating and, above all, to communicate and engage. Psychology can be both surprising and fascinating.

Returning to the point made at the start of this preface, I am now in a position of easily identifying those aspects of psychological research that (in my view) have been, let us say, less than riveting. They are simply all of those parts of psychology *not* included in *Applying Psychology to Everyday Life*, but the thought of writing a book about them is also less than riveting. This was the better way to do it.

CHAPTER ONE

Psychology in life

Some examples

Jeff is a man in his forties, happily married with a growing family. Currently, he is in the neurological ward in a hospital, recovering from the effects of a particularly traumatic car accident. Driving home in murky conditions, he was sideswiped at great speed by a young man who had been banned from driving. He had stolen a car and simply lost control on a bend travelling much too fast for the road conditions. Jeff suffered a broken leg, a broken arm, several broken ribs, a punctured lung and considerable brain damage.

All the breakages have recovered and the lung is mending well. Jeff has had brain surgery and again, from a surgical or medical viewpoint, his scars are healing well. However, some of the time he is unable to recognise his wife, his children, and other members of his family and his friends. He can remember how to clean his teeth and all of the events of the day, but he cannot remember much of his previous life. This is extremely upsetting both to him and to his family and friends. The specialists who are dealing with Jeff keep talking about the effects of brain damage and what functions might or might not recover in 'cases like yours' and the likelihood of one part of the brain taking over from another.

Mary is an air stewardess, working on a domestic route, having had considerable previous experience on international routes. She has just arrived at her flight for the morning. She had been called in suddenly, although not expecting to be rostered on, because three other people had telephoned to say that they were sick. She is feeling very under par. The previous weekend, her boyfriend of some three years said that he thought that they should have a time apart for two or three months because 'things didn't seem to be going very well'. And in the middle of the night, her period had started, waking her with a series of very painful cramps. She had been suffering from endometriosis for some time and it seemed to be getting worse.

Mary only knew the other two cabin crew vaguely and, anyway, is not the type of person who would seek sympathy from others. She feels grey, and slightly feverish. Her clothes feel simultaneously too tight and too loose and she feels that her make-up is a mess. She quickly checks herself in the mirror as the passengers start to board the plane. She doesn't like what she sees but cannot see anything precisely wrong with it. She walks out into the cabin. 'Miss, Miss . . .' The first request comes from a middle-aged man, slightly flustered at not being able to find the seat that he thinks is listed on his ticket. Mary turns on her usual beaming smile and leans over the man, reaching for his ticket. 'Can I help? What seat are you heading for?' Her voice is calm, quiet and reassuring.

Nathan was a farmer living in New England in the 1700s, shortly before the American Revolution. Chance led him into an affair with the wife of another farmer who lived a short distance away. He and she were obsessed with each other, so much so that the caution with which they had begun the affair gave way to the taking of increasing chances. The inevitable happened and they were caught.

The local people were outraged and subjected Nathan and his paramour to a tirade of public abuse. They were condemned and derided by everyone in a clamouring mass of arm-waving abuse. Eventually, stocks were constructed and they were each clamped into the stocks and left in the centre of the local village for three weeks, for all to see and for all to vilify verbally and through pelting them with rotten food, offal and dung. Each day, the local minister spent some time with them, asking them to abase themselves in the eyes of God and the people. They did so with increasing fervour until finally they were released. It was as though they had been branded with their shame for the remainder of their lives.

Charlie is an 18-year-old golfer who is showing enormous promise in his game. He has won a number of local championships and is on the verge of national selection. However, he has developed a problem that he cannot seem to deal with. His long game is fine but the nearer he gets to the green, the more he finds his game difficult to control. So his putting is suffering. On the green, he cannot seem to relax; his arms stiffen up, his body feels as though it is always slightly in the wrong position and he has begun to miss putts that a few months ago he was able to achieve easily.

Fortunately, Charlie's new coach has had a great deal of experience with this sort of thing, something that he describes to himself as 'freezing'. He always deals with it in the same way, although suiting exactly what he says and does to the person he is dealing with. He has given Charlie some training in relaxation and has been getting him to visualise being on the putting green and making various putts while he is in the relaxed state. The moment that Charlie says that he is feeling anxious, the coach stops him from thinking about the putting and gently gets him to relax again.

This process has worked well over some days and now the coach has Charlie on the golf course and is starting to take him from green to green and putt to putt in increasingly difficult circumstances. All the time, he is taking things very slowly and gently and having Charlie calmly visualise what he is going to do before allowing him to give it a try. It seems to be starting to work quite well.

▶ What is psychology?

Although the four examples just described might be said to be about psychological matters, are they? The first one is about brain damage, damage to the central nervous system. Jeff is being looked at by specialist neurologists. There is something physically wrong with him. The electrochemical connections in his brain have been damaged and so his memory has become systematically impaired.

In the second example, Mary is seen as putting on a special display of emotion because she has to for her job. She is 'putting on' her emotion and her social behaviour in the same way that she might put on her make-up. This type of job-related emotion work might well be seen as within the domain of the sociologist or anthropologist rather than the psychologist.

In the third example, Nathan is being socially shamed, one of the major ways of social control for misdeeds in pre-Revolution New England. Interestingly, after the Revolution, this type of social control gave way to guilt as the main mechanism. So, public prostration was replaced by privately admitting one's culpability to God. This might be about emotion, but surely it is in the domain of the historian.

Finally, Charlie, the young golfer with a putting problem, is being helped by his coach. As will be seen in Chapter 18, the coach is certainly using a variation on a psychological technique to try to help with the putting, but he is nevertheless clearly coaching. He is not a psychologist and nor would he think of himself as 'doing psychology'.

In short, psychology overlaps with many other areas of study or even areas of life and work. Perhaps in part because of this, a definition has proved difficult for more than 100 years. Nowadays, it is usually defined as: *the scientific study of behaviour and mental processes*. Some years ago, behavioural purists wanted the definition to embrace only behaviour, but the vacuity of that was eventually realised. There is clearly more to the human condition than behaviour. Also, the word psyche has an interesting background; it is a mixture of mind, spirit and, originally, even air (the other sense of spirit). It is perhaps reasonable that psychology should be concerned with such aspects of life as well as with behaviour.

The 'scientific' part of the definition, at a basic level, refers to empiricism. In other words, the idea is that psychology should proceed in such a way as to be verifiable by observation or experience, that is, by data that come from the senses. The alternative is to derive information simply from theory or from logic. This is not to say that psychologists ignore theory or logic but that they tend to agree that their fundamental information should come via empirical means.

The fact that psychology is such a broad subject and that it is usually regarded as dependent on empiricism is simultaneously a strength and a weakness. The strength, as many academic psychologists would point out, is that it has its basis squarely in the scientific endeavour and so there is an emphasis on methodological rigour and great care is taken not to over-generalise, that is, not to 'go beyond' the observations made. The weakness is that this approach has tended to make psychology a rather arid and cautious discipline, one that has not led to as penetrating an understanding of the human condition as might be expected.

Interestingly, the humanities (many of which have little or nothing to do with empirical science) are best described as those subjects that are concerned with what it is to be human. Psychologists are frequently concerned more simply with what humans do rather than with the human condition. This can make the subject somewhat disappointing to the beginning student who seems to want rather more than this. For many students, one of the core reasons for studying psychology is to find out more about oneself and others and to find things that might be useful as one goes about one's daily life. All too often, such knowledge is not to be found in psychology texts.

One point to bear in mind is that understanding of what it is to be human comes not just from the humanities (such as history, languages and literature, the classics and philosophy) but also from art (in its widest definition) and litera- ture. These, it should be said, are not empirical endeavours – they do not follow the precepts of the scientific method. However, whatever techniques their prac- titioners use must in the end derive from empirical observations. What else is there? It is hard to conceive of a human being born with no capacity to receive *any* sensory input who is then able to think. In this sense, pure thought is not possible; surely, also, consciousness is not possible without sensory input. So, the entire human endeavour is ultimately based on sensory input or empirically derived data. However, it does not necessarily follow from this that all that it then remains to do is follow some rather narrow methods in order to gather and view any information that might be available.

▶ Psychology going wrong

If you were to pick up a textbook written over 100 years ago by William James (1884), and assuming that you are even slightly interested in psychology, there is a strong likelihood that you would rapidly become engaged with the book. Certainly, James was writing well after science and the scientific method had begun to have an impact on the world, but they had not yet begun to really affect psychology. This happened in the 1920s with the rise of behaviourism.

By contrast, if you were to pick up a psychology text written during the past, say, 20 years, you would be likely to have one of two possible reactions. If it were one of the huge (usually American) introductory texts, you might well be interested in its glossy and highly illustrated layout and you might well be interested in the occasional snippet of information it contained. If it were any other text in psychology, you would put it down rapidly. It would be difficult to understand and would not give you much in the way of insight into the human condition, even though from a science perspective it might contain 'good' science.

The push given by behaviourism to psychology in the direction of scientific rigour was perfectly understandable, but within a few years it became too much even for academic psychologists. They needed something more than behaviour. Thus came cognition (thinking, memory and the like); in fact, it had never been far away, previously having been mainly in the domain of the philosophers. However, the cognition that developed was very much informed by the science that had been advocated by the behaviourists. This has led to something approaching 100 years of increasingly impressive scientific methodology and huge areas of academic psychology that are almost impenetrable to anyone other than those already expert in it. A further problem is that when the results of these endeavours are watered down sufficiently to be understood by the 'intelligent layperson', they often do not seem to amount to much. The content of some of the self-help books that are often vilified by the scientific psychologist can be far more engaging and frequently seem to have more to say about the nature of what it is to be human.

So, did psychology lose its way, somehow? Did it go wrong? The answer is both yes and no. Certainly, the emphasis on scientific rigour has led to a degree of respectability for 'psychology-as-a-science' that would otherwise have not developed. It is worth bearing in mind, however, that psychology is still not regarded as being particularly scientific by 'real' scientists such as physicists and chemists and even biologists on a bad day. On the other hand, much of psychology, it has to be said, viewed from the perspective of a person who has to study it just for one year, for example, is deadly dull. Many of the interesting things that they would like to know are simply not written about and the result is disappointment and the vague wish that they were doing something else.

▶ Common sense

One of the problems is common sense. Psychology was defined by one scurrilous student as the 'laborious discovery of the obvious'. The difficulty is that most people think that they know a thing or two about psychology – in the sense of real-life psychology – and so they do. Most people circumnavigate the waters of everyday life quite well and to do this they must know a reasonable amount about their own reactions and those of other people. Many generations of this type of knowledge are sometimes referred to as common sense.

In some instances, the scurrilous student is right. Applying scientific methods with care and precision can be a time-consuming and an exacting business. So it might well take a long time to 'prove' something that everyone already knows only too well. For example, most people would not be surprised to find that psychologists have found that behaviours that are rewarded tend to occur again. Or, to take another example, that without putting in a great deal of effort it is difficult to remember more than about seven items in one go. It did take a long time, however, to establish these fairly obvious 'facts' and all the conditions that surround them.

On the other hand, many things that psychologists have found out are less common-sensical. For example, if you want somebody to keep on doing something, would you give them a reward every time they did it or not? This is not an easy question to answer. However, the answer, long since established empirically, is very clear – you would only give them a reward some of the time, not all of the time. The question then becomes, how often and when?

All of which means that people tend to have one of two reactions to what they find in psychology texts. On the one hand, they find it quite obscure and difficult to understand and start to query its relevance to themselves and to humanity in general. On the other hand, they tend to dismiss it as all too obvious, saying that's just common sense. Occasionally, they find something in the middle that attracts their attention.

▶ The present book

This book set out to be a diatribe on where psychology had gone wrong. It was going to be a critical study of 100 years of psychology and a consideration of the perils of over-'sciencing' a discipline at the expense of interest and understanding. Turning this on its head, and taking a positive stance, the aim became one of describing in everyday terms just what psychology had got right. In fact, returning to the previous paragraph, there are many things within psychology that *are* interesting and that *are* highly applicable not only to the human condition in general but also to the life of any one person in particular.

Since psychology (and, indeed, almost everything else) is ultimately empirical, it is grounded in everyday life. However rarefied the methods that research psychologists use, their starting point is observations that they or others have made of the everyday human condition. It is assumed, therefore, that anything worth describing in this context should not only derive from everyday life, it should make some sense in everyday life and furthermore should, in some way, be applicable to everyday life. Fundamentally, psychology should be a useful subject. The result of reading a psychology text should be not only to be better informed about some aspect of what it is to be human, but also one should be able to take that knowledge and make some use of it in improving one's own lot or the lot of someone else.

Another way of describing what follows in this book is that it is, in the eyes of the writer, made up of all the interesting bits of psychology. It is intended for anyone who either wishes or is forced to study psychology for a year as part of some other qualification they are pursuing. They may never read any psychology again. If so, I would like to give them a large set of facts, ideas and suggestions that not only make more than common sense but also that they can use in their own lives. As a by-product, it may well also help them to pass whatever examination they have to take. If the aim of the book is successful, then anyone who has read it will, in fact, go on to read more psychology, for no reason other than interest. They will, however, have to choose carefully.

The question remains as to what has been left out of the book. There are various possible answers to this. It would be possible to list topics such as the theoretical details of colour vision (one of the most difficult areas of psychology to understand, in my view – a bit like physics) or the hundreds of studies that have been conducted on rats learning in laboratories. This type of list would be quite lengthy. Another answer would be to point to the content of almost any of the articles that could be found in recent issues of the many hundreds of academic and professional journals published each year. They would be unintelligible to anyone other than those already versed in whatever area they cover. Occasionally, but not often, there might be a little nugget of interesting and applicable information that can be found therein. This book is a systematic mining of those nuggets. I hope you enjoy it.

CHAPTER TWO

Emotional life

Recognising feelings and emotions

Scenes from life

You wake up covered in sweat and shouting. You turn to the clock and see that it is 3.15 a.m. although you can barely focus on the display. It just seems like a red blur that you have to screw up your eyes to see. You don't know whether you are hot or cold, although the pillow and bedclothes are ringing wet. You remember shouting out but have no idea what you shouted. You are trembling and can feel your heart pounding. You have vague memories of the most frightening nightmare but cannot really bring that into focus either. Eventually, you sit up, switch on the light and the reality of your bedroom comes crashing in and it is most welcome.

Imagine that you are 22 years old and have recently completed your university studies. You are on your way to a job interview, dressed in your best clothes. You feel very good as you walk towards the rather imposing office block. It is still a few hundred metres away and you check your watch, feeling a slight sense of urgency. You do not want to be late and you are not quite sure where to go when you get to the building. You speed up your pace slightly and stride out a little, wondering what the interview will be like, whether there will be any tests, and how you will acquit yourself. Suddenly your foot slips on something on the pavement and you begin to slide. You try to right yourself but both feet go out from under you and you make a three-point landing on the pavement with your hands and bottom. You slide along slightly in a puddle of something entirely disagreeable. You get to your feet, embarrassed as people look at you. You look down at your hand and at your clothes and find that they are heavily smeared with . . . .
. . . . . you fill in the blank.

You are at work. It is lunchtime and you have stayed behind to catch up on some work while you eat your sandwiches. It is quiet in the open-plan office and you work away in your section, making good progress. There

9

seems to be nobody else around. You find that you need something from the stationery cupboard at the other end of the office and so quietly walk down the central aisle. As you near the end, you hear two voices coming from one of the cubicles. You cannot help overhearing what they are saying. In fact, they are talking about you and agreeing that you are one of the most pleasant people to work with that they know. What would you feel on hearing this? What would you do?

Or, imagine the same situation but you heard them agreeing that they couldn't stand you and regarded you as having an entirely overblown opinion of yourself. What would you feel on hearing this? What would you do?

Without emotion, life would be dull. Emotion colours everything that we do. Emotion is always present in one form or another as a basic aid to our survival. It is our emotional reactions to the world that allow to us determine which parts of it are safe for us and which are dangerous, which will bring happiness and which will bring sadness or anger or depression. Emotion is both a very basic and primitive part of our existence and also a very sophisticated and important part of our survival. At the most fundamental level, emotion provides us with information about ourselves that is essential in our struggle to deal with daily life.

Ask some friends or members of your family to say what they think emotion is, or even to define it if they are able to. If you consider what they say, you will find that it consists of a number of components that they or you can more or less put in order of importance. These will include: feelings, changes to physiological state, behaviour (particularly facial expression) and cognitions or thoughts and memories. Some of them will have also said something like, 'Emotion is when . . .' or 'I feel emotional when . . .' In other words, they will have described the social contexts in which emotional reactions occur.

▶ The basics of emotion: feelings

Although some of the fundamental approaches to emotion are clearly scientific (as they are throughout psychology) and therefore rest very much on measurement, there are many other ways of gaining insight into emotion. The folk or everyday psychology of emotion has much to offer as also does the portrayal of emotion throughout the arts, particularly in literature and drama. Also, emotion is widely studied by anthropologists, sociologists, philosophers and even historians, as well as by psychologists.

Anybody who discusses emotion mentions feeling. Feeling is the subjective side of emotion, the aspect of it that seems to be most directly within our experience. There is a large discrepancy between psychology texts and self-help books with respect to how much they mention feeling. Feelings are absolutely integral to daily life and also have a central place in popular psychology books of the self-help variety. However, there is little mention of feelings in academic texts. The reason is that there is no direct way of measuring feelings and many psychologists are so concerned to preserve the scientific status of their discipline that they become uneasy if they try to deal with feelings. In other words, ironically, they shy away from their own emotional reaction.

Phenomenological psychologists attempt to study subjective experience and consciousness, and those of this persuasion who study emotion tend to do so with the belief that emotions are meaningful events that are there to be understood by those who experience them. The most obvious way of assessing subjective experience is through questionnaires. A good example of this approach is given by Scherer, Wallbott and Summerfield (1986) who conducted a huge cross-cultural questionnaire study of emotion on sample populations throughout Europe. They concentrated on joy, fear, anger and sadness, four of what are regarded as the fundamental emotions. They found a wide series of similarities across the cultures but also some interesting differences between the emotions. For example, anger seems to be experienced less intensely than the other three emotions. Also, fear can last from a few seconds to about an hour, anger between a few minutes and a few hours, joy from an hour to a day and sadness from one day to many days. (For interest, take note of your own emotional reactions on the next occasion that you are requested to complete a questionnaire.)

▶ The basics of emotion: behaviour

Behaviour is obviously involved in emotion – we can see others (and ourselves) behaving emotionally. For the most part, however, the gross behaviours of emotion, such as running in fear or striking out in anger or jumping up and down with pleasure, have been studied very little in humans. There are some studies of reactions such as the frustration effect in laboratory rats, but their relevance to the human condition is marginal. Throughout a long history, the study of emotional behaviour has mainly been concerned with emotional expression, particularly, and not surprisingly, in facial expression.

As well as providing very intimate information to us about ourselves, emotion is also a social phenomenon. The facial expression of emotion conveys crucial information to other people and we gain crucial information about others by studying their facial expressions. We depend on our 'reading' of other people's emotions for the continued ease of our social intercourse. Just think for a moment of how difficult telephone conversations can sometimes be, in comparison to face-to-face conversations. This is simply because there is much less information available on emotional reactions, tone of voice being the only possibility. There is the possibility, however, that blind people become adept at recognising emotion through intonation of voice.

As a moment's reflection will show, our emotional expression and communication are non-verbal. We make judgements about another person's emotional state by looking at their body language. This is a very complex skill that we seem to acquire and use unconsciously. Of course, there are exceptions to this among those people who consciously manipulate body language (and hence emotional expression) for professional reasons: actors, salespersons, cabin stewards on airlines, for example. So, these skills do not have to be unconscious, but they are frequently so routinely used that they can become automatic.

There are huge individual differences in these abilities; some people are far more adept at emotional expression and its recognition than others. Also, some of us are more openly expressive than others and not all emotions are expressed, even facially, on all occasions. Whether they are or not is a matter of the regulation of emotion (see next chapter).

The key question about the recognition of emotion in others is: how good are we at it? (This leaves aside the matter of how good we are at recognising emotion in ourselves. Again, this will be dealt with in the next chapter.) Generally, we are not overly successful at judging emotional expression without some knowledge of what surrounds its occurrence. So, for example, if we were suddenly confronted with a disembodied face, emoting for all it was worth, we would not be very good at 'reading' its expression – quite apart from being startled into terror by such an apparition. It is possible, however, that television has had some effect in widening our capabilities in this respect.

Normally, we have some knowledge of the events that led up to the expression, some knowledge of other responses going on at the same time (bodily and physiological reactions) and knowledge of events that follow the expression, such as the reactions of other people. Frequently, there are also others who are interpreting the expression at the same time as we are. All such items of knowledge allow us to check the emotional expression we are looking at.

In general, many people are reasonably accurate in recognising the emotional expressions of others. This is, perhaps, not surprising since it is a skill that has considerable survival value and which has been honed for a long time. Moreover, there is overwhelming evidence that many of the facial expressions of emotion are universal or at least they have been found in all the cultures that have been studied.

Psychologists who work in this area are convinced that the basic emotions (see later for a discussion of these) are interpreted similarly across all cultures. They are therefore believed to have a firm genetic basis, to be hard-wired throughout the human species. However, each culture has developed its own rules for the display of emotional expression. So, for example, anger might well be represented by similar facial expressions throughout all the cultures in the world, but it may well be more or less readily expressed from one culture to the next. Such differences also occur sub-culturally. For example, in Western cultures, anger is typically expressed more openly and forcefully by men than by women. Or, to take another example, in some cultures (e.g. for Muslim women) excessive display of emotion is considered to be immodest.

▶ The basics of emotion: physiology

Think of the last time that you were angry or afraid, or anxious, or felt a pang of guilt or a twinge of jealousy. The stirred-up feelings that you begin to experience are the beginnings of physiological arousal. Arousal is integral to emotion. As we experience an emotion, particularly if it is strong, then we can feel the changes to our breathing, sweating, pulse rate, muscle tone, and so on. We might feel 'butterflies in our stomach', 'our heart lurching into our mouth', 'steam coming out of our ears', and so on. Even the smallest emotional reaction has an attendant physiological arousal.

These reactions are the autonomic nervous system (particularly the sympathetic branch) preparing us for emergency action. Not for nothing are preparatory emotional reactions known as being concerned with fight or flight. All emotion is about dealing with sudden changes in the environment, evaluating their significance for us and preparing ourselves to deal with them. We become aware of the reactions of our peripheral (autonomic) nervous system in emotion. We can feel our heart racing whereas we cannot feel the parts of the brain that are implicated in emotion sending out their signals.

If you compare the bodily responses you experience in anger and fear and in happiness and sadness, they will probably seem different to you. This apparent difference in physiological reactions between the emotions led many researchers to consider that there might be specific bodily patterns of response associated with each emotion. Ever since William James's time (the 1880s), we have known that physiological arousal is a necessary part of emotion, so the search for specific bodily mechanisms involved in this process has been carried out for 120 years, but without much success. There appear to be some broad differences in heart rate between happiness, surprise and disgust, on the one hand, and anger, fear and sadness, on the other. But in general any differences between the emotions physiologically are swamped by individual differences in reactivity from one person to the next.

William James (1884) created a long-lasting puzzle with his theory of emotion, of sufficient moment to describe in brief. The common-sense view of emotion is that we perceive something that causes an emotional reaction, and that causes us to do something. Somebody says something insulting to us in public, we flare up in anger and bite back with a sharp retort. James put things round the other way. He suggested that our bodily reactions follow directly from our perceptions and that the feeling of these bodily changes is the emotion. So, somebody says something insulting to us in public, we bite with a sharp retort and the feedback that comes from doing this *is* the emotion. In reality, it is probably a mixture of both types of directionality that occurs in emotion.

The physiology of emotion goes much deeper than the autonomic nervous system. It is clear that emotions have a biological base, one that is grounded in evolution as a fundamental aspect of our survival mechanisms. Although the arousal aspect of emotion might occur peripherally, the integration of emotion happens in the central nervous system. Subcortical mechanisms are involved as

also is the limbic system and the frontal lobes of the cortex. Of particular importance is the amygdala, an area of the limbic system that appears to be crucial to
emotion. To the extent that emotions are hard-wired, then they must be located
in the limbic system.

▶ The basics of emotion: cognition

It is clear that emotion and cognition are intimately intertwined and that emotion
and motivation are also connected. It is difficult to understand emotion without
considering cognition. Imagine that you have just woken up on the morning
when you are due to have root canal surgery. You have not experienced this
before but many of your friends have and they all speak of it, wincing with
expressions of mild horror. You get up and find that you are very tense, so much
so that breakfast is an impossibility. Even coffee is hard to take and only seems
to make matters worse. This experience builds up until you are sitting in the
dentist's chair waiting for the onslaught.

Clearly, this is an example of anxiety and one that is shared by many people,
and it seems equally clear to understand. However, consider the elements that
go to make up the reaction. It is your *beliefs or knowledge* about the nature of root
canal operations that lead to the anxiety. You have considered what is to come
and judged how it is likely to affect you. The result is anxiety. The emotional
reaction has followed on the heels of cognitions in the form of beliefs and knowledge. If you had already experienced a root canal procedure and found that it
was easy and painless, then your beliefs would be different and you would not
be anxious.

As much as any other psychologist it was Stanley Schachter (1964), throughout the 1960s, who made it clear that there is an intimate connection between
emotion and cognition. His two-factor theory was very straightforward. A necessary part of emotion is arousal of the sympathetic nervous system. In other
words, emotion cannot occur without this arousal. However, these states of
arousal differ from one situation to the next, so we interpret the arousal according to our beliefs, knowledge or expectations about the situation. So, our experience of emotion, according to this view, depends on both physiological arousal
and cognition. Going back to your impending root canal procedure, both the
arousal and the beliefs are easy to see.

Schachter and others conducted many studies to test this theory. Although
many of the studies were ingenious, they did not prove that emotion necessarily
depends on arousal and cognition. For example, it is possible to induce arousal
through cognition, say, by reflecting on what your reactionary father said to you
last time you spoke to him. Or it is possible to produce a sort of physiological
tranquillisation cognitively, by imagining a quiet country place when you feel
anxious. This is all part of emotion regulation, to be discussed in the next
chapter.

While it is clear that arousal and cognition can and do combine in emotion, exactly how is not yet known. Think of this problem. If cognitions are used to label arousal and so lead to subjective feelings, these links must be learned. If we have to know something about the world before being able to label our feelings about it, then how can the young child feel anything before knowing the label for that feeling? Of course, young children do have emotional experiences. Indeed, very young children often seem to have very little else.

There are many ways in which cognitions might be linked to emotion. For example, our memories have emotional aspects that colour our present reactions. If, on the last three occasions that we went to a party, we had an unpleasant time, the next invitation to a party is likely to lead to a negative reaction, or our emotions might affect our cognitions. For example, if you have just fallen in love, with all the attendant emotional turmoil, this colours most of your thoughts. Or if you have just had an inordinately frustrating day at work and this has left you feeling constantly irritable, this will influence the way in which you think about things throughout the evening.

However, the main way in which cognitions and emotions are linked is through *appraisals*. When anything happens, we evaluate what it means for us, its significance to us – this is an emotional appraisal, or an appraisal that leads to an emotional reaction. These appraisals are believed to help us in making fine distinctions about our emotional experiences or in determining the extent or the intensity of the emotion. For example, seeing a $100 note on the pavement would produce a very different emotional reaction from seeing the same note in a pool of vomit. Or being told off privately for a work mistake that should have been avoided would produce a very different appraisal than being condemned publicly.

Some psychologists believe similar emotional experiences and expressions follow similar appraisals and also that each emotional experience is unique because each appraisal is unique. This might sound convincing, but what happens if a person does not have the cognitive capacity to make a particular type of appraisal? Are they able to experience the emotion? For example, knowledge of art presumably allows finer appreciations of works of art. Without such knowledge, would a person's emotional reactions to the work be different?

For psychologists who are concerned with such matters, a key issue has been whether or not cognitive appraisal is *necessary* to emotion. There are (at least) two sides to the matter – appraisals always precede emotion, and cognition and emotion are independent (although often related). If you are standing waiting to pay in a cafeteria with a laden tray and someone crashes into you from behind, sending everything flying, your reaction is likely to be instantaneous and to occur without apparent thought. But it might be argued that you have made an instant, very primitive appraisal. Also, it is obvious that some cognitions occur unconsciously and that some emotions occur without conscious involvement. This makes the issue even more complex.

In the end, there is a very complex interplay between emotions and cognitions. Compare the instant reaction to a sudden loud sound in the night and the complex mixture of thoughts and feelings you have if your fiancée has just ended the relationship. Compare jumping out of the way in the road as the brakes squeal behind you with the appraisals that you make when a member of your family has died. The links between emotion and appraisal go in both directions and become very intricate. They are always intertwined, but whether or not they are necessary to each other is another matter.

▶ The specific emotions

In everyday life, the specific emotions are very important to us. We don't just feel 'emotional', we experience anger or sadness or joy or guilt, or whatever it might be. Emotions exist in quite discrete ways although they can also appear in very complex mixtures. So, for example, we might well experience sadness in a very pure form if our dog has just died or we might experience a complex mixture of sadness, anger, anxiety, jealousy and even guilt and shame if our relationship has just ended.

Are some emotions more important than others? When we are in the all-encompassing throes of a particular emotion, it seems as significant at the time as any other. We might be as wracked with envy over a rival's promotion as we are consumed by anger over a social slight or trembling with anxiety at the thought of an impending speech. However, there is one sense in which some emotions do seem to be more important than others, in that they are more basic to survival. For example, fear is probably more linked to fundamental survival than is envy, or joy/happiness is more important to survival than pride.

The usual list of primary or basic emotions is: fear/anxiety, anger, sadness and happiness, with disgust sometimes added as a fifth.

Fear is perhaps the most straightforward emotion of all and is clearly grounded in biology, for survival. It is very distressing and is directed towards some specific object or event, alerting us to potential danger and mobilising us to flee, to escape. It is at its most obvious when physical danger is present but becomes considerably more subtle with all the learned fears that are created by modern society. Here the range might go from fear of failure to fear of walking into a room full of people.

Anxiety is arguably the most commonly experienced emotion and is certainly among the most studied. Most of us experience anxiety to some degree nearly every day. It is a feeling of apprehension about something that lies ahead and at mild levels can be extremely motivating, in a positive way. For example, you are likely to perform better in an examination or an interview if you go into them with a moderate level of anxiety. Too low or too high a level of anxiety detracts from performance. However, we all differ considerably with respect to what is moderate in this context. Moreover, when anxiety levels are abnormally high, this is thought to be the basis of much that can go wrong or be harmful to us.

The experience of anxiety provides us with good information that something is wrong and needs fixing. In the extreme, it can be debilitatingly unpleasant. In its extreme acute form, it is a panic attack, something suffered at some or other time in life by a surprising number of people. On the other hand, if a high level of anxiety is chronic, that is, it continues for some time, the almost inevitable result is depression. It is a case of unpredictability in life leading to uncontrollability.

This brief discussion of anxiety 'going wrong' by being too high points to the broad issue of whether or not emotions in general can be abnormal. The answer to this is squarely 'no'. An emotional reaction is an emotional reaction – it cannot be wrong. So if someone says to you that 'you shouldn't feel angry' or 'you shouldn't be sad for so long' or 'I should have thought that you would have been happier than that', and so on, this is complete nonsense. You are experiencing whatever emotions you are experiencing and every one of them is providing you with information.

So, emotions cannot be wrong. It may be that your *expression* of a particular emotion might be inappropriate in the context. It might not be regarded as seemly, for example, to give open vent to your anger at a board meeting or to continue grieving too openly for too long over the death of your cat. But the *experience* of such anger or grief is simply the experience and there is little you can do about it other than to give it due attention.

In general, if any of the specific emotions occur too little or too much, if they occur at unusual, inappropriate times and places, then they are doing little good for us or for those around us. This is even so with the positive emotions. Imagine what it would be like to be ecstatic for days. It would be debilitating in the extreme.

Imagine that you work with a team of people and do your absolute best to contribute to the overall good. You speak up whenever there is a point to be made but whenever you do one of your colleagues tends to speak over you and drown you out. On the rare occasions when you manage to make your point, the same colleague brings it up a few moments later as though it was his or her idea. *Anger*, like fear, also mobilises us for action, in this case defence rather than escape.

Anger is clearly related to aggression but they are not one and the same. It is possible to be aggressive without being angry and it is equally possible to be angry without becoming aggressive. However, the two (the emotion of anger and the behaviour of aggression) are linked and are biologically based, with obvious survival value. Anger always results in a much increased burst of energy and, although biologically based, is seen by some psychologists as largely socially constructed. That is, some people might be temperamentally more prone to anger than others, but the extent to which they express this is probably socially determined. In our culture, for example, boys are encouraged to express their anger more openly than girls and a far greater proportion of men than women are made to take anger management courses. These are learned differences, not differences of biology.

Imagine a family sitting watching a television documentary about the terrible deprivations that are suffered by children who live in countries wracked by famine. Or think of your reactions when you lose some favourite object. *Sadness* might be described as somewhat purer than the other negative primary emotions. It is made up of a mixture of down-heartedness, being discouraged, loneliness and feelings of isolation. It tends to follow the loss of something that was dear to us, whether this is a job, a house, a loved one, a favourite car, or even something like time. Unlike fear, anxiety and anger, the main effect of sadness is to slow us down rather than speed us up. In the extreme, sadness takes the form of grief, although grief is made up of much more than sadness alone. It also embraces anger, disgust, contempt, fear, guilt and even shyness, protest and despair. In this sense, it is not an emotion but a state comprised of a constellation of emotions that vary from time to time and person to person. Not all those who experience grief will necessarily experience all these processes and those who do might not experience them in the same order or over the same time period.

You have been meaning to do a large job in the garden for some weeks. You eventually get round to it and spend the entire day digging, weeding and clearing up. As twilight approaches, you finish the job and stretch your back, looking round at the cleared garden and the completed job. You walk quietly indoors, looking forward to a glass of wine and a quiet evening. The only primary emotion that can be described as positive is *happiness* (there are simply fewer positive emotions than negative ones).

Talking of happiness, joy, elation, euphoria, etc., seems to be talking of variations on a theme or positions on a dimension. It is a very difficult emotion to pin down because it can have so many different meanings, even involving sadness in some cases. Think of the strange mixture of happiness and sadness in nostalgia, for example.

If you think about the conditions that bring about happiness, they often involve the possession of something or some quality, often (although not always) a thing or a quality that we have and others do not or that we have now when we did not previously. In other words, happiness is relative and depends on a perceived change in circumstances. Although some people might be generally more content (temperamentally) than others, a state of happiness or joy or elation cannot go on for long. If one won Lotto every week for a year, the elation would begin to pall after a few weeks, even for the most avaricious. Nothing stays the same, least of all emotional reactions.

Sometimes included in the list of primary or basic emotions (in that it seems to have a clear biological basis) is disgust. Imagine that it is lunchtime and while you are talking you put a forkful of lettuce into your mouth. You bite into something soft and succulent that you realise should not be there. You spit out a half-eaten slug. Disgust is about rejecting anything that is bad, harmful or noxious from possible ingestion into or even proximity to the body. This gives disgust a very obvious survival value. However, at the human level we learn to be 'disgusted' at a wide range of things that have to do with moral values and even aesthetic appreciation. This might range from a reaction to an art work to responses to how some people treat their children or animals.

Related to disgust is contempt. In the way that disgust involves an essential 'spitting out' of something from the mouth, contempt involves a sort of looking down the nose at something. One psychologist even referred to contempt as 'dis-smell'. Something that is held in contempt is beneath our attention.

The far more negative emotions of *jealousy* and *envy* also depend on comparisons between what one has and what others have. The word jealousy is often misused. It is impossible, for example, to be jealous of another person's car. Jealousy is about the possibility of losing another person's affections because they are being directed towards a third person. Interestingly, there is a general female/male difference with respect to jealousy. For the male it tends to be about sexual interest and for the female it is about the emotional aspects of the relationship. Envy, more simply, is concerned with wanting something that someone else has, whether it is an object (such as a house or car or set of clothes) or a quality (such as high intelligence, or creativity or a good singing voice or sporting ability).

In some ways, the most interesting emotions of all are what are referred to as the *self-conscious* emotions. These are: *embarrassment, pride, shyness, guilt* and *shame*.

You have begun a new job and are attending your first meeting. It is important that you create the best possible impression. You have just been welcomed by the chairperson and settle back into your seat, hoping to sit quietly and learn. Just as the chair is about to begin the first item, your cell phone shatters the silence.

You go shopping for your usual groceries at the supermarket. You live close by so it is not far to walk. You have been very busy and so are in a bit of a daze, but you manage to go round and collect all that you need. Five minutes later you realise that you have arrived home pushing a supermarket trolley full of goods for which you haven't paid.

You and your wife or husband are attending the school play. Your 7-year-old son or daughter has been given a part and this is the first time he or she has performed anything in public. You are amazed at how well they do and what a success the play is.

Imagine a man in his late teens who usually travels to work on the same bus at the same time each day. Quite often on the bus there is also a young woman whom he admires. He glances at her from time to time over the top of his book and thinks that she is lovely. One day she happens to be sitting next to him, looks over and says, 'What are you reading? That looks interesting.' He blushes to the roots of his hair and can barely stammer a reply.

From these examples, it should be clear why these are called the self-conscious emotions; they all make reference to the self in some way and how the self is performing in some social situation. (In the case of the example of pride, the reference was to how proud the parents were of their child.) So, to some extent all these emotions depend on the evaluations made of us by other people, either at the time or more generally.

Embarrassment, guilt and shame are, perhaps, the most important of the self-conscious emotions because they are to do with social control. They give us information (and also give the information to others through our reactions) about the extent to which we are conforming to social rules and standards.

Embarrassment is the simplest of them and need not be an entirely negative emotion; one can be amused at one's own embarrassment. It is mainly about making a social gaffe of some sort, or, to put it more formally, of not fulfilling a social role properly, losing self-esteem and leading others to form what one believes might be a negative social impression of one. Think, for example, of a situation in which it is important that you make some smooth social introductions and halfway through them you forget one of the key names (somebody you know perfectly well) and simply cannot think of it for the life of you.

Guilt follows the transgression of a rule that comes from an authority. In order to experience guilt, one has to be accepting of the authority. So, for example, if a teenager is told off for coming home late but no longer accepts that his (or her) parents have any rights to say so, then no guilt will be felt. The essence of guilt is that one has caused harm, either by doing something that one should not have or by not doing something that one should. Perhaps the most significant aspect of guilt is that it involves possible reparation. It is usually possible to right the wrong that has been done.

Shame is much more fundamental because it concerns one's beliefs about oneself as a whole, not about some simple transgression. And it cannot be put right. If one does something that causes shame, the shame stays – the matter cannot be put right because it is about one's character. At least the process of putting it right might take some time. When feeling shame, all the person wants to do is to find a rock to crawl under or a hole to swallow them up. In some ways, it is the most debilitating of all the emotions.

Shame occurs when the person is exposed in some way. The obvious example in our society is sheer physical nakedness, at least in situations in which it is not encouraged. But any exposure of one's flaws will do the trick, particularly if one has been brought up in a particular way. Compare, for example, the difference between a child being told, 'No, you should not have done that because it would hurt your brother. Don't do it again' and 'Why on earth did you do that? You must be bad through and through. What's wrong with you?' The first type of telling off would be engendering guilt and the second shame.

More than all the other self-conscious emotions, shame relies on a basic evaluation of the self by the self. And what is regarded as shameful varies from time to time, from society to society or culture to culture. It is at the core of social control. Putting people in pillories or stocks was an attempt at social control through shame, as is publishing the names of bad debtors in supermarkets or those who have been convicted of drunken driving in the newspaper.

It is also important to point out that it is thought that the self-conscious emotions do not develop until a child has developed a 'theory of mind'. That is, until the child understands that there are other people and that they have their own minds with their own particular viewpoints that might well be different from the child's.

► Emotion and gender

To finish off this chapter it is important to say a little about the relationship between emotion and gender, a topic that has already been touched on. The Western stereotype is that women are irrational and emotional and men are logical and rational. What truth is there to this?

It is true to say that women, in our society, are more emotionally expressive than men and that they are better than men at expressing some emotions (sadness and fear, for example). Men, by contrast, are better at expressing anger. 'Better' in this context means can express it more openly and readily so that it can be more easily recognised. It is also apparent that women and men do not differ much in what they report of their emotional experiences. However, girls are brought up to account more for their emotions than boys. Moreover, they are encouraged (by their mothers) to be more responsible than boys for the emotional reactions of others as well as for their own.

By contrast, boys tend to be encouraged almost to deny their emotions, and certainly not to explore them. Given these differences, it is hardly surprising that the stereotype has developed as it has. One has the impression that the stereotype is changing in some segments of society through the influence of the feminist movement and suggestions for anger management and emotional sensitivity training for men.

► Summary

■ Emotion is difficult to define but always consists of feelings, behaviour, physiological change and cognitions and always occurs in a particular context which influences it. Its major function is to give information to the individual about their interaction with the world.

■ From an everyday perspective, the core aspects of emotion are to do with its expression (largely, although not solely, by the face) and its recognition.

■ Feelings are the basic subjective elements of emotion. They are difficult to study because of their subjectivity. Their duration and intensity differ from emotion to emotion.

- In human beings emotional behaviour has mainly been studied with respect to facial expression. The expressions for the various emotions seem to be universal although the rules for when and how much to express the emotions vary from culture to culture.

- Physiological arousal is thought to be, but has not been proved to be, a necessary aspect of emotion. Both the autonomic and the central nervous systems are implicated in emotion although there is little to support the idea that each emotion has its own particular pattern of physiological response.

- There are intricate relationships between cognition and emotion, some psychologists believing that emotion cannot occur without cognition. The major form of cognition involved in emotion is the appraisal of the significance of stimuli for the individual. Whether or not cognition is necessary to emotion remains a moot point.

- There are four or five basic emotions, basic in the sense of being clearly biologically grounded and important to the evolutionary survival of the individual. These are: anxiety/fear, sadness, anger, happiness/joy and disgust. Others include: contempt, envy and jealousy.

- The socially constructed and self-conscious or self-referent emotions are: pride, shyness, embarrassment, guilt and shame. Some of these emotions, as well as giving information to the individual, also function as mechanisms of social control.

- The stereotypes concerning the difference between men and women in emotion in Western society are partly borne out. Although women are not more emotional than men, they are encouraged to express emotion more than men and to be more responsible for its control both in themselves and others.

▶ Questions and possibilities

- Thinking of the specific emotions, are some of them more important at home than at work? Which? What causes these differences?

- Do the people that you know differ in how well they can recognise emotional expressions in others? What causes these differences?

- Almost certainly, some people that you know are more emotionally expressive than others. Why?

- Do you think that it is possible to tell what somebody else is feeling from observing their emotional behaviour and change in their physiology?

- Is it more or less difficult to remember something that has happened that was very emotional than something that was not?

- Have you experienced any emotions that seem to have arisen without cognitions being involved? If so, what has made this happen? What is the difference between these emotions and those that clearly involve cognition?

- Do you know anyone who has never experienced shame, or guilt? If so, why do you think that they haven't? In what ways is their life different from yours?

- Do you experience some emotions more than others? Why?

- Have you observed any differences in emotion between the sexes? What are they and why do you think they exist in the people you have seen?

- What effect do you think it has to 'keep a poker face'?

- How important are the expression and recognition of emotion in your job?

- In what situations are you able to 'be yourself' emotionally? What are the differences between these situations and those in which you feel that you have to exercise firm control over your emotional expression?

- How important do you believe emotion to be in decision-making?

CHAPTER THREE

Emotional life

Regulating emotions

Scenes from life

Imagine a 15-year-old boy, voice broken, shaving now and then and testosterone rampant. Emotionally, he is all over the place, trying to come to terms with budding adulthood but still feeling like a child some of the time. He is going through a period of resenting his parents, not only because they are still to some extent controlling what he does, but also simply because he does not like the way they live their lives. In fact, he is resentful of many things, including not having very much money, being fed up with school, having less than what he regards as appropriate success in his fumbling attempts with girls, and so on.

Recently, he has been spasmodically stealing money from his mother's purse when he happens to see it and she is not around. There are no great amounts of money involved, but he has not been as clever as he imagined and it has been noticed. One evening after a particularly quiet meal, he gets up to leave the table and his father tells him to stay where he is; they have something to talk to him about. His father then tells him that they are aware that he has been stealing from his mother and asks him to give an account of himself. He feels dreadful inside, a mixture that he cannot name of anxiety, guilt, the usual resentment and a strange sort of belligerence. He resolves to show his parents nothing of this but to lie and to control all of his expressions in order to be convincing.

Picture a woman in her early twenties, slim, good-looking and perpetually on a diet of some sort. Her health is not wonderful because she is semi-starved for much of the time, and then binges and purges occasionally. Her immune system is not coping very well, so she seems to be attacked by whatever bug is going around and she often feels listless and without energy.

Many of her social interactions pass in a sort of daze. Often she finds that she does not quite understand what people mean, particularly if they talk about emotions. So, for example, if someone says to her, 'I don't feel that good today, I'm just anxious all the time', she hasn't noticed anything different about the person. When she is with her family, she feels that she does not quite understand what is going on. She feels different and somewhat isolated but doesn't know how to express these feelings. They just make her feel like eating and then, when she eats, she feels that she is out of control. She constantly feels hollow and alienated, never knowing whether or not she is happy. In fact, as she sometimes thinks to herself, she does not know what happiness is.

Think about the following phrases: Don't give way to your emotions. Keep a stiff upper lip, a poker face. Don't let your heart rule your head. Big boys don't cry. It's important to let off steam. Don't be silly, you shouldn't be feeling angry (or sad, or happy, or guilty, or jealous . . .). The strength of our emotions and our attempts to control them become an automatic part of daily life, growing up and general social control.

▶ Detecting lies

A good way to begin thinking about how we regulate emotion is to consider the question of attempting to detect lying. We would all like to be able to do it from time to time, since both honesty and deceit are so commonplace in daily life. A foolproof method of lie detection has been sought for many years – there are numerous occasions when the legal representatives of society would very much like to know whether or not someone is telling the truth. There are also quite a few occasions when ordinary members of society would like to know if their elected representatives (in the form of politicians) are telling them the truth.

Over the years, people have been interrogated, tortured, put into ducking stools, and so on. The modern equivalent of this is the lie detector or polygraph. This is based on the idea that someone who is lying is making an attempt to regulate their emotional expression, but that it is difficult to regulate the psychophysiological side of this. So, if there is physiological arousal underlying an otherwise bland exterior, this will show up in measures of heart rate, blood pressure, respiration, sweating, and so on. The general method is to ask people ordinary questions when they are relaxed, in order to establish a baseline. Then, they are asked, 'Did you shoot the vicar with a blow-pipe as he stood in the pulpit delivering his sermon?'

It is hard to know whether or not this is a good thing, but the polygraph does not work all that well. It is possible to learn to control one's psychophysiological responses, there is no particular pattern of responses that means 'lying' and, moreover, if someone's responses go haywire in reaction to a pointed question, this does not necessarily mean they are guilty.

Currently, then, there is no foolproof method of lie detection. Perhaps this is just as well. The use of such a method would be fraught with ethical difficulties. Would people be given lie detector tests at job interviews? Would they be used routinely during the family evening meal? Would parents give such tests to their children?

▶ Emotional intelligence

Emotional intelligence and its potential impact on daily life at home and at work have been much discussed recently. It is to do with a set of skills that everyone possesses, to some degree; in this it is similar to general intelligence. These skills concern how we deal with any information that is relevant to emotion. In more detail, our emotional intelligence is made up of how we judge emotion and express it, how we make use of whatever information we gain from emotion, and how we regulate emotion in adaptive ways.

There are huge individual differences in emotional intelligence, particularly in the way in which people appraise and express emotion and how they use the information they derive from emotion. Think, for example, of the differences in these respects that there are between members of your family and your friends and people that you work with. Particularly important, however, is the manner in which we regulate emotion – this is significant throughout our development, from early childhood onwards, especially concerning our well-being. The major question here is: how do we learn to regulate our emotion?

Interestingly, at one extreme there is a condition known as *alexithymia* that essentially is equivalent to having an extremely low emotional intelligence. An alexithymic person has great difficulty in processing emotion information and in regulating their own emotion. He or she has a limited understanding of blends of emotion, a limited awareness of how to describe complex, different-iated emotional states, an inability to see emotional subtleties and no awareness of the complexities of the emotional life of others. In other words, the emotional system of an alexithymic person seems to be dissociated.

Gross (1998) has done much to conceptualise the ways in which we attempt to regulate emotion. He lists five types of regulation process:

1 *Situation selection* – we can approach or avoid people or places or objects that we know lead to pleasant or unpleasant emotional experiences for us.

2 *Situation modification* – we can focus on whatever is leading to the emotional experience and change it to our advantage.

3 *Attentional deployment* – this simply means putting one's attention elsewhere, away from the emotion-evoking situation, by distracting oneself, concentrat-ing hard on something else, or merely by ruminating or worrying.

4 *Cognitive change* – this involves altering our appraisals or evaluations of something in order to alter its emotional impact; it would include all of the psychological defences (see Chapter 17) and the making of downwards social comparisons (they are all worse off than me anyway).

5 *Response modification* – in everyday terms, this is the most common form of emotion regulation; it happens late on in the situation and might involve drugs, alcohol, exercise, therapy, food or outright suppression.

Whether or not we regulate our emotions depends on our own emotional awareness (part of emotional intelligence) and how we think about our own moods. Also, we need strategies to use that can affect our feelings. So, for example, we might make ourselves feel good by helping other people, or by leaving the more pleasant things that we have to do until later in the day. (Of course, some people might start off with the more pleasant tasks and never actually get round to the less pleasant ones.)

Emotion regulation is learned to begin with in childhood, as the ability to reason develops and as children begin to realise that emotion is something that can be changed. The capacity to regulate emotion depends partly on temperament but also very much on the development of language because that provides access to the social influences on emotion.

If emotion regulation is low, then the child (and later the adult) is likely to be uncontrolled, unconstructive (socially), aggressive and susceptible to circumstances such as social rejection. If the level of emotion regulation is high, then general socio-emotional competence is increased. As our ability to regulate emotion grows, so too does the way in which we think about emotion. This is also influenced by the way we are brought up, in particular, the type of attachment that we experience early on in life (see Chapters 6 and 14).

Emotion regulation tends to continue its development throughout the lifespan, older people generally being better at it than younger people. One of the major ways in which the elderly regulate their emotion is through being highly selective in their social encounters. They try to restrict these to people who understand them and with whom they feel safe in shared intimacy and emotional expression. Emotion regulation is important to staying positive throughout the vicissitudes that inevitably come with increased age.

One important area in which emotional intelligence and regulation have been studied recently is the workplace. For years, work was seen as the place where only 'rationality' could drive what occurs. It was regarded as unprofessional to be otherwise, which meant, of course, that women (since they are more 'emotional') were regarded as less professional. So, emotion regulation was seen as very important to the workplace, simply through its suppression.

Recently, this view has been shown to be the nonsense that it obviously is. Emotion has a key role to play in the workplace and many (if not all) decisions are essentially emotionally based, the 'rational' gloss being placed on them afterwards. Current thinking is more along the lines that directness, openness and spontaneity are important to workplace productivity and well-being, this being a long way from emotion suppression.

Emotional intelligence has been shown to be highly relevant to success at work, success being indicated by both increasing status and by well-being. A number of matters are relevant to any consideration of this sort, however. For example, emotion regulation is related to dependency and dependency can take many forms in the workplace. Also, emotional expression and emotion regulation or management are based on social rules, some of which might be specific to a particular place of work. For example, air cabin crew have evolved a way of being emotionally engaged when dealing with passengers that is entirely different from their behaviour towards one another when they are off duty.

To take one example, there is an interesting relationship between emotional intelligence and style of leadership. A basic distinction is between transactional and transformational leaders. Transactional leaders work through the use of rewards and punishments; leadership for them is a question of transactions. Transformational leaders work through affiliation, affection and general emotional involvement; they tend to be charismatic. They have visionary goals, challenge the status quo and concern themselves with individual needs.

Transformational leaders tend to have skills that overlap considerably with those of emotional intelligence. They are positive and sensitive, with good language skills, and high self-esteem. They are intuitive and maintain close relationships with members of their group. So, in emotional intelligence terms, they are in touch with their own feelings, honestly, they show empathy and excite emotional commitment. They are emotionally stable and encourage a similar stability in others through mood and stress management. They tend to be pleasant, more emotional, more altruistic and less aggressive than transactional leaders.

▶ Emotions and health

Emotion always serves the function of giving information. It can be extreme, unusual, debilitating, painful, and so on, but information is always being provided. Emotional reactions are always simply emotional reactions; they can never be abnormal. However, traditionally, emotions have been seen as contributing to the neuroses, the psychoses, to the affective disorders (such as bipolar disorder), to psychopathy and to excessive (or minimal) eating, alcoholism and drug abuse. But even in psychiatric conditions, emotions are perfectly normal with respect to what brings them about. They are just what they are, with no values attached to them. However, it is reasonable to say that emotions can be dysfunctional or dysregulational.

Stress

A core concept in emotion dysregulation is *stress*. Stress has been defined in very many ways, but the general way of looking at it nowadays is that it involves an interaction between the individual and the environment. So, some people might be more prone to stress reactions than others but these reactions are prompted by particular types of environmental stressors.

The person who has done most to further our understanding of stress is Richard Lazarus (1991, 1993, 1999), who makes his far-reaching exposition of emotional in general through an analysis of stress and coping. He regards stress as an unfavourable person–environment interaction that can take the form of harm (psychological damage from, say, loss), threat (the anticipation of harm) and challenges (demands that we feel able to cope with).

In general, if we are stressed by something, then our aim is to alter either the circumstances or our interpretation of them, in order to make them more comfortable. This is *coping*. Coping can be either and/or problem-focused or emotion-focused. For example, we might be stressed by a situation at work that we think about and decide is due to some miscommunication. We determine that we might be able to sort it out through discussion. This would be problem-focused coping. On the other hand, the problem might be insoluble in this way because one of the people involved is impossible to communicate with, whatever attempts are made. This might be because there is a huge difference in power. Then, all we can do is attempt to deal with the emotional impact of the stress – emotion-focused coping. In practice, many instances of stress are dealt with by a mixture of problem-focused and emotion-focused coping.

Stress, then, is always followed by attempts at coping. It depends on an appraisal that either something can be done about the situation or that nothing can (and so the focus must be on emotion regulation). Some of the coping strategies that people use are stable and some are not (thinking positively, for example, seems to be stable), and, interestingly, there are no female/male differences in reaction to similar stressors. The particular strategies that people use in stressful situations change from time to time. For example, problem-focused coping might work well for a while and then have to be replaced by emotion-focused coping. Most important of all, the precise form of coping strategy used (and hence a determinant of emotional reactions) depends on the stressor, the individual's personality and the area of life involved (e.g. well-being, health, social functioning, and so on). For a more extended discussion of stress and health in general, see Chapter 17.

Psychosomatics

Psychosomatics is a loose heading under which to consider the important links between emotion and physical illness. A core example concerns the relationship between emotion and pain. A common reaction to pain is fear. What does this pain mean? What are its implications? Is this the beginnings of a heart attack? Have I got lung cancer? This prompts a hyper-vigilant way of paying attention to whatever happens in the body and a keen concern to escape from it all. Then, if the pain becomes chronic, general emotional distress results and, if it continues unrelieved, one result can be anger. From quite a different perspective, pain can sometimes relieve guilt. 'I have done some wrong to these members of my family and so I am now suffering the pain I deserve.'

Emotion can be involved in any medical condition. For example, a broken leg can lead to anger and frustration, anxiety, fear, sadness, and so on. Or it may be that one's emotional condition was a precipitating factor in whatever led to the leg being broken in the first place. But the most problematic circumstance comes with the idea of psychosomatic disorders, in which the disorder is clearly physical (migraine, skin rashes, indigestion, peptic ulcers, asthma, genito-urinary conditions, and so on) but the causative factors seem to be emotional. The emotion most commonly implicated is anxiety. The extent of the emotional is hard to determine, one view being that *all* illness has an emotional component, causatively. For example, long-term stresses may well have a deleterious impact on the efficacy of the immune system and thus leave a person more vulnerable to infection.

One of the basic views of how links between emotion and physical illness might work is that severe or prolonged environmental events interact with factors internal to the person (such as particular weaknesses in one's bodily system) to produce high arousal and hence intense emotion. With such high arousal, the usual adaptive responses become less efficacious. This process can become self-perpetuating and if it continues for long enough, there can be anatomical changes with resultant illness.

Added to these ideas is the notion that if particular organ systems are affected by specific emotions, this eventually produces wear and tear on these organs. Moreover, a person's belief system might simultaneously affect their emotional reactions and their health. Furthermore, if particular emotions are either expressed or suppressed, this may also affect health. (This is in accord with the general view that it does one's health little good to constantly suppress emotional reactions.) Perhaps the most important factor here, however, is time. Changes in health are to do with long-term changes in organ systems; long-term aspects of emotion are clearly linked to personality and so this must also be taken into account when considering effects on health.

Writing and narrative

In the past few years, Jamie Pennebaker (e.g. Pennebaker & Segal, 1999) has produced a fascinating and important series of research findings on the links between health and narrative as mediated by emotion. They have significant implications not only for possible types of therapy but also for self-care. The basic assumption of this work is that to tell stories is natural and assists us in understanding, organising, remembering and integrating our thoughts. It makes the emotional effects of life's events more manageable and so improves predictability and feelings of being in control.

The generic experimental procedure is straightforward. It involves bringing participants into a laboratory and inviting them to write about a topic for 15 minutes a day for four days. They are assured that the writing will be anonymous and that they will be neither assessed nor given feedback about it. Members of the experimental group are asked to write about one or more traumatic experiences they have had and members of the control group are asked to write about something non-emotional such as the decor in their living-room. The general and much repeated finding that results from this simple procedure is that, in comparison with the control group, the experimental group has many fewer visits to medical services during the following months, their general physical health is improved, and, if they are students, their grades are higher. In general, their life changes for the better.

People from many walks of life seem to benefit from this writing exercise. It has been shown to lower the use of medication, reduce pain and improve the immune system. The precise content of the writing is unimportant, although it is important to use it to explore emotions and thoughts about emotions.

Pennebaker's preferred explanation of these results is that the conversion of emotions and the images associated with emotions into words changes the organisation of thoughts and feelings into something that is more coherent than previously. This is supported by the fact that the more positive emotion words used in the narrative and the more moderate negative emotion words, the better the outcome. This is, perhaps, all based on the perennial search for meaning and understanding that seems to be part of the human condition.

We ask questions of ourselves constantly. Why did he look at me like that? What did she mean by that? Why do I feel so uptight today? Why am I so averse to religion? Why do I become so uneasy if I am asked a direct question in public? Why don't I like to be told that I have done something incorrectly? Why doesn't anyone seem to like me? Why can't I seem to form a steady relationship?

Creating a story or narrative from the answers to such questions, particularly a story based on our own experiences, helps to organise and simplify them. This increases our understanding of the issues and makes everything more coherent. So, a sense of closure comes and we can move on. In the end, writing such emotionally based personal narratives appears to lead to increased insight, self-reflection, optimism and an increased sense of self-esteem. In other words, it provides a very adaptive coping strategy. It can be used as a form of everyday therapy that could be extremely beneficial.

▶ Emotion in the arts and in sport

The regulation of emotion always occurs in some context or other – it has to. Many of these contexts involve either leisure or work (discussed earlier in this chapter). Other than family life (which might be regarded as a mixture of leisure and work), these two together characterise what can loosely be termed culture. In other words, this is a combination of the customs and achievements and style of a particular group of people. This section, then, is to do with how, *in practice*, people regulate their emotional lives, for emotion certainly permeates all aspects of culture.

The links between emotion and the arts are obvious and yet quite difficult to understand. For example, think of your emotional reactions when you read a novel, go to a play or watch some modern dance. You might react emotionally to the work itself, and to the performance in the case of the play or the dance, or to the particular characters in the novel or the performers on the stage, or to the emotions that they are apparently experiencing. Art can be abstract and yet we still react emotionally to it. Art can represent very negative emotions (as in the case of a tragedy, for example) and yet overall we might react positively to it, as a work of art.

In fiction, emotions are portrayed, described and analysed through the characters, but the reader's emotion is also played upon through the manipulation of events. Startling events occur and characters react emotionally and then do other things that regulate their own emotions in some or other way. So the reader comes to have his or her own emotion regulation practices endorsed or negated, or new possibilities suggested. Also, however, for the reader, engaging with a work of fiction might well represent a way of emotion regulation, a way of escaping from the emotional turmoil of daily life. It barely matters what the fiction is – heart-rending romance, swashbuckling adventure, spell-binding historical intrigue – but the reader is always invited to suspend disbelief (in the fictitious events) and to suspend reality. Then, one can identify with larger-than-life heroes whose experiences abound with emotional satisfaction.

In fact, it is this identification that is at the core of our responses to fiction and our use of fiction to regulate our own emotional lives. If we can find no way of identifying with the characters, then the fiction falls curiously flat; it seems lifeless. If we can identify and then become absorbed in the fictitious lives, the emotional effects of what we have read can linger for some time, either positively or negatively. We can be emotionally uplifted by fiction or we can be depressed for days.

In passing, it is interesting to note here a problem which has beset philosophers for some time. When we are made emotional by fiction, what is it exactly that we are made emotional about? We know that a work of fiction is fiction and we know that what is happening to the characters is fictitious, so why do we still react emotionally? We don't actually believe in the existence of fictitious characters and yet we have emotions for them. This is sometimes termed the paradox of fiction.

Perhaps even more problematic in this regard is our emotional reaction to televised events. We react emotionally to fictitious events on television, but somehow keep them at a distance because we know that they are on the flat screen. What about when the events are emotionally uplifting or harrowing and come from scenes in real life? What, then, are our emotional reactions? Do we learn to limit these reactions and hence generalise from this to daily life? In other words, do we become habituated emotionally by the overexposure that comes through television?

To take another example of emotion regulation through the arts, music has much of its effect through emotion. Simply watch a crowd at a classical concert or a rock concert or even a head-banging crowd at a rave and the emotional effect of music is obvious. But, again, how does it work? From time to time, many of us will play music to fit in with our mood or to change our mood, or whatever, but how does this work? Do particular types of rhythm or speed or rising tones have particular emotional effects? Sometimes, a piece of music will produce a chill down the spine, a physical shiver. This seems a very basic, primitive sort of reaction. What is this tapping into? Is this bringing up some basic evolutionary process, such as a mixture of warmth and coldness or approach and withdrawal or rejection?

Much as is the case with music, emotional reactions to drama are obvious – drama depends on them. There are two aspects to this, however: the emotional reactions of the audience and the emotional involvements of the actors. With respect to audience emotional reactions, there is a similar problem to that with literature – we *know* that what we are observing is not real – they are only actors, after all, and it is only a play – and yet we become emotionally captured by what happens to the characters. It even happens in opera, in which the stories tend to be so simple as to be comedic.

The interesting question about actors' experience of emotion, which might also apply to acting-like situations (teaching, selling, running a meeting, and so on), concerns the extent to which the actor actually experiences (or should experience) the emotions being portrayed or projected. It could be that there should be emotional involvement, or emotional detachment or some sort of self-expression (with the character disappearing behind the actor). This type of analysis is carried out by Konin (1995). In each of these cases, the actor has to be both involved with and not involved with the emotionality of the character being portrayed.

The result is an extraordinarily sophisticated type of emotional regulation, involving four levels simultaneously. There is: (1) the private person with private emotions; (2) the actor with the emotion involved in the acting; (3) an inner model of the play with its intended emotion; and (4) the actual character as performed with the attendant emotions. This is very complex and must occasionally go very wrong, for example, confusing the actor's 'real' life with the character's. Konin suggests that these complexities lead to an overriding emotional reaction that is based on challenge. So the performance itself becomes a source of emotional reaction. It is interesting to speculate about the extent to which this very intricate type of emotional regulation occurs in our daily lives in circumstances in which we are required to project an image of some kind, either at work or even at home.

Whatever is going on with respect to our emotional reactions to art, almost certainly some type of empathy is involved, either with characters or performers or even with a piece of work itself. So, for example, it is possible to 'feel into' a work of art on canvas and to feel some type of empathy for what is being portrayed. All this is enhanced or inhibited by whatever is important to the person at the time, whether this is a social role or a particular way of looking at the world. This type of influence on our reactions changes from time to time and from culture to culture. Our reactions also depend on how close or how distant we allow ourselves to be from the work of art in question.

Sport

Although sport is about performance, it is obvious that what makes the performance is the emotional reactions to it on the part of both participants and observers. Almost any emotion can impede sporting performance. Go to play any sport while in the grip of some or other emotion (anxiety, anger, jealousy, guilt, even an overabundance of joy or elation) and your performance is likely to suffer. On the other hand, a moderate level of anxiety and perhaps a general background state of happiness are likely to enhance sporting performance.

From the point of view of the spectator, although at an intellectual level it is possible to appreciate a fine sporting performance, it is the emotions that are generated that make what is observed come alive. To identify with a team and support it can evoke enormous highs and lows of emotion. To identify with an individual athlete and watch a triumphant performance can uplift the spirit.

Ultimately sport is about winning or losing, doing well or doing badly, and the value judgements associated with this inevitably lead to positive or negative emotional reactions. There are some very straightforward patterns that arise emotionally. Winners are likely to feel positive – it is so obvious as to almost go without saying. Losers, by contrast, might feel a mixture of surprise, anger, sadness, or even fear (of never regaining the ascendancy). If one loses a sporting encounter and attributes this to internal causes ('it was my fault because . . .'), the result is likely to be burgeoning depression. If these internal causes are seen as uncontrollable, an inevitable part of simply being the person, the likely result is shame. If the result is externally attributable ('I lost because the weather was so bad, the equipment was faulty, I'd eaten something that disagreed with me . . .'), then the result will be much less negative. The general point here is that the intense emotional investment that there is in sport makes the experience powerful.

Talk to a jogger or runner about why they run and one point that always comes up is that it makes them feel good to have been for a run (or it might be a swim, an aerobics class, or whatever). Why does exercise make people feel good? Why does too much or too intense exercise sometimes lead to negative emotional reactions? There are a number of possible reasons for exercise leading to emotional outcomes. It could be, for example, because we make positive attributions about having exercised – we are doing ourselves some good, we've lost some weight, we are strengthening our heart, and so on.

Also involved might be the straightforward links that come from conditioning. For example, a person might have conditioned links formed between exercise, looking good and feeling a heightened sense of self-efficacy. This effect (and others) in exercise and sport comes about through a mixture of the psychological and the physiological.

The emotional involvement in spectator sport is a huge and under-researched topic. It is clear that sport generates considerable arousal in spectators. While this might be entirely positive to begin with, it can also turn in more negative directions, both emotionally and behaviourally. For example, the anger generated in parents watching their children play rugby or soccer can be palpable and can even turn to violence towards other parents, the referee or in some cases their own child. Furthermore, the anger-fuelled aggression at soccer matches, particularly in the United Kingdom, is very well documented, if not as well understood. This capacity for arousal to spill over into violence is not restricted to soccer but from time to time can be seen in the spectators of many types of sporting encounter.

In the end, it is hard to conceive of sport, whether as a performer or as a spectator, without emotion being integrally involved. In fact, the sight of an apparently emotionless tennis player or the soccer player who doesn't show jubilation at success is slightly unnerving. Our expectations are for emotional reactions both within sport and to sport.

▶ **Summary**

- The detection of lies is based on the use of the polygraph, which in turn is based on the idea that when we attempt to control our emotional expressions and behaviour, we might give ourselves away psycho-physiologically. For many reasons, including huge individual differences in reactivity, the polygraph is not foolproof.

- Emotional intelligence (EI) is made up of the ability to judge emotion, to express emotion, to make use of emotional information and then regulate emotion. There are large individual differences in EI.

- There are many ways to regulate emotion, depending on altering the situation, attention, appraisals and responses.

- Emotion regulation develops throughout the lifespan but derives largely from childhood, particularly the early attachment relationship.

- Traditionally, emotion in the workplace was contrasted with rationality. It is now known to be highly relevant to success, impacting on such things as leadership style.

- Emotion is linked to health, often through stress and coping, the latter either being problem-focused or emotion-focused.

- There are huge links between emotion and pain and emotion is involved in all medical conditions, either as part of their cause or as a result.

- There are special links between emotion and writing. Writing about emotional events can alleviate their effects and can even affect the immune system.

- Emotion is involved across all of the arts – literature, drama, music, dance, painting, etc. It is involved both from the perspective of the artist and the observer.

- Emotion in art probably works through some kind of empathy and has intriguing problems associated with it. For example, why do we feel emotional about something that we know is not 'real'?

- Emotion is an integral part of sport, in both the participant and the spectator.

▶ **Questions and possibilities**

- What emotion regulation techniques do you use at home and at work? Do they differ in the two situations? How might you improve them?

- How good are you at detecting other people lying or in some other way attempting to dissemble about their emotions? How do you do it? How confident are you?

- What coping strategies do you typically use at home and at work? Do you prefer to be problem-focused or emotion-focused? Which do you think is the better?

- Have any of your family had psychosomatic disorders? What is it about their emotional experiences that might have brought them about? What other instances can you think of in which emotion and health are linked?

- Try writing for 20 minutes or so about some negative emotional experiences that you have had recently. Do this for 20 minutes on four successive days. Then observe what effects this might have on you throughout the next few days and weeks. How do you think such effects might be working?

- Do you have emotional reactions to art? What brings them about? Are your experiences different with regard to different types of art? What is your answer to the question of how we experience what seem to be genuine emotional reactions to things that we know to be unreal?

- What is more important in reacting to art, the emotions or knowledge about the art and artist?

- If you play an instrument or have acted or danced, etc., has doing so evoked emotional reactions in you? What are they? How do they come about? When you watch other people doing these things, are the same sorts of emotion aroused in you?

- What emotions have you experienced when playing sport, or watching sport, or watching your relatives or friends play sport? Have you had emotional experiences that interfere with your sport? Do you derive emotional experiences from sport?

■ Make a list of the occasions when you have felt emotionally high during or after playing sport and a list of occasions when you have felt down. What are the essential differences between the occasions?

CHAPTER FOUR

Motivational life

Hunger, thirst and sex

Scenes from life

You have just finished a satisfying breakfast and feel reasonably full and comfortable. The pleasant aftertaste of coffee lingers on. You have plenty of time and it is a pleasant day, so you decide to walk to work. Twenty minutes along the way you pass a bakery and the smell of fresh bread and cakes fills the air. You start to salivate and instantly feel that you could do wonders with a custard square. At one level you know that you are full and at another you feel hungry. What has happened? How can you feel hungry and not hungry at the same time?

Imagine a young woman who is overweight. At least she is overweight as she sees it; she is definitely not comfortable whenever she looks in the mirror. She worries about whether or not she will continue to fit into the particular clothes size that she normally wears. She worries about what she looks like from behind or from the side and can never quite see enough in the mirror or never get what she considers to be an honest answer from anyone.

So she diets, she restricts her food intake severely and, sure enough, she begins to lose weight. But it is very difficult. Her thoughts constantly turn to food or even to drink. Thoughts of food interrupt her work. She becomes irritable and scratchy, snapping at her friends and colleagues and then instantly regretting it. She finds herself buying magazines about food and taking pleasure from reading recipe books. She stares at food advertisements on the television. In general, her life becomes dominated by the thought of food, its preparation and particularly by whether or not she should eat it and how often and when and where. Why is this happening? Why has food and eating and all that surrounds it taken over her way of life?

Imagine that you are a student, writing an essay for biological sciences. It is a hard but interesting topic on evolution in the modern world from a sociobiological perspective. It exercises you but you work hard at it and successfully produce the 2,000 words required. You print it out and give it to your flat-mate to read over to see that it makes sense and to point out any obvious grammatical errors.

After a few minutes your flat-mate starts giggling and then snorts with laughter. He points out that you have consistently used the word 'orgasm' when you clearly meant to use the word 'organism'. Why might you have done this? How could you have done that? Clearly, you know both words and the difference between them, so what happened did so unconsciously.

You have to write a report at work. It is about the financial implications of some new developments that are going to take place and, for you, it is an incredibly boring topic. But it has to be done. You have been putting it off for days, but now you surround yourself with necessary papers and determine that you won't look up until it is done. After an hour or so, you have to stop. Your head is aching and the muscles in your neck and shoulders have stiffened into knots. You break for 10 minutes and then get back to the report. After another hour or so, you more or less finish a first draft but rather than feeling a sense of satisfaction, you feel drained, tired and restless. Your headache is worse and your shoulder muscles have become one big knot. Time to go home.

At home, things feel no better and you cannot face getting yourself any food. So you make a cup of tea and think that you will try to settle your mind (and body) by reading a little more of a half-read novel that you have been enjoying. More than an hour later, you wonder where the time has gone and how easily you have become absorbed. Your headache has passed and your shoulder muscles feel considerably freer. What makes the two types of reading that you have been doing so different? Why is one absorbing and the other not?

Motivation is basic to everything that we do. We need motivation to get started on anything, from eating to working, from canoodling to painting a picture, from playing a musical instrument to playing a sport. And once we have started something, we need the other end of motivation to stop doing it otherwise we might go on doing it forever and never start anything else. In fact, some people do seem to become obsessed with doing a few things over and over at the expense of the remainder of their lives. This is an example of when a mixture of motivation and emotion has gone wrong in some way.

We spend a great deal of our lives reflecting on why we or other people do what they do? Why did she say that? Why didn't he look at me this morning?

Why was I so snappy with my parents when I didn't mean to be? Why do I keep putting off writing that thank you letter or digging the garden or phoning my friend?

Thinking about motivation is thinking about what gives behaviour its purpose and its direction. It is also about what sustains us in doing whatever we might be doing. Essentially, motivation is about goals, setting them, keeping them, dropping them and dealing with them when they conflict. So, like emotion, motivation provides the energy of life.

▶ Some basic definitions

As with various areas in psychology, there are a number of basic words to do with motivation that are used commonly and sometimes confusedly. It is important to distinguish between them:

- *Needs* are deficiencies in whatever we require for survival, the most fundamental being oxygen, closely followed by food and drink. If oxygen is in short supply, we are impelled to do something about it, fast. In an everyday sense, of course, the word need is used more loosely, to mean something that we feel is pressuring us. I *need* to rest, I *need* to see my mother, I *need* to go to work early today.

- *Drives* are either the state of energy that goes with needs (physiological drives) or derived states of (psychological) energy that are learned (say, the drive for money) rather than built in (say, the drive/need for food). In everyday usage, again one can see the impulsion involved. I was *driven* to do that means that I had little choice.

- *Motives* are the background conditions that might lead to energy being channelled in particular ways. So, my motive might be to be successful in life, for example. This would have all manner of implications for what I would do, the decisions I would make, and so on. In other words, it would channel my energies in a very different direction than if my motive were, say, to be liked by everybody.

- *Goals* are whatever we are striving to achieve or accomplish, from having something to eat, to buying another car, to being a better person. They can vary from short to medium to long term, from writing the next word, to getting through the day without having a cigarette, to wanting to be still alive at 90.

- *Desires* are strong feelings of wanting or wishing or craving and *wishes* are expressions of desires or hopes. Although used often in everyday life, these two words are not much used by psychologists. Because they refer to subjective states of feeling, they are harder to pin down objectively.

- *Instinct* is the most difficult of the motivation words to define. At the everyday level it is used often. For example, the sports commentator might say, 'He made that pass instinctively.' This means that the pass was made easily, automatically, with great skill and with a seemingly intuitive knowledge of the state of the game. However, at a technical level the word refers to behaviours that are built in, always appear in a similar form and are specific to a species. So, a spider builds a web instinctively and a bird's mating display might be instinctive. It is unlikely, though, that there is any equivalent instinctive behaviour in human beings. Some people might argue that a mother's reaction to her newly born child is instinctive, but certainly not all mothers react in the same way and even when they do, they express it in myriad forms. In general, instinct has been found to be a not very useful construct in giving accounts of the 'why' of behaviour.

The need for oxygen apart, the basic necessities of life seem to be food, drink and sex, although not always in that order. Our requirements depend on our state of deprivation.

▶ Hunger

We need to eat to live and for most people the feeling of hunger is a regular and very familiar occurrence. But the mechanisms that control hunger are a very complex mixture of the physiological and the psychological. There is the intake of necessary energy in the form of calories and there are fat deposits and general metabolic rate. There are also external, psychologically mediated factors such as the sight or the smell of a favourite food. This might well tempt us to eat even though we have recently eaten.

The complexities of the mechanisms that control eating and satiety (the cessation of eating – we do need a mechanism to stop us eating as well as one that prompts us to eat) are not surprising. We need a wide variety of foods to survive and so must have a mechanism that allows choice to be made, that allows food preferences to develop usefully. We need a system that automatically turns us away from poisonous foods and that allows us to follow a balanced diet.

To take an obvious example of built-in *food preferences*, it is built in to most people to prefer sweet- to bitter-tasting substances. This is adaptive. Most poisonous substances are bitter and we reject such substances by spitting them out and registering disgust (a primary emotion). By contrast, generally, sweet things contain more calories and thus have a higher food/energy value than bitter things. In this sense, they are better for us.

This difference also provides an interesting example of how modern culture can clash with the built-in exigencies of evolution. Food manufacturers have capitalised on our preferences for sweet things and advertise in such a way as to constantly tempt. Unless we guard against it, we are thus in the position of easily eating far more sweet stuff than is good for us, the results being tooth decay, obesity, increased risk of heart disease, and so on. In one sense this all follows from the exploitation of an inherited taste preference which was (and potentially still is) of adaptive, evolutionary value.

Not all food preferences are built in. Our bodily system is flexible enough that some preferences can be acquired through learning. For example, first tastes of coffee or alcohol or even yogurt or blue cheese are frequently not much enjoyed. But they can be rapidly acquired and last throughout life. Similarly, if on the first occasion you taste, say, a peanut butter sandwich, something independently occurs to make you nauseous, then there is a high likelihood that you will have acquired an instant aversion to peanut butter sandwiches.

Internal and external influences

Bodily control of eating occurs both in the central nervous system and the peripheral nervous system. There are centres in the hypothalamus that determine the starting and finishing of eating. However, there are also peripheral mechanisms involved. The *glucostatic* theory suggests that the level of blood sugar is important and the *lipostatic* theory suggests that the amount of fat in the body is crucial. *Set-point* theory has it that the number of fat cells in the body is set either genetically or very early in life and remains constant. So, a person with a higher set point has more fat cells and will tend to eat more than a person with a lower set point. This person will find it relatively hard to diet or to lose weight.

Similarly, there are peripheral mechanisms that help us to stop eating once we have started. Sheer stomach distension is the most obvious example. We feel less like eating if our stomach is full than if it is empty. Feedback from the full stomach goes directly to a nucleus in the hypothalamus, a nucleus that is known to be involved in the cessation of eating.

Bodily control is not enough to account for why we eat and why we stop eating. External factors also come into play, stimuli from the environment that we become aware of through our sense organs. So, the sight and smell and taste of food influence whether or not we feel like eating and how much we eat. Also involved are such things as the time of day, the company we are in and whether or not we are stressed or anxious. We tend to eat more in company than when alone and most people tend to eat less when highly anxious than not, although some people eat far more then.

As Stanley Schachter (1964) showed many years ago, our eating is under the control of a mixture of internal physiological cues and our interpretations of external cues. The balance between the importance of these cues varies from person to person. So, some people are more under external control for their eating and others more under internal control. It is never the extreme; both sets of cues are always involved but the balance varies. The 'externals' are more likely to be overweight or constantly dieting than the 'internals'.

Schachter demonstrated this in many ways. For example, he found that people who are overweight are more likely to overcome the effects of jet-lag than those of normal weight – they simply find it easier to eat at the same time of day as everyone around them. Or, counter-intuitively, he found that overweight Jews are *more* likely to stick to a fast day than Jews of normal weight. No doubt, this finding would extend to non-Jewish people as well.

Eating disorders

In Western society, currently, slim is beautiful, although there is a little evidence that this might be changing and the more robust look of 30 years ago is beginning to be in favour once more. However, the pressures of society (fashion, television, the corporate world, etc.) have been huge for people (mainly, but not solely, women) to stay slim or to become slim.

Reasons for being overweight (however this is defined – usually by life assurance companies dealing with actuarial risks to life) are genetic or because of overeating, or both. Increased calories will lead to increased weight, but two people taking in the same amount of calories may well gain weight at different rates, or one might gain and the other not. We cannot control our personal genetics so the only possibility is to control how much we eat and how much we exercise – that is, the balance between calories in and calories out. And the problem for most overweight people is that they are more under external control and they tend to eat more when experiencing any sort of increased emotional arousal.

People vary enormously with respect to how restrained their eating is. Some constantly restrict their intake and others never do; most of us fall somewhere between these extremes. There is one huge irony involved in severe food restriction or dieting. People who train themselves to ignore feeling hungry or feeling that they want to eat also tend not to be able to recognise their feelings of being full. So they tend to eat a great deal once they start. Thus severe dieting often leads to an *increase* in weight. For example, the person who manages to eat nothing all day will often then eat more in the evening than she (it is usually 'she') would have, had she eaten moderately throughout the day.

In the extreme, when eating goes wrong, the disorders of *anorexia nervosa* and *bulimia* can develop. There are many reasons for this, some of them stemming from patterns that are laid down in early childhood, from family background, from personality, and so on. These disorders can be extreme and life-threatening and those who suffer from them need a great deal of help to control or overcome them. It is not, as some people think, a matter of simply starting to eat or starting to eat sensibly, in other words, of 'pulling their socks up'. It is far more complex than this.

How to lose weight

Bear in mind that one of those unpleasant rules of life is that it is easier to put weight back on than it is to lose it. This means that if you want to lose enough weight to alter your body shape, then you will have to make a *permanent* change in your life-style. And this can be expensive. Eating less and running on the spot are probably not enough. A balanced, restricted diet and the membership of a gym or equipment to use at home or even running shoes can cost a great deal. So, if you start, start seriously.

It is important to put controls in place. For example, if your downfall is dairy food, then don't have any in the house. If you live with other people, either family or flat-mates, then you might have to enlist their aid in this. Or, to take another example, don't go to the supermarket when you have not eaten all day. Go soon after you have eaten and you will be less tempted to buy items that you 'should' not. Also, the type of food we eat is important to consider. How hungry we feel depends on what we eat as well as on how much we eat. So, it is better to eat those types of foods that are less easily changed to fat, for example.

Cutting down intake is not enough, however. We have to use up more calories than we take in and it helps in doing this to establish an exercise programme. Here there is another irony. At first, restricting intake seems easier than exercising, if you are used to doing neither. But rapidly, exercising becomes easier than restriction. The first meal is easier to miss than it is to take the first run, but the tenth meal is harder to miss than it is to take the tenth run.

Finally, one of the most important points to realise in attempting to lose weight successfully is to be reasonable. If you go to extremes, if you try to restrict and exercise too much and too fast, the chances are that you will fail. You'll binge and make matters worse. And this type of lack of success is very dispiriting; you might even turn to food as a source of comfort!

It is important to make reasonable changes to one's habits, one's typical way of being around food. So, for example, it might be important to lay down a rule *never* to eat between meals, and to only eat at certain places at certain times and never at others (in front of the television, for instance), and never to miss a meal entirely. It is only through approaching weight loss in a reasonable way that you will be likely to succeed. It is possible to make permanent changes to one's eating and exercise habits but to attempt to do so in an unreasonable way is likely to end in failure.

▶ Thirst

Water, like food and oxygen, is necessary to survival. In fact, we would die sooner through a lack of water than a lack of food. Again, then, like hunger, thirst is a basic, built-in need that is based on a deficit. Water is not something that we see in the environment that suddenly has great allure and draws us towards it. It is something that we are primarily impelled from within to seek if we have been without it for some time.

Again, like hunger, thirst depends on a mixture of changes that occur inside the body and events in the world at large that we learn to interpret in particular ways. So, if we have been without liquids for some time, if we have been eating foods (like salt) that absorb liquids, if we have been working hard in the heat and so losing bodily moisture, if we have been losing blood, and so on, then we will feel thirsty and seek some liquid. As most of us have experienced from time to time, however, there is far more to thirst and drinking than this. For a multitude of social reasons we tend to take in far more liquids than we need, usually in the form of alcohol or mild stimulants such as coffee or tea or soft drinks (that might also be sugar-filled).

At the bodily level, thirst comes about following the depletion of water both inside and outside the cells of the body – *the double-depletion* view. A lack of water leads to reduced volume of water in the body in general and an increase in the concentration of water in the body cells. If laboratory rats (such studies are not done with humans, for obvious reasons) are deprived of water and then given water either within their body cells or outside their body cells, it is clear from the amount that they then drink that intra-cellular fluid is more important than extra-cellular fluid.

Just as with food intake, we need a mechanism to stop us from drinking once we have started. There seem to be three such mechanisms, centred in the mouth, the stomach and the cells, respectively. Of relevance are numbers of laps and swallows in the mouth, the distension of the stomach and an inhibitory mechanism from the cells.

Again, just as with hunger, thirst also depends on our interpretation of various environmental factors such as how long it is since we last drank, the time of day, the taste of the liquid and even our perception of how much is available. Interestingly, taste is very important to liquid intake. At low concentrations, any of the four major tastes (sweet, sour, bitter and salt) improves the palatability of water. When the concentrations rise, then sweet predominates, something known only too well by the manufacturers of soft drinks.

Alcoholism

Ironically, it is the depressing effect of alcohol that makes it so enjoyable. It is a cortical depressant and so depresses those parts of the brain that control judgement and inhibition. With judgement impaired and inhibitions (particularly social inhibitions) reduced, we are free to do all manner of things that we normally would not, even though the temptation is there. Moreover, at a physiological level, alcohol is *anxiolytic*, that is, it helps to reduce anxiety. It is no wonder that people tend to enjoy alcohol (even though most of us do not like the first taste of it – the taste is acquired) and then some people become addicted to it.

We all have urges, some of them not regarded as socially appropriate and so they are often inhibited. Alcohol tends to release us from such inhibitions, allowing us to be more aggressive, more extraverted, to eat more and, of course, to go on drinking even more. As well as releasing our inhibitions, alcohol also acts as a relaxant, slowing us down physically, even though it might not seem so to do. Thus, for example, we tend to drive faster but react more slowly after drinking alcohol. Alcohol also affects memory, making it difficult to remember things that happen or that we learn when under its influence. Memory and retrieval of memory are partly dependent on our physical and psychological state at the time (see Chapter 13).

In small amounts, it is clear that alcohol can be a social lubricant, but in larger amounts it is enormously costly to society in many ways, from deaths on the road to the social and economic costs of alcohol-related diseases and alcohol-related behaviour. In the extreme, when addiction occurs, this is alcoholism, the causes of which range from early childhood learning and opportunity to the possibility of an alcoholic personality. There is certainly strong evidence that some people are more prone to the effects of alcohol than others, Asians, for example, are affected far more readily than Caucasians; this comes from an in-built physiological difference.

Moral judgements made about alcohol consumption in society point to the confusion that exists. These range from the idea of total prohibition through to there being no laws at all about alcohol consumption. Alcohol is an integral part of our society with enormous economic interests in it. And there are very few people who do not drink alcohol at some time or another. From a motivational point of view, this is an example of one of our basic needs becoming distorted and in some cases out of control. Of course, though, there are also enormous costs (economic and social) of distorted eating behaviour (under-eating or over-eating) and, as will be seen shortly, distorted sexual behaviour. In fact, when taken to the extreme, the results of any human motive can become harmful to the individual or to society.

▶ Sex

The urgency that sometimes attends sex might make it appear to be necessary for survival but it is not necessary in the same way that food and water are. It is necessary for the survival of the species but not for the individual. Like hunger and thirst, sex has both internal and external mechanisms of control but it is not based on deficit or a basic bodily need of the individual. Sex is also different from hunger and thirst in that it frequently involves more than one person, of necessity. However, sex is usually regarded, with hunger and thirst, as one of the three basic drives.

Sexual motivation is based on a mixture of hormones and beliefs about matters such as attractiveness, romance, moral strictures, and so on. This is, of course, at the human level. Animals below the human level are not much dependent on romance and morality. Androgens (testosterone, from the testes and the adrenal cortex) and oestrogens (oestradiol from the ovaries and the adrenal cortex) are the sex hormones. They appear in both sexes but the androgens mainly in males and the oestrogens mainly in females. The hypothalamus and the pituitary gland are concerned with the release of these hormones into the blood-stream. (In passing, it is worth remembering that the hypothalamus is involved in hunger, thirst and sex as well as being implicated in emotion.)

The human sexual response follows a relatively unvarying pattern. It is a four-stage process.

1 Excitation – increased blood flow to the sex organs after the sex hormones have been released.

2 A plateau – when nothing much changes.

3 Orgasm – rapid breathing, rhythmic pelvic movements (and bodily pleasure).

4 Resolution – the body returns to its pre-excitatory state, something that happens immediately for males whereas for some females does not occur until after the experience of multiple orgasms.

Beliefs and values

Putting the *form* of the human sexual response to one side, sexual motivation in humans seems to be largely dependent on beliefs that are shaped by society, many of them being established early in life. These tend to be in the form of *scripts* about sex that are based on love, romance and fantasies. These centre around masturbation to begin with and then develop through dating, necking, petting, and so on, whether they are heterosexual or homosexual. Sex might be grounded in hormones for its impetus but for its precise form we need the sexual scripts that come from society.

One of the more interesting aspects of sex comes from the typical male/female differences in sexual desire. In women it is less dependent on hormones than it is in men. In other words, men are sexually driven more by their bodily reactions and women more by their social reactions or beliefs. Whether one can conclude from this that women are slightly more advanced than men in an evolutionary sense is a matter to conjure with. And then there is the question of sexual orientation, the morality (and laws) surrounding which have changed dramatically during the past few decades. This has usually been in the form of legalising homosexuality and ensuring that discrimination does not occur on the basis of either gender or sexual orientation. Of course, to enshrine this in the law is quite different from ensuring that it never occurs; this is far more difficult to achieve.

Sexual extremes

Just as with hunger and thirst or eating and drinking, the sexual drive and sexual behaviour can become dysfunctional. Such dysfunction might take the form of becoming problematic for the individual in that it is unsatisfactory or impossible in what might be regarded as the 'standard' or normal ways. This is to be descriptive. But the topic of sexual dysfunction frequently also becomes highly emotive. It is imbued with strong value judgements and shades into the so-called perversions. It includes many practices or behaviours that some people regard as distasteful (but that others clearly enjoy) and in the extreme is seen as immoral and even illegal and punishable.

As with so many aspects of human behaviour about which value judgements are made, the more extreme forms of sexual behaviour depend on some or other idea of normality. As is discussed in Chapter 16, the definition of normality and abnormality is no easy matter. In various societies at various times, for example, paedophilia, incest and rape have been regarded as acceptable and heterosexual behaviour has been considered normal and acceptable only within limits. To take typical Western society at present, in most countries homosexual behaviour is not illegal (although some people would regard it as abnormal), although a few years ago it was illegal. Heterosexual behaviour is not permitted under particular prescribed ages.

Even for the most free-thinking person it is hard to consider paedophilia and rape dispassionately. The value judgements are almost part of the very concepts in much the same way that it is difficult for a person who knows about World War II not to see a swastika unemotionally or to hear the name Hitler without having a negative reaction. What about voyeurism and sodomy, sadism and masochism? What do you think of people whose sexual gratification can only come through their own pain or the pain of others? Is it even possible to think about prostitution without making a value judgement about it, positively or negatively?

These difficulties, based as they are on the moral order of societies, point to the fact that sex is not simply a matter of a biologically based urge. It is also highly dependent on learning and cultural influences. The particular settings in which sexual practices take place and develop and the moral order that surrounds them have very strong influences. To put it at its simplest, merely because children are procreated by heterosexual behaviour does not mean that this is the only 'right' sort of sexual behaviour. In the extreme, the value judgements that tend to envelop all considerations of sex are even made with respect to whether or not some or other sexual behaviour should be considered 'normal' or not.

To move into some of the details of sexual dysfunction, motivation is clearly involved on some occasions – for example, frigidity or orgasms that go awry in some way in women, and impotence, on the one hand, or premature ejaculation, on the other, in men. Here it is easy to see that there could be either bodily factors or sociocultural influences involved.

To take an obvious example, men's capability to have an erection is likely to decrease with advancing years, hence the widespread use of drugs such as Viagra. This is not a matter of waning desire (although desire may indeed wane) but simply a change in a bodily mechanism that can be temporarily reversed by the judicious use of drugs. On the other hand, frigidity or the apparent impossibility of becoming sexually aroused in a woman might have nothing to do directly with bodily function. Rather, it may be based on unfortunate previous sexual encounters, a matter of learning.

With other types of sexual dysfunction or abnormality, motivation is involved in a different way. Take, for example, voyeurism (sexual fulfilment coming from watching others engage in sexual behaviour), fetishism (sexual fulfilment being based on some non-sexual object), or sado-masochism (sexual fulfilment being based on inflicting pain either on oneself or on others). The motivational reasons for the development of such behaviours could include almost anything and are dependent on the details of the precise experiences that the individual might have had. How such behaviours are regarded varies from place to place and time to time and depends somewhat on their extent. Regarded as foibles, each of them has its place in the sex industry, but taken to extremes they become illegal.

Considering the extremes, possibly the most extreme sexual behaviour is rape, the forcing of sexual attentions on another person. It is not only male to female, but may be male to male or female to female and in some cases even female to male. But most rape is of females by males and is a matter of massive everyday concern to women. As with murder, the majority of rapes are carried out by someone known to the woman.

Again, the motivation involved in rape can be very complex and based on a wide variety of possibilities. However, it seems that it almost always involves power (see Chapter 5). The following are all factors in rape: anger; contempt; sadism; a man thinking that it is his 'right'; a man believing that in reality the woman wants the sexual encounter just as much as he does, and so on. The place of motivation in rape is frequently a matter that concerns the legal process. It is notoriously difficult to find out whether or not rape has occurred and even to define it in the first place (where does it begin and end?). It becomes even more difficult to establish a person's motivation for rape. It is not simply a matter that a person may lie or be mistaken but may genuinely be unaware of their motivation for rape (or, indeed, for anything else) (again, see Chapter 5 for a discussion of unconscious motivation).

Finally, there is the question of homosexuality which many people would even take objection to finding in a section entitled *Sexual extremes*. Perhaps the most important thing to say about homosexuality is that it is not a matter of choice or of being self-indulgent or of, in some way, going astray, any more than hetero-sexuality is. Nor, in spite of a modern myth held particularly among homophobic men, are homosexuals more or less promiscuous than heterosexuals. In fact, sexual orientation is an interesting subject in its own right.

Sexual orientation is not one thing or the other – we are not either simply male or simply female – and nor is it based entirely on genetic make-up or on our experiences. We all have both male and female or female and male characteristics, but in varying degree or amount. The range goes from people who are exclusively heterosexual to those who are exclusively homosexual, with most people occupy-ing a mixed territory in between. It is also surprising to learn of the number of people who appear to be exclusively heterosexual who have had some or other homosexual experience at some point in their lives, even if as children.

Sexual orientation is a little like handedness. Most people are right-handed, some 10 per cent are left-handed and some are ambidextrous, all of these to varying degrees. Thus it is with sexual orientation; most people are heterosexual, some are homosexual and some are bi-sexual. It is, perhaps, worth pointing out that the fact that everyone has his or her own mixture of male and female characteristics is not just a matter of sexual proclivity but also is part of what might be regarded as 'typical' male or female behaviour or style.

▶ Addiction

Discussion of the more extreme forms of eating, drinking and sexual behaviour prompts thoughts about addiction. In some ways, addiction might be said to represent one of the most powerful forms that can be taken by motivation in that it is characterised by a craving, an extreme desire.

The term addiction is used in two ways. More formally, it tends to be restricted to dependence on drugs, including psychoactive drugs such as heroin or cocaine, and also drugs such as alcohol and nicotine. These are drugs on which the body becomes dependent, in which a clear physiological mechanism is involved. However, at a psychological level, it is also possible to become addicted to almost anything. Certainly, the craving that some people have to gamble or to amass money, that others have to exercise, that some have to follow their sexual predilections and that others have to collect stamps look very much like addicted behaviour.

A problem with what might be termed psychological addiction is the extent to which physiological mechanisms are involved. On the one hand, the bodily dependence that develops on, say, morphine or alcohol can be assessed. On the other hand, there must be a bodily involvement in gambling or in collecting stamps, in that there is a bodily substrate to everything that we do, but it is less obvious.

For behaviour to be referred to as an addiction, it needs to be compulsive and the craving that goes with it also needs to be compulsive. So, merely to be highly interested in something is not to be addicted, whether it is in stamp-collecting or social drinking. But either can become addictive, if the collecting or the drinking *have* to occur for the person to be (briefly) satisfied.

Although any compulsive craving can alter the course of a person's life, the addiction that is involved in psychoactive drugs is more extreme. This can become overwhelming and life-threatening. There are three reasons for this:

1 Psychoactive drugs work directly on the brain mechanisms of reward, setting them off in a super-active way. This, in turn, leads to powerful memories of the pleasure involved.

2 If the person stops taking such a drug, the lack of activity in the reward centres and the 'drug-opposite' bodily processes that start up lead to some extremely unpleasant withdrawal symptoms.

3 Such drugs cause permanent changes in the reward systems so that even if the person has managed to go through the horrors of withdrawal, there will remain some level of craving. The relevant brain structures have become sensitised and so relapse remains a possibility.

Clearly, these physical extremes are not involved if one gives up stamp-collecting or taking six spoons of sugar in one's tea, having collected stamps and taken sugar in tea compulsively for years. But it is nevertheless possible to experience similar effects to that of giving up a psychoactive drug, albeit in more minor form.

In passing, in this context, the question might be asked – why is it so difficult for many people to give up smoking? It is not that nicotine is a psychoactive drug, like heroin, nor can one become quite as dependent on it as is possible with alcohol, nor does it stay in the system as long after ceasing to smoke and nor are the withdrawal symptoms so marked. The problem is association. For many people, smoking becomes associated with so many other activities that the moment one of these activities is engaged in, it acts as a sort of prompt to light up. So, for months or even years after giving up, an infrequently experienced situation, even one experienced vicariously in a movie, might create the old urge.

▶ Homeostasis

A final word in this chapter on the basic motives or needs or drives is to do with balance. A homeostatic mechanism is one that keeps something in balance. Thus it is with the basic needs such as for food and drink and oxygen, and, perhaps, for sexual release as well. A homeostatic system is always based on negative feedback. So, for example, if we have not eaten for some time, this is reflected in various bodily and psychological mechanisms (negatively), the information goes to the controlling mechanisms in the brain and we are prompted to eat, simply in order to get the system back into balance. A thermostat is a homeostatic mechanism. If the temperature drops below a set amount, this (negative) feedback goes to the system which then sets the heating to come on to bring the temperature back to the desired level.

So, much of our basic motivational systems is based on this type of balance. The ideal is a sort of middle way that is maintained by a homeostatic mechanism. Depletion or deprivation feeds back negatively, producing a state of drive which has to be reduced in order to return the body back to its balanced state. Then, overall, there must be some other mechanism that keeps some sort of balance between the various needs and drives. Something must ensure that we do not eat, drink, make love, make money and collect stamps, all in the same breath. Possible mechanisms to deal with this overarching balance are discussed in the next chapter.

▶ Summary

- Motivation is the energy of life, prompting us both to start and to stop doing things. Important basic concepts in motivation are: needs, drives, motives, goals, desires and instincts.

- The bodily needs, based on what is necessary to live, are for food, drink and, to some extent, sex.

- Hunger is determined by a mixture of internal and external factors and even food preferences are sometimes built in (sweet versus bitter, for example) or are learned.

- The major eating disorders are anorexia and bulimia and attempts at weight control have to be based on the idea of permanent changes in life-style to succeed.

- Like hunger, thirst depends on a mixture of internal and external mechanisms and, again like hunger, can go wrong, this usually taking the form of alcoholism.

- Sex is necessary to the survival of the species rather than the individual and is driven by hormones, on the one hand, and cultural beliefs, expectations and values, on the other. It can take a wide variety of extreme forms, each of which can be driven by a wide variety of motives.

- The most extreme form that motivation can take is addiction. Although formally applied to drug dependency and strict physiological mechanisms, addiction can also occur at the psychological level, gambling providing one example.

- The basic needs work according to homeostatic principles. That is, a homeostatic mechanism keeps the system in balance by prompting the body to respond to negative feedback.

▶ Questions and possibilities

- Make a list of your personal needs, drives, wishes and desires. What are your major motives in life? What order would you place them in?

- Do you think that you are prompted to eat, drink or have sex generally more by internal cues or external cues? Are you the same or different than your family or friends in this? What do you think makes the difference and what are the possible effects of being internally or externally oriented?

- Have you made attempts to control your weight? If they haven't worked, why not? If you would like to control your weight, draw up a weight control programme for yourself based on the principles described in this chapter.

- What are your views on alcohol? On marijuana? Why is drinking alcohol legitimate but smoking marijuana not in some countries?

- What are your own sexual preferences? What are your views on the more extreme forms of sexual behaviour? How do you think that your views have been formed? Are they changeable?

■ Are you addicted to anything? Work or money, for example? Do you some-times crave certain things? If so, why does this happen at some times and not at others?

■ What would happen if our needs were not controlled by a homeostatic system?

■ To what extent do you think that it might be useful to extend the idea of a homeostatic physiological mechanism into daily life, with the aim of achieving a balance in all that you do?

CHAPTER FIVE

Motivational life

From sensation-seeking to self-actualisation

Scenes from life

You are 18 and bored. Your job in an office is monotonous with little variation from one day to the next. Even the people that you work with seem to have no sparkle. And your social life is not much better, having a routine sameness about it. So, even though you look forward to what each weekend might bring as a break from the humdrum workplace, you end up on Sundays feeling listless and with little energy to get up and do anything. Underneath it all you are constantly restless.

You are living with someone whose circumstances are very similar to your own, but who seems to be completely content with things as they are. Seeing this only seems to make you even more restless. You *have* to do something about it, so you start playing a series of practical jokes at work. On behalf of your workmates, you put fictitious advertisements in the lonely hearts columns, you have items delivered to people who do not want them, and one night you even go into work and board up somebody's doorway.

This is not enough, though, so you also to start to liven up your weekends. You commit yourself to a sky-diving course and during the evenings you start to say evermore outrageous things when out with friends. All of this makes you feel much more alive; suddenly life seems more worth living again even though you are frequently in trouble. In fact, if you are found to be behind the practical jokes at work, your job will be gone. Meanwhile the person you live with cannot believe what has got into you; 18 is definitely too young for a mid-life crisis.

Picture a woman of 35 or so standing in the kitchen, doing the dishes. It is a spring morning and the sun is streaming in through the window. Her husband has just gone off to work after a loving farewell and a thought about what they would be doing in the evening. Behind her, the two young children are playing, the usual sort of altercations rising and falling as they do. As she feels the hot, soapy water running over her hands and slippery, sparkling dishes emerge to drip on the tray, her thoughts turn to the day ahead – shopping, off to the park with the children, thinking about organising a birthday tea for the following week.

As she stands there she is suddenly overwhelmed by a feeling that all is absolutely right in her world. Life could not be better than it is. Gazing through the window, she even feels a sort of affection for the muddle of a garden that she never seems to have quite enough time to deal with. The feeling goes on, giving her a sensation of fulfilment and purpose. Colours and sounds seem sharper, even the smell of the dish-washing liquid smells good and the bubbles in the bowl swirl around like rainbows captured in minuscule globes. This is a moment that Abram Maslow would describe as a peak experience; a time of complete engagement with the world as it is for someone who is self-actualised.

George is in his forties, the CEO of a large organisation. He is a man of energy with what some of those around him see as a great zest for life. In fact, he communicates very little with his wife. He talks to, or perhaps at, her but rarely listens and never tells her what he is feeling about himself or her or their children. The children are in their teens and George provides them with anything they need, although being very careful not to spoil them by giving them whatever they want. He admires and encourages their successes, becomes irritated with their failures and has very little idea of their opinions, beliefs and values.

George is driven by his work. There is nothing he likes more than clinching a deal that makes more money for his firm, except, perhaps, to exercise his authority in sorting out disputes. He sees himself as a great pragmatist, a realist with his feet on the ground whom people will listen to. In fact, he deals with work problems by the exercise of sheer power based on a belief in his own essential rightness. After clinching a deal or telling people 'how it has to be', he feels curiously enlivened, full of a restless sort of energy. Recently, he has begun taking the occasional hour off in the afternoons to visit a prostitute.

After the basic needs have been satisfied, motivation becomes even more complicated. Although, like everything else, it must have a physiological substrate, it is no longer grounded in bodily change; it is now purely psychological. And the range of motives that appear to drive human behaviour is enormous. However, they can be roughly categorised, put together in a hierarchy of motives that makes sense of all the complexities involved. This categorisation will be returned to at the end of this chapter. First, though, it is important to describe what makes up complex human motivation, from curiosity to sensation-seeking, from play to work, from power to affiliation, and from conscious to unconscious influences.

▶ Being curious and seeking sensations

To be human is to be active, to explore, to play with our world. Our basic state is not one of torpor but of curiosity and the seeking of novelty, within limits of relative safety. Even the couch potato likes to change channels from time to time. This is what has been called *intrinsic motivation*. Much of what we do or do not do is the result of being rewarded or punished for it. But playing and being curious need no external reward; the reward seems to be built into it.

This is very adaptive. The more we can understand, master and manipulate our environment, so the better we can survive in it. Acquiring a new skill is pleasurable in its own right. Learning to ride a bicycle or to type is not merely satisfying because the one moves you about faster than walking and the other allows a better form of communication. To have acquired these abilities simply seems to be satisfying in itself. The child might say, 'Look, Mum, no hands' for the external reward that comes from the mother's mixture of horror and pride, but riding also brings a great feeling of pleasure in its own right.

To turn the coin over, the other side of curiosity is boredom. Most of us have experienced this occasionally, from long grey afternoons during the school holidays when all friends are away and all books have been read, to, well, pretty much the same thing in adult life. The feeling of boredom is one reflection of our need to explore or to be curious, but it is when this need is being frustrated.

Of course, too much of a new thing can become overwhelming, although how much is too much varies from person to person. There is a balance for each of us between a liking for the familiar and a desire for the novel and we spend much of our lives trying to find that balance. Being stuck in the same old groove becomes enervating and having too much change and unpredictability generates anxiety.

There are huge individual differences in sensation-seeking, what is exciting for one person being boring for another and what is adventurous for X seeming to be pointlessly dangerous to Y. As with so many aspects of psychological functioning, there is no right or wrong here, there are simply individual differences in what is ideal for each person.

▶ Flow

What is it, then, that makes something more intrinsically motivating than something else? It has long been known that unpredictability, complexity and novelty make things seem more compelling. Again, however, what is a comfortable level of unpredictability, complexity and novelty for you might be altogether too much for me.

Of particular interest in this context is the idea of flow, developed by Csikszentmihalyi (1990). We experience flow or flow time at those moments when we seem to be able to accomplish whatever we might doing with minimal effort. We are simply in fine control of what we are doing. Time passes without it being noticed. People report this state of flow to be very pleasurable. However, presumably it is only afterwards that the pleasure comes, since during the experience we are completely absorbed.

The pleasurable experience of flow comes about in conditions of optimal challenge. This simply means that the challenge of whatever we might be doing exactly equals our ability to do it. If the task is too easy, then the result is boredom, whereas if the task is too difficult, the result is uncertainty and anxiety. Think of any of your daily jobs and it is easy to realise how well these concepts apply to them. It is as though one only becomes aware of the passage of time when there is an imbalance between the demands of a job and one's abilities to do it.

The intrinsically rewarding nature of curiosity and sensation-seeking can be unpacked a little further. A sense of *competence* is also important. The more we perceive ourselves as being competent at whatever we are doing, then the more intrinsically rewarding it becomes. Similarly, if we believe that we are in charge of what is happening to us, in other words that we are *self-determined*, then again intrinsic motivation increases. This means that we believe that we can initiate our own behaviour and choose our own goals.

▶ Work and play

Most of us work, usually, but not always for money. Other than to survive, why do we do it? What are the links between motivation and work? In general, work provides a way to satisfy various needs – for competence, for achievement, for affiliation, for power (these are discussed later).

Self-determination is integral to how hard we work. Generally, if we can set our goals, set our own times of working, and change what we are doing from time to time, then we will tend to work harder than if no such flexibility is possible. Similarly, our beliefs in our abilities have an effect on how well we do. If we believe that we can work at a particular pace and in a particular way to achieve something, then this tends to become a self-fulfilling prophecy.

Everyday workplaces are interesting because they provide an obvious forum for a mixture of intrinsic and extrinsic motivation. Certainly, people work for money or for goods or for some form of payment – extrinsic motivation – although this also comes in the form of social contacts. However, the work might also be satisfying in its own right and some people do settle into jobs that they enjoy, the payment they receive being almost a bonus to the intrinsic satisfaction they derive from the work. The most obvious example of this in the modern world comes from the large numbers of people who do voluntary work; helping others is a curious mixture of intrinsic and extrinsic motivation.

On the other hand, play seems to be entirely intrinsically motivated. Many young animals (not just humans) play and seem to do so for nothing more than the pleasure it brings. Yes, it helps in the development of skills and of finding things out, but basically it appears to happen for its own sake.

For humans, play does not stop with the end of childhood. Play is such an important aspect of adult existence that it always becomes heavily institutionalised. There is art and music, there is sport and pastimes, there is the enormous holiday and tourism industry. Of course, all the varied activities that make up human adult play become work for some people – professional sportspersons and artists, for example. But for most people they retain an amateur (that is, a play-based) status. The interesting question is whether the professional tennis player or artist, golfer or musician is playing or working, being driven by intrinsic or extrinsic motivation. The answer is that it is probably a mixture of both.

Most people work to live, part of such living being the opportunity to play. That is, people work for obvious extrinsic rewards, the partial result of which is to provide the opportunity to do something that is intrinsically rewarding. Of course, it is not either one or the other, but a question of the balance between extrinsic and intrinsic in the various activities. The ideal is when work and play coincide and do so at a level in which there are many opportunities for optimal challenge and the experience of flow.

▶ Success, friendship and dominance

Everyone is away and you have just spent a long, wet weekend by yourself. Nothing has happened. All sport was cancelled, you could not find a video that you had not seen or a book that you had not read. The television appeared to be unwatchable and the newspaper depressing. Everyone you tried to telephone was out (and no doubt having a good time). You are stir crazy and, desperate for human contact, you go out and spend time wandering around the supermarket simply for some human contact, for the sake of hearing someone say 'have a good day', ironic though it might be in the circumstances.

Many of our motives or needs are social. We are a gregarious species, although, as with everything, there are huge individual differences in the amount of contact we need. But it is not just a matter of needing social contact, but that this contact can take so many different forms and can satisfy so many different needs. Some of these social needs have been studied in detail because they seem to be of more general importance than others. Three of them are to do with achievement, affiliation and power.

The strength of achievement motivation has long been assessed by so-called *Thematic Apperception Tests*. These take the form of a series of simple pictures portraying people engaged in something or the other. Respondents are asked to make up stories about the pictures, the contents of the stories then being evaluated for themes related to achievement. Distinctly different stories are told by those with a high need to achieve than those with a low need to achieve. Of course, having a high need to achieve does not necessarily mean achieving great success in life.

Of possible importance here is whether a person wishes to achieve in order to prove something to someone else or to himself or herself. In other words, is it for recognition of doing well, or not? In either case, actual ability by itself is irrelevant; the result also depends on the nature of the task. Moreover, people vary considerably with respect to whether they are motivated to achieve for hope of success if they do or fear of failure if they do not.

Affiliation seems to be basic to human motivation. Most people are gregarious; they seem to need the contact of others. Just as with other human behaviours, there are enormous variations in the strength of the drive to seek contact with others. Affiliation is related to attachment (see Chapters 6 and 14) which is fundamental to so many aspects of our social and emotional development. Friendship and association with others are to do with developing a feeling of security socially and with the search for intimacy in social relationships.

It has also been established that there is a link between anxiety and affiliation. We tend to seek the company of others when we feel isolated and fearful. Interestingly, if we are fearful of the situation that we are in and are sharing this situation with strangers, the strangers rapidly become friends, at least for the time being. Think of the rapidity with which conversations are struck up when the lift becomes stuck between floors or the train between stations. Also, it is likely that people who share some extreme physical dimension would also more rapidly establish social contact than those who do not; the very tall or the very short, for example.

As a final example of a social motive, we all vary with respect to our liking for *power*. This is concerned with wanting to be dominant and/or to be recognised as of high status or good repute. Those with a high need for power tend to have high blood pressure and high catecholamine levels, which means that they are relatively argumentative, tend to be angry, play much sport and have trouble sleeping. Of course, as well as there being large variation in the need for power, there is a similarly large variation in how people use whatever power they might have. At one extreme are social goals and at the other personal ambition and aggrandisement; very different styles of leadership might result.

▶ Motivation and thinking

As well as being linked with what we do socially, motivation is also linked with thinking. These are complicated links, but one in particular is worth describing since it forms such a common part of everyday life. *Cognitive dissonance* occurs when we hold two beliefs that don't match up – this produces in us a strong drive to do something about it. Our thoughts lead to motivation.

I am out drinking with friends and the wine is affecting me. I have my car and want to drive home for convenience, but I know that my driving will be impaired and I might cause an accident. This is cognitive dissonance, a state that is pushing me to do something about it simply in order to reduce the dissonance. What to do? Get a taxi; stop drinking and start eating; drink some coffee and let time pass; tell myself that I am actually a better driver after a few drinks; or go on drinking so much that I forget about the consequences. All of these ways out are solutions that help me to get rid of the dissonance caused by the two conflicting pieces of knowledge or belief. Of course, some are more socially acceptable than others.

The conditions under which cognitive dissonance is most likely to occur are: when you think you have made free choices; the decision is significant and hard to alter; you feel responsible for any outcomes; and, finally, if you have put a lot of work into something, you will value it more. This is why initiation ceremonies work – if I had to go through all this pain and torment, it must be worth it. All such thoughts are not necessarily conscious, of course.

▶ Do we know what drives us?

A couple are having a slight altercation; not exactly a row, more a minor skirmish in what they see as the battle of the sexes. It is over one slight area of difficulty in their lives, a not uncommon one. Although Jane is not very fond of her mother, she does have some regard for her and generally holds that 'She is my mother after all, and you only have one mother and you don't want to live with regrets after she has gone, and she's getting on.' Jack does his best to tolerate his mother-in-law but actually cannot stand her presence in the house; he sees her as a moralising nuisance. Jane thinks that it is time that they had her to stay.

Jane and Jack bicker throughout the evening but eventually reach a compromise. They will invite her, but it won't be until next week and they'll make it clear that they have things to do and that she can only stay for a week. Jane writes the letter of invitation, gives it to Jack to post in the morning and they go contentedly to bed, having stuck to their usual principle of never going to bed disgruntled.

Sometime early in the following week, Jane is puzzled that she has not heard from her mother and says to Jack, 'It's strange that we haven't heard from Mum. You did post that letter, didn't you?' 'Yes, of course, I did. She probably just hasn't got round to replying.' But it has pricked Jack's mind. Did he really post the letter? When he tries to think about it, he cannot remember putting it into the postbox. His stomach sinks and he quietly goes to check the pocket of the jacket he was wearing at the time. There is the letter, slightly crumpled. He walks back in to see Jane, clutching the letter and wondering how to explain himself.

Norman is in his fifties and is a fairly successful businessman. He is quite driving and tough-minded but has a kindly side. He tends to treat his employees well and generally is a good, tolerant husband and father, although he is clearly the boss and likes to be thought of in that way.

He and some of his senior managers have been conducting interviews for a relatively high-level appointment in the company. They have spent the afternoon seeing the final three short-listed candidates and in the view of all but Norman, one of them has emerged as the clear front-runner. They have been extolling his virtues to Norman and he can see, to some extent, to what they are saying, but nevertheless feels very uneasy about the applicant. He cannot quite pin down why but goes on to talk about how he might not quite fit into the company and expresses his worries about whether everyone would get on with him well enough.

One of the others starts to describe the applicant's obvious good qualifications and experience and general affability and then says, 'Well, the only thing that I can think of that might stop him from going down well is that he is homosexual. But no one here is bothered by that, are they?' They all agree with him about that and Norman suggests that they sleep on it and make the decision the next day.

On the way home, stopped briefly at the lights, Norman idly looks over at the car beside him and receives a huge smile from the young man who is driving. He smiles back and drives on when the lights change, feeling slightly uneasy and having no idea why.

We do not always know why we do things. This has been known from the time of Freud's (1933) writing. One of Freud's greatest contributions to knowledge was his idea that motivation is frequently unconscious. We sometimes do things and cannot readily explain why and sometimes other people call into question any explanations that we might give.

To understand unconscious motivation, it is necessary to understand something of the unconscious. Freud suggested that the personality is made of three energy systems – the id, the ego and the superego (see Chapter 10). And the unconscious part of the personality is where basic instincts and impulses are stored (the id) and where there are demands made on how we *should* behave (the superego). Meanwhile, it is the ego that keeps us in touch with reality.

A basic question is: how do we know that there is an unconscious if it is unconscious? The main indications of it are all indirect rather than through straightforward measurement, as might be expected. They are through: *free association* (saying whatever comes to mind, uninhibitedly, without censorship); *analysis of dreams*; *projective tests* (vague materials on which the person puts his or her own interpretation); *slips of the tongue* (Freudian slips); *accidents* (Freud believed there aren't any); *humour*; and *hypnosis*. This might seem to be an unusual mixture, but will make more sense as the matter of defence mechanisms is considered.

▶ Defence mechanisms

One definition of defence mechanisms is that that they are learned responses to stressful situations that are not based on a realistic evaluation of the circumstances. Stress and uncertainty lead to anxiety and the straightforward way to deal with this is to face the source of the anxiety and either do some problem-solving or, if this is not possible, then to engage in some emotion regulation (see Chapter 17). However, this is sometimes too difficult, especially if the situation arises early in life, so we build barriers or defences against the anxiety, treating the symptom rather than the cause. Such defences are short-term solutions that are adaptive in that they take the pain away but they do not provide long-term solutions.

The defence mechanisms tend to occur in combinations rather than singly, but they can be grouped into a number of major types, most of which were originally mentioned by Freud. These categories depend either on the degree of their potential harm to the individual or, as will be seen, on the degree of their social acceptability. As the defence mechanisms are described below, it would be useful to consider examples of each of them that you might have observed in yourself or in other people. You will have seen them all at some time or another.

1 *Compensation* is a very common defence mechanism and tends to be socially acceptable in that it is a way of simply making up some deficiency in life. A schoolboy might, for example, make up for poor sporting skills by developing a ready wit. Somebody who cannot find a job that matches their abilities might develop other interests that help to fulfil their potential. Clearly, these examples *are* defensive but they are only of benefit to the individual. Compensation becomes problematic when it goes to the extreme. Compensating for disadvantages by lying, cheating or stealing, for example, benefits nobody. Compensating for a physical disability by developing a caustic tongue eventually makes matters worse.

2 *Sublimation* is similar to compensation but is believed to result from a frustrated sex drive. So, a person who cannot for whatever reason gain sexual fulfilment might push that latent energy into some creative intellectual activity such as writing. Again, this might very well be highly adaptive and socially acceptable but it is a defence against the anxiety that develops because of the sexual frustration and, of course, does nothing to solve that problem.

3 *Rationalisation* is something most of us engage in at times. We explain things away, apparently quite rationally but without taking account of the underlying

motivations. I'll eat this extra helping; being overweight never did anybody any harm. I might as well continue smoking; you've got to go some time in some way. I'll take the car today; it might rain. In these cases the 'real' motivation is, respectively, I really like the taste even though I am not hungry; I am addicted to smoking and need the next cigarette; I really feel quite lazy today. To admit these underlying motivations would be to allow anxiety in. The rationalisation is a protection from this.

4 *Identification* is again something that we all do frequently. For example, we identify with characters in films, on the television, in books, on the stage, and so on. We also identify with those who are significant to us, such as parents or mentors. This is a perfectly normal part of growing up and living. However, it can become a defence mechanism if it is too extreme; for example, if a mother tries to live her life through her daughter, encouraging her daughter to do things for her (the mother's) sake rather than the daughter's. Or, for example, if a young man can only live an anxiety-free life by dressing like a Hell's Angel.

5 *Projection* is a matter of pushing onto other people wishes, desires, thoughts or beliefs that are our own, but which it would cause too much anxiety to admit to. For example, the latent homosexual might see homosexuality wherever he looks and cast it in a negative light. Or, at an even simpler level, a very anxious person might see all those around her as being highly anxious.

6 *Egocentrism* is the increasing of one's own significance way beyond what is appropriate. Of course, most of us do this in a minor way from time to time, but when it is done in the extreme and in the service of anxiety-reduction, it becomes a defence mechanism. It can be seen as the extreme form of attention-seeking ('Look, Mum, no hands') and, of course, usually has the opposite effect to that intended – it puts people off.

7 *Regression* is a dropping back into a form of behaviour more appropriate to an earlier stage of development, even childhood. A person might go to bed rather than face the world, or break down in tears rather than admit to something. Interestingly, the regression might also be to a less advanced or more primitive form of motivation. For example, a woman might over-eat instead of facing her social problems or a man might start regularly drinking alcohol in order to dull the anxieties generated at home.

8 *Dissociation*, as the name suggests, is the splitting of various aspects of a person's life. If two behaviours or two motives are in conflict but expressed or held by the one person, this produces great uncertainty/anxiety. Dissociation allows them to be held simultaneously. For example, a man might be the mildest of husbands and fathers but believe the only way to be at work is ruthless. The anxiety that this obvious contradiction might generate can be warded off by dissociation.

9 *Repression* is an unconsciously motivated forgetting. Again, this is something that we all do to some extent. However, in the extreme it can stop the person from realising that there is even a problem that has to be dealt with – the entire problem is repressed. This is clearly maladaptive. It is one thing to forget to post a letter inviting your mother-in-law to visit, it is another to forget to pay the mortgage when the bank is threatening to foreclose.

10 *Negativism* has straightforward roots in childhood, referring to incorrigible opposition. To constantly say 'No, I won't' can put an adult in a terrible position in that it becomes impossible to escape without considerable loss of face. This possibility in itself will generate anxiety and lead to even more defensive, perhaps negativistic, behaviour.

11 *Fantasy* is the final defence mechanism that in its milder forms we are surely all used to in a daily (if not hourly) sense. Day-dreaming is an escape from reality. If it becomes extreme and habitual, if a person is only off in a make-believe world rather than facing the anxieties of daily life and its problems, then it becomes a defence mechanism.

Defence mechanisms then involve the expression of unconscious motivation. We all engage in them in their milder forms and their roots in childhood are easy to see. But in the extreme they are defensive reactions to facing up to the uncertainties and anxieties that arise in everyday life. They allow an escape from reality and so provide a short-term solution to problems. In the long run and in the extreme they are mostly maladaptive and harmful. Some defence mechanisms, however, might be described as more mature than others, such as sublimation or humour (this can easily be a defence against anxiety as well as those already described). Such defences might be unconsciously motivated but they are much less harmful to the individual than some of the others, such as dissociation or repression might be. It is, perhaps, important to remember, however, that because defence mechanisms are unconsciously motivated, they are not a matter of choice.

▶ Motives in order: how to become self-actualised

It should be clear by now that what makes people do things, keep on doing them and eventually stop doing them is a large topic. The list of human motives could be seen as endless, especially taking into account the possibilities of unconscious motivation. So the question becomes: is there a way of putting all of this in a reasonably coherent order, at least to describe it if not in an attempt at explanation?

By far the most important and influential way of ordering motivational life was put forward by Abram Maslow (1954, 1971). His hierarchical view of motivation has permeated thinking throughout many areas of psychology, including the applied world of industrial/organisational psychology, and has had influences beyond psychology, in education, for example.

To say that motives are arranged hierarchically means that needs/drive/ motives at lower levels have to be satisfied before those at higher levels can be addressed (Figure 5.1). For example, if we are hungry, then we will not be much bothered about self-esteem. If we do not have a roof over our heads, then we will not be much concerned with whether or not everyone likes us.

The basic needs are clearly physiological (as discussed in the previous chapter), then come those based on safety and security, love and a sense of belonging, followed by self-esteem. Then, via the fulfilment of cognitive and aesthetic needs, the final level is the need for self-actualisation. At the lower end of the hierarchy, basic motivation depends on deficiency (in whatever we have to have for survival). As the hierarchy is climbed, so there becomes an increasing dependence on psychological growth rather than merely dealing with deficiencies.

Psychological health also comes into the reckoning in this hierarchy. Although deficiency needs dominate (and for some people in some parts of the world, they remain paramount), a person is not psychologically healthy until some of the growth needs are being fulfilled. It is simply rare for this to happen without deficiencies first being met. There are exceptions, however. The image of the artist or writer who continues to work although penniless comes to mind. Also, there is the aesthete who starves in the wilderness while pondering beauty or the saint who might lead a physically deprived life in the service of others.

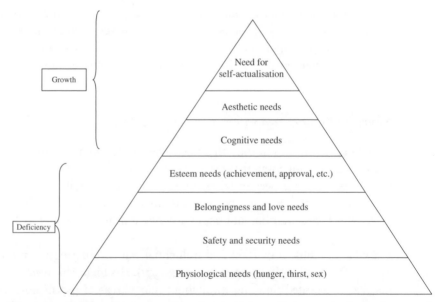

Figure 5.1 Maslow's hierarchy of needs in which needs low in the hierarchy must be satisfied before those that are higher.

The most compelling aspect of Maslow's hierarchy of motives is the idea of self-actualisation. This is concerned with the fulfilment or realisation of self-potential. This does not mean high achievement, power, success or status. It is both simpler and more complex than that. It concerns our ability to fulfil whatever potential might be within us, whether it is to play a musical instrument, run a marathon (or a mile), write a well-constructed sentence, or even do the washing-up as well as we could do it.

Imagine a woman in her thirties, married with two young children. It is Sunday in summer. Her husband is playing in the garden with the children and she can hear their laughter. She is sitting, relaxing with a cup of coffee, quietly looking forward to the remainder of the day. Suddenly, it seems to her as if everything is right with the world, everything seems to be in front of her with great clarity. She is lost in the present and could not feel better.

Or think of a 17-year-old lad who is driving his first car. He has scrimped and saved for it and his parents have matched his money so that he could buy it. It is old but sleek and he is immensely proud of it. He is going to drive it round to show his girl-friend and take her for a drive. He snaps the car into third gear to take a corner and does so smoothly and with no discernible awkwardness. He breathes a huge sigh of contentment.

Or picture a teacher in front of her class. The children have been difficult and the topic in which she has been trying to interest them is also difficult. There comes a moment when she sees how it might be achieved, how their attention might be captured. She asks someone a question, receives the answer she wants, asks another and can feel the atmosphere in the class begin to change. Twenty minutes later the lesson is over, everyone is surprised by the ringing of the bell and, as the children file out, she leans back contentedly at a job she knows has been well done.

These are all descriptions of what Maslow called *peak experiences*, moments when everything seems to be absolutely as it should be. The world is right and one's place within it is exactly as it should be. Such moments characterise people who have become or who are becoming self-actualised.

Self-actualisation depends on a number of so-called meta-needs; these are needs that occur at a higher order than most and would presumably only be found in humans. They include: truth, goodness, beauty, wholeness, transcendence, aliveness, uniqueness, perfection, completion, justice, order, simplicity, comprehensiveness, effortfulness, playfulness, self-sufficiency and meaningfulness. The idea is that as long as all our lesser needs have been met, then we will try to fulfil these and any similar needs on the way to becoming self-actualised.

Maslow's idea of self-actualisation is very compelling and appears to be something that could be sought, particularly if it leads to the highly enjoyable peak experiences. Maslow argued, though, that only as few as 1 per cent of the population become self-actualised. This seems to be unlikely if it is such a built-in aspect of motivation that it prompts good psychological health. Surely a greater proportion of us than 1 per cent become self-actualised, even if only from time to time.

In spite of his 1 per cent idea, Maslow did also list some ways in which self-actualisation might be achieved. These are in the form of strategies that one might use in life. They each involve making a basic decision about how to conduct oneself.

1 To consider life to be made up of a series of choices that can move one in the direction of growth.

2 To be non-conformist.

3 To construct an environment in which peak experiences are more likely to occur. It is worth noting that peak experiences seem to be akin to 'flow', which occurs when one's skills equate with the demands of a task. If this is so, then finding such tasks would help to set up such conditions.

4 To give up any defences; this would presumably include those that are unconsciously motivated.

5 To be honest, especially with oneself.

6 To find oneself, which surely links with being honest.

7 To throw oneself whole-heartedly into any experience.

8 To do the best one can towards being whatever one wants to be.

These eight rules might also be said to lead towards developing a creative outlook on life, or even, to some extent, on developing a Buddhist perspective (see Chapter 11). The evidence for the idea of self-actualisation is not strong but the concept is convincing in the everyday sense. Ideas such as psychological growth and health might be a little vague but this does not mean that they are not compelling. Maslow's ideas were among the forerunners of what in recent years has come to be called positive psychology. This is a humanistic, whole-person approach based on an optimistic view of what it is possible to become and to achieve in life.

▶ Summary

- Much of the more advanced form of motivation is based on curiosity and sensation-seeking. It is built into us to be curious and to seek meaning in the world. We differ with respect to how much we do this, how much we seek sensations (and take risks) and how well we can tolerate boredom.

- Flow occurs when the challenges of a situation or task exactly balance with our capabilities to meet them. It happens when a challenge is optimal and results in us being lost in the moment.

- Most creatures play and human beings play a great deal. The motivation in play is built in or intrinsic, as though the activity is being engaged in for its own sake. The motivation for work is extrinsic, although the ideal occurs when someone earns money for doing something that he or she enjoys as though it were play, that is, it is intrinsically motivated.

- We all share, to some extent, a mixture of broader social motives, such as for success, friendship or dominance (or status).

- Cognitive dissonance occurs when we hold to beliefs about ourselves that are inconsistent. This produces a strong force to change simply in order to reduce the dissonance.

- Much of our motivational life is unconscious; we do not always know why we do what we do. The idea of unconscious motivation is used to help account for the development of defence mechanisms that we learn early in life to protect us from uncertainties and anxiety. They only provide immediate and incomplete solutions to problems, even though they might be long-lasting.

- The most influential way of giving a complete account of motivation comes from Maslow's hierarchy of motives, based partly on deficiencies and partly on psychological growth. The hierarchy culminates in self-actualisation, which develops in the service of various meta-needs and is characterised by peak experiences, states which are somewhat similar to flow.

▶ Questions and possibilities

- Make a list of whatever activities you find highly interesting and another of those you find very boring. Is there a difference in their intrinsic and extrinsic motivation?

- How would you develop any of your daily activities at home or at work in order to increase the likelihood of experiencing flow time? Would you concentrate on altering the task or altering your personal skills?

- What are your major social needs or motives? Are they the same as those of your friends and family? Do your social needs differ at home and at work?

- Think of people that you know who work hard. Why do they do it? What about people you believe to be lazy? Why are they lazy? What is laziness? Why do you sometimes work hard and sometimes not?

- Collect some examples of cognitive dissonance that you have seen around you. How do those involved reduce the dissonance?

- What defence mechanisms have you experienced? Find examples of the various defence mechanisms in the people you know.

- In general terms, how important do you think unconscious motivation is? How can we ever know about it?

- Think of anyone you know that you would describe as self-actualised. What are they like? What is it about them that prompts you to think that they are self-actualised? Are you now or have you ever been self-actualised?

- What do you think of Maslow's ideas about how to increase the likelihood of becoming self-actualised? Could you put them into practice, if you don't already? Do you think that they would work?

- Have you ever had peak experiences? If you have, then think about the circumstances that led to them and consider whether or not you could make them happen again.

CHAPTER SIX

Social life

Forming and maintaining relationships

Scenes from life

Charles is a 23-year-old rather shy and inhibited man. He lives with a male flat-mate and has a good, steady job in an office. The prospects for career advancement are reasonable although not startling and Charles has a number of outside interests, all of which tend to be pursued alone – reading, running and hiking or walking in the countryside when time off allows. He gets on well with his parents and visits them quite regularly. Like him, they tend to be quiet people who keep themselves to themselves. So far, Charles has not had a girl-friend. He finds it difficult to talk to women and can never seem to strike up the necessary boldness to invite a woman whom he likes out for a meal or to go to the cinema. He hasn't spent much time wondering why this is so, just putting it down to his inherent shyness and quietly hoping that some day something will happen and a relationship will develop for him.

He works in a high-rise building and at the start and end of each day uses the lift to get to the seventeenth floor. It is always crowded and Charles usually travels silently, keeping his eyes fixed to the floor indicator as it moves up and down. Conversations sometimes go on around him in the lift but he finds it difficult to engage in them even when it is with people that he knows. Descending one day after a busy day at work, his thoughts veering off to what he will read that evening and whether or not he will go for a run, the lift suddenly stops between floors. It is crowded as usual and the unscheduled stop instantly causes a small hubbub of conversation, frustrations and witticisms flying around. Charles stays quiet.

After a few minutes, the lift has still not started. Once or twice it has juddered a little, but the collective sigh of relief is quickly stifled as the descent does not begin. Charles can feel the tension in the lift beginning to mount. Voices are beginning to be raised and become a little more shrill. Charles turns and sees next to him a young woman whom he has seen occasionally travelling up and down in the lift. She looks worried and glances up at Charles and says, 'This is annoying. I hope it starts soon. I have to get home to see my mother. She's not been well.' Charles can hear the strain in her voice and finds himself saying, 'I'm sure it will be alright. It will start in a minute.' He feels slightly excited and does not notice that he has spoken quite normally to the young woman, without his usual shyness. He thinks to himself how attractive she seems, in a quiet, understated way.

The lift does not begin its way down for another 40 minutes and in that time, Charles and the young woman gradually have more and more to say to each other, ignoring the complaining, joking voices around them. As the lift reaches the ground floor, Charles finds that he is experiencing an odd mixture of excitement and disappointment. As they make their way to the front doors of the building, Charles asks the young woman if she likes the movies and whether she would like to go with him some time. She immediately says how nice that would be and they finally swap names and make a date for the following evening. Charles makes his way home feeling a sense of quiet elation.

Imagine a 3-year-old girl, Gail, lively, intelligent and reasonably alert and aware as 3-year-old girls can sometimes be. She spends most days at home with her mother, who decided to take a few years out of her career in order to bring up her children. Gail is the first and another is on the way. Gail does the things that 3-year-old girls do. She plays with dolls, enjoys building things with Lego, enjoys her first brushes with learning to read; she paints, she uses crayons, she plays with friends. In all of this she is encouraged by her mother who consistently helps her and actually plays with her.

When things go wrong and she is frustrated or hurts herself or is upset by other children, her mother is always there to give comfort and warmth and to reassure her. Sometimes her mother tells her off but this is usually in the form of helping her to rethink something she has done. Even when Gail has transgressed some family rule and been 'naughty', her mother deals with this in the same way. She is firm but never rejecting; she draws clear boundaries for Gail but always remains a source of comfort to her. Everybody describes Gail as a happy child.

Gail's overriding image of her mother is of someone who is warm and kind and who smells nice and is always doing interesting things with her. Without yet knowing what 'feeling close' to someone means, she feels close to her mother. Her mother enjoys Gail's company and is looking forward to the birth of her next child. She is content with spending the next few years with her young children and then resuming her career later, if that is what seems right at the time.

Now imagine this same 3-year-old Gail, just as alert and intelligent and again with a mother who has taken some time out of her career to have children. However, she was less keen on having children and became pregnant with Gail by accident. There are times when she enjoys Gail's company but other times when she resents having to be at home, particularly when she sees her contemporaries forging ahead with their careers.

Gail plays at home and with friends, just like the first Gail, but she is much more alone when she does. Her mother spends less time with her and is generally less encouraging of what Gail does. She is simply more absorbed in her own world. When Gail hurts herself or when things go wrong or she is frustrated, her mother sometimes is there to comfort her and sometimes just seems to ignore her or tell her to go away. Sometimes when she breaks a family rule, when she is 'naughty', her mother is quite forgiving and at other times she loses her temper and tells Gail what a thoroughly bad child she is. There are few boundaries set for Gail, or at least the boundaries shift from time to time unpredictably.

Gail's overriding image of her mother is of someone she desperately wants to please but does not know how to. Sometimes she seems to get on with her well and sometimes she doesn't and she never knows what it will be like on any particular day. She is very tentative when she is with her mother and is starting to constantly look at her mother's facial and bodily reactions before she does something. She has no idea that this is what she is learning to do but nevertheless she is doing it. Sometimes she is happy and sometimes she isn't and she is sometimes experiencing strange feelings of discomfort inside and gets a very upset stomach. Everybody describes Gail as a rather moody child.

For all but the most isolated individuals, social relationships are an integral part of life. Human beings are gregarious; they are social animals. The occasional person who seems to shun the company of others tends to be regarded as abnormal, although there will be far more about what is and is not abnormal and how abnormality is defined in Chapter 16. The question of how we form and then maintain relationships is extraordinarily complex. A good place to begin is with the idea of liking.

▶ Liking

Why do we like some people more than others? Why do we find some people attractive and others not? How is it that we can meet someone and instantly dislike them and meet someone else and find that we are immediately drawn to them? There are many reasons for these reactions, but mostly they can be gathered under four major topics. The important point to bear in mind is that the question of liking and disliking (and even loving) other people is not based on something mystical or unfathomable.

The first and in some ways the most obvious determinant of liking is *physical attractiveness*. Some people might not rate it highly or might say that other aspects of people such as their warmth or generosity or whatever are more important, but in practice it counts. Simply looking at studies that have been carried out on the characteristics of a person's first and subsequent dates, sheer physical attractiveness is more significant than intelligence, social skills or personality.

Of course, the question of defining attractiveness is not straightforward. To a large extent it is culturally determined and so attractiveness varies from place to place and from time to time in history. In Western society, for example, compare the rather fuller-figured look that was considered to be the epitome of attractiveness in women in the 1950s with the very slender look that supplanted it throughout the latter part of the twentieth century.

However attractiveness is defined, it is important in dating not least because a person's social standing increases if he or she is seen to be dating a more attractive person. On the other hand, attractiveness is regarded as less important when choosing a permanent partner. It is then that the other personal characteristics such as intelligence, social skills and personality become more prominent. It is interesting that, by and large, we end up with partners who are approximately our equal in physical attractiveness.

Again, in Western society there appears to be an interesting gender difference in the importance of attractiveness. Physical appearance is less important to women than it is to men. This may well be to do with the way in which gender roles have developed culturally. Women are supposed to be and to remain young-looking and attractive and men are supposed to be mature. Taking it to the teenage level, girls are supposed to be beautiful and boys are supposed to be associated with girls. Clearly, where such differences exist, they are the result of social learning and the modelling of social roles. They are not inherent.

Cutting across any possible cultural determinants of attractiveness is the much less subtle, more direct factor of physiological arousal. Much as in the first example from real life at the start of this chapter, physiological arousal of any sort makes men more sexually responsive to attractive women and less to non-attractive. The stopping of the lift between floors would raise physiological arousal and thus embolden the young man in a way that had not previously been possible for him. This was first established with a clever field study that involved having an attractive young woman stop men to ask them some survey questions either when they were on a high, swaying suspension bridge or when they were on a low, steady bridge. More of the men from the higher bridge telephoned the woman afterwards to ask her for a date.

There are a number of ways of accounting for this. It could be that the person misattributes his arousal to the presence of the woman rather than to whatever is really causing the increase in physiological arousal. Or it might be the transfer of excitement or even the facilitation of one type of response by another. Whatever the explanation, the effect is worth bearing in mind for both men and women, either to keep alert to what might be happening to them or even to make some use of the effect.

Proximity is also important as a determinant of liking. The best predictor of friendship patterns is how close people live to one another. Friendships tend to be made between people who live next door to one another or those who live opposite one another. Of course, there are exceptions but generally the rule of proximity holds.

Related to proximity is *familiarity*. Sheer exposure to other people increases our liking of them. This is, perhaps, one reason why proximity is important. The closer we are to someone else physically, then the more frequently we are likely to see them and the more frequently they see us, then the more likely they are to like us. A rule that can follow from this is that if you are interested in forming a close relationship with someone else, then it is worth being persistent and simply being around them frequently. This is not, of course, a recipe for stalking.

The final and, perhaps, the most important of the determinants of liking is *similarity*. Similarity in attractiveness has already been mentioned, but there is also similarity in race, religion, social class, educational level, intelligence, and so on. This is to do with weighing up whether or not the other person will want to be with us. So, in general, we have partners who are similar to us in many characteristics.

When liking becomes love and, perhaps, marriage or committed partnerships, then similarity in preferences for daily activities also becomes important. In practice, the similarity factor works well because social norms and situations tend to throw similar people together. There is very little evidence to show that opposites attract despite the perennial conversations that centre on the possibility, but an interesting theory that embraces this possibility is discussed at the end of this chapter. In general, if you want people to like you, then quite apart from the way you behave, it is important to spend as much time as you can being physically close to people who are similar to yourself in attractiveness and as many other characteristics as possible. As will be seen later, liking can then develop into closer and closer relationships and love may ensue.

▶ Attachments

Any close relationship is based on forming an attachment. To a greater or lesser extent we all form attachments throughout our lives. Some people form attachments easily and firmly, others have great difficulty in forming attachments at all. Some people form many somewhat superficial attachments and others form lasting and deep attachments. Some people seem to be fickle in their attachments and never to commit fully to close relationships. Why should there be these differences? Where do they stem from?

Not everything goes back to the early years, but some things clearly do and attachment patterns are among them. Our capacity to form attachments later in life depends heavily on the type of attachment experiences we had in the first few years of life. John Bowlby (1973, 1980) was the psychologist whose name is most readily linked with the importance of our early attachments. It was he that first drew attention to the importance of these initial social encounters, but others have developed the ideas considerably.

Essentially, three patterns of attachment have been identified and these are discussed further in Chapter 14. Of course, the subtleties of an individual's experiences are more profound than would simply be describable in three categories, but, nevertheless, to a greater or lesser degree, they do represent the only possibilities. Attachment is either *secure* or it is *insecure*. If it is insecure, then it takes the form of being either *avoidant* or *anxious-ambivalent*. The training ground for two of these types is portrayed in the second of the two examples from real life at the start of this chapter – the secure and the anxious-ambivalent. For the most part, the initial attachment, whatever form it takes, is to the mother, but it may be to the father, or grandmother or to some other caregiver or in some instances might be to multiple caregivers.

Securely attached babies seem delighted when their mothers return from being out of the room; they protest if she leaves and they search for her when she is not there. They clearly demonstrate their firm bonds of attachment (and affection). The insecure avoidantly attached babies rarely cling to their mothers and do not become upset if she leaves the room. They appear to be indifferent to her and show no pleasure if she returns after being away.

The insecure but anxious-ambivalent type of attachment is a mixture of the other two. Such babies cling to their mothers but they do not take pleasure in her return after being out of the room, continuing to cry if they have been upset. They give the appearance of being disorganised, negative and very anxious.

The picture of these three types of attachment comes largely from a series of investigations carried out over the past two decades using what is called the 'strange situation test'. Essentially, this involves observers watching an infant's reactions to mildly unusual and disturbing ('strange') situations in a room in which the mother is also present and can be used by the child as a way of relieving stress. It is important to note that much of the importance of the initial attachment depends on the sensitivity of the caregiver. If she (or he) is sensitive to the child, then a secure attachment can be readily formed even though (s)he is not available 24 hours per day.

Following this brief description of early attachment styles, the important question is, how do these relate to the formation of relationships later in life? Essentially, those who have had a secure early attachment are much more likely to form secure committed relationships as adults, whether these are romantic or simply based on liking, attraction or friendship. Again, as the names suggest, those who have early avoidant attachment tend to avoid close relationships as adults and those who have had anxious-ambivalent early attachments tend to have difficulty in forming adult relationships and when they do, not to be fully committed to them.

Love will be discussed in more detail later in Chapter 14, but it is worth making brief mention here of one set of ideas that are based on seeing adult love as a basic attachment process. The idea is that there are four possible patterns of adult attachment and that these follow from the possibility that any one of us will have a particular level of dependence on other people and a particular level of the degree to which we seek or avoid intimacy with others. This, in turn, might depend on whether our image of ourselves is positive or negative and whether our image of other people is positive or negative.

The secure style of adult attachment comes in a person who enjoys and seeks intimacy but who does not depend on others for their own positive self-view. There is a dismissing (avoidant) type of attachment and a fearful type, both of which avoid intimacy, although the dismissing person still depends on others for their own self-view. The person who is 'fearfully' attached tends to avoid closeness or intimacy in case the result is disappointment. The preoccupied style of attachment is characteristic of a person who depends on other people and seeks them out but, nevertheless, remains insecurely attached.

A final point about the relationship of early attachment to later attachment is that it is not set in cement. Although early attachments are the breeding round for later attachments, it is possible to learn to be securely attached later in spite of early insecurities. Similarly, and unfortunately, it is possible to learn to become insecurely attached because of one's adult experiences with attachment.

Role models

There are other influences on the question of whom we like and dislike or with whom we form intimate relationships other than our early attachments. These influences come from our culture, whether it be the broad culture within which we live (say, Western or Eastern society) or the more narrow sub-culture within which we spend our formative years. Cultures and sub-cultures have their customs and values; they have their heroes and their villains. They have their leaders and followers. In short, all cultures have those who provide role models for others.

In a simple and relatively restricted society, these role models come largely from close family members and friends. However, in a more complex society, they come from the mass media, from literature, and from advertising. To take the obvious examples in the Western world, the cinema and television have an enormous influence. It is not by accident that eminent sportspersons or others who are in the public eye are persuaded to front the advertisements for various products. This is in a clear attempt to persuade us all to buy whatever it might be *because* X has endorsed it. If the captain of the national team uses it, then it must be good. And the captain of the national team, whatever the sport, is a role model.

Moreover, television and film drama not only reflects society but also helps to shape it. So, again our television heroes provide role models for how to look, how to behave and for the type of person with whom we might most like to develop a close relationship or attachment. Ask anyone in the Western world in the last few years if they would prefer to 'go out with' someone who had abdominal muscles that looked like an old-fashioned wash-board than with somebody who had no such muscular definition and the chances are that they would say 'yes'. Ask somebody in Polynesian society the same question and the answer might be different.

In summary, our liking and disliking of other people depend on physical factors such as proximity, familiarity, similarity and physical attractiveness. The way in which we form attachments once we have established whether or not we would like to become attached to someone depends largely on the nature of the attachments that we formed early in life. However, the patterns of liking and disliking and the general overall attractiveness of various characteristics and types of person are also determined by very broad cultural values, beliefs and opinions.

▶ Love, intimacy and much more

Our initial attachments in life come about through force of circumstance. Then our later attachments start with liking that is based on attraction that is, in turn, based on the many factors already discussed. Sometimes liking develops even further and we find ourselves 'in love' or having 'fallen in love'. This seems to be a very different state from simply liking someone. And its opposite is hate which is much more than dislike. There is an active urgency about love (and hate) that is not there in liking (and disliking). There is also almost always a large increase in intimacy. What is love and why does it seem to be qualitatively different from liking?

The *sociobiologists* argue that love might be little more than the human word for the pair-bonding that goes on throughout much of the animal kingdom. So, from an evolutionary perspective, human beings bond into long-term heterosexual relationships in order to ensure that their children survive until reproductive age. Thus the species is prompted to continue.

This evolutionary-based argument is taken further. What they refer to as mating strategies differ between males and females. From a male perspective it is an evolutionary advantage to impregnate as many women as possible in order to optimise the chances of passing on their genes. From the female perspective it is an evolutionary advantage to select a mate who is both willing and able to protect and raise her children, thus increasing the likelihood of her genes being passed on. So, in behavioural (and somewhat judgemental) terms, men are likely to be more promiscuous and less discriminating than women in their search for sexual partners. It also suggests that men prefer more fertile (therefore, younger) women and women prefer higher status and better resourced (therefore, older) men. By and large, it does seem to work out a little like this, at least as far as preferences are concerned.

This is all very well from a biological or evolutionary perspective and perhaps begins to account for some of the urges for sheer sexual activity that occur, but there is far more to love and intimacy than this. To begin with there are various types of love, not all of them involving a sexual encounter. Consider these examples.

> *A young couple have been worried about their first child's first day at school.* He has been a quiet child and they think of him as being quite sensitive. He is very close to them and they are concerned that he will be unpleasantly buffeted about by the demands of school. He goes in readily enough in the morning but with some backward glances at them that they interpret as a sort of wistful longing. They decide that they will both meet him after school and wait anxiously for the children to come out. Their son comes bouncing out and rushes over to them talking and laughing. He is obviously very happy and they glance at one another over his head as he prattles on.
>
> *Picture a young man of 17 or so.* He has seen the woman of his dreams who seems to be like an amalgam of all of his favourite film stars. She is a few years older than him and she lives close by so he can see her quite often. He believes that she is the most wonderful being he has ever seen and simply wants to be able to gaze at her occasionally. He knows that she is beyond his reach but he does not mind this. He does not lust after her; in fact, the idea of that type of intimacy with her seems quite wrong to him. But he can think of little else than her.

Love might reasonably be said to be involved in both of these situations, but they are very different types of love. And in their turn they would differ from the type of love one might feel for one's parents or for one's ageing grandmother, or for one's new partner or for one's partner of 20 years. In and of itself love is not an emotion; it is far more complex than an emotion, even though emotions (such as anxiety) can be quite complex. It certainly involves emotion, or perhaps it is better to say, many emotions. Whatever form it takes, it seems to involve attachment, loyalty, protectiveness and nurturance, although romantic love is special because it also involves sexual behaviour, which love for one's parents or siblings and so on does not.

For many years, psychologists left the topic of love strictly alone, regarding it as in the domain of novelists, poets and philosophers. In other words, they threw it squarely into the too-hard basket. More recently, though, some psychologists have begun to engage with the study of love, appropriately enough, since it is one of the most significant aspects of human life. Concern to study love, whether with field research or in theoretical terms, also fits with a gradually developing movement in academic psychology to consider what some call positive psychology.[1]

One of the foremost psychologists to have studied love is Richard Sternberg (1986). He attempts to bracket liking and loving and has created a three-part or triangular model of them. The three parts are: intimacy, passion and decision-commitment. Each of these three parts can vary in both quality and quantity, of course, but their general presence or absence leads to the various types of liking and loving that are possible. As can be seen below, these types are, perhaps, better described as kinds of love relationship rather than kinds of love. The eight kinds of love relationship are:

1 *Non-love.* This is the extreme, describing a casual relationship in which there is neither intimacy, nor passion nor commitment.

2 *Liking.* Liking is what we experience with some friends and acquaintances and involves only an increase in intimacy. There is no passion or commitment, although it might be argued that it is perfectly possible to be committed to a friend and their welfare.

3 *Infatuation.* Infatuation involves passion but neither intimacy nor commitment. As children or teenagers we might experience infatuation with some adult, say, a school-teacher, or we might become infatuated with some unobtainable person such as a film star or television personality or even the perfectly happy wife or husband of someone round the corner.

4 *Empty love.* This is an interesting category that involves only decision-commitment, but with no intimacy or passion. Like infatuation, it tends to be in one direction, that is, to be unreciprocated. A relationship based on empty love is hard to imagine.

5 *Romantic love.* Romantic love is what most readily comes to mind when the word love is mentioned. It involves intimacy and passion but not necessarily any commitment. It is what characterises many short-term romantic encounters, even those that last for only one night. In such encounters there is always an increase in intimacy and passion, otherwise they would not occur.

6 *Fatuous love.* Again this is an interesting and, perhaps, a rather rare type of love relationship in that it involves passion and commitment but with no intimacy. It is descriptive of the type of relationship in which the sex is good and the people are committed to a long-term relationship but in which there is very little intimacy. Fatuous is a good word to describe such relationships since they are probably doomed to failure at some time.

7 *Companionate love.* Here there is intimacy and commitment but no passion and is, perhaps, the position of many reasonably successful marriages. The passion has gone but the intimacy and commitment remain. Clearly, however,

if a relationship started off in this way it would seem as if there were something missing; and there would be.

8 *Consummate love.* Finally, there is consummate love, which involves all three of intimacy, passion and commitment. This is how many long-term relationships begin or how they develop in the early stages. Some remain like this.

Although Sternberg's model is compelling, it is definitely a model that is viewing love as one or other kind of social relationship. It takes little or no account of the emotional turmoil that might be going on surrounding the relationship. Nor is it easy to use to describe love for one's grandmother or son, or uncle. The closest category for these would, perhaps, be companionate love, but this does not capture the differences between the love one experiences for one's son and one's grandmother.

Some psychologists have begun to ask whether or not love is the basic emotion that it appears to be to many people in everyday life. Ask people what the two fundamental emotions are and they might well answer: love and hate. Of course, both love and hate have their entrenched and highly significant emotional aspects, but psychologists tend to argue that they (particularly love) are too complex socially and too long-lasting to be seen as basic emotions. They are, perhaps, made up of a mixture of many basic emotions. Love in some form (be it simple attachment, the providing of care or nurturance, or sexual attraction) seems to be universal. However, what is missing even in this type of description is whether or not there is some fundamental emotional aspect to love that is neither seen nor experienced in any other emotional context.

Perhaps the answer to this type of question could come from looking at the difference between love and the state of being 'in love'. There is an obvious high emotional component to the state of being in love and this is an aspect of love that is concerned with romantic attachment, the passionate desire to be constantly with or engaged with another person, sexually and usually in other ways. Apart from the sexual aspect there may be little to distinguish this state from any type of attachment and the feelings of intimacy and closeness may be very similar within any strong social bond.

Marriage

In Western society, love and marriage tend to go together, although not necessarily. It is certainly possible to be in love and even partnership with someone without being married to them, but the common expectation is that such relationships tend towards marriage. However, that love is not a necessary condition for marriage can be seen in those societies (for example, Indian and Japanese) in which marriages are frequently arranged, the two partners having seen little, if anything, of each other before marriage. They have had no occasion to form any kind of attachment, not the least one that is based on a romantic entanglement. Nevertheless, on average, such marriages are as long-lasting as those that follow from romantic attachment.

A possible reason for this lack of difference between the longevity or success of the two types of marriage is that passion fades. It is rare to find a relationship in which the sexual attraction or physical passion remains at the intensity with which it might have begun. For success, marriage (or any other long-lasting) partnerships have to cope with waning passion and to develop more in terms of equality (in interests, values, attitudes, power, intimacy, and so on) between the two persons involved. This is as likely to come about in arranged marriages (in which passion might develop for a while a little later) as it is in Western-style marriages.

The important question in everyday life is, what is the recipe for a successful marriage or long-term partnership? Many (half to two-thirds) marriages fail and in some of those that do not actually end, the partners are not happy. Interestingly, a key component for success is liking rather than love. Partners in successful marriages say that they very much like each other; they are 'best friends' or very good mates. They confide in each other and seek advice from each other. They might argue but they do so with goodwill and with a push towards being constructive rather than destructive. They talk about 'we' and 'us' and value their interdependence as much as they might also value a measure of independence, an independence that they respect in each other and allow room for.

The partners in successful marriages genuinely listen to each other, rather than thinking about their own problems or what they are going to say when the other person stops talking. They don't 'bring up the past'; they don't attempt to 'win' in any sense in the relationship and don't see themselves engaged in a battle of the sexes. All of this type of interpersonal behaviour (based on liking rather than passionate love) requires considerable work, work that is more often, although not only, begun and maintained by the woman than the man in the relationship, if it is heterosexual. In our society, girls are brought up to assume such responsibilities and boys are brought up to allow girls to assume them. Of course, there are exceptions but this seems to be the general rule. One outcome of this rule is that when a marriage begins to falter or become discordant, the woman tends to feel unhappier about matters than the man.

A time of particular stress for many marriages is when there are children. Although, in some ways, children can increase the bond between the couple, their advent nevertheless creates particular pressures, both interpersonal and economic. In current Western society, this is particularly the case when a couple has been used to two incomes and now, suddenly, there is only one but with an extra drain on resources. The arrival of children also means that there is less opportunity for intimacy and the various problems of bringing up a child may also lead to conflict between a couple. The implication is not that part of the recipe for a successful marriage is not to have children but rather that like many other aspects of marriage, the having and upbringing of children require a great deal of sensitive work to be accomplished successfully. All of the relationships within a family unit are to do with attachment, the importance of which cannot be stressed too much.

Love again – a genuine theory

Robert Solomon (1994) is a philosopher who has written for many years on topics also of interest to psychologists. In 1994 he produced a stimulating book on love, representing a genuine attempt to create a theory that makes both philosophical and psychological sense. His theory rests on the core belief that a theory of love is, in fact, a theory of self, but a theory that involves the notion of a shared self. This, in turn, reflects Plato's view that love is to do with the joining of two souls, an idea that began with Aristophanes who argued that love is an attempt to find the other, 'missing' half of oneself.

Solomon then suggests that love is about attempting to define oneself in terms of another person. He also points out, reflecting an idea put forward by historians of emotion, that love, as we think of it, is a relatively modern notion. It is an idea, in Western society, that two separate and autonomous persons are free to make choices, among these choices being that of (romantic) partner. For the partnership to work, however, as Solomon sees it, there has to be the tension that comes from relatively opposed forces. So, if one seeks a relationship with a person who has complementary characteristics to one's own, this leads to an increasing *excitement* simply because of the tension that then exists with respect to one's autonomous self. For example, if you are a rather placid person who seeks certainty in life, you might well be attracted to a more outgoing person who is comfortable with uncertainty and who likes to move things on. This is simultaneously filling in a missing part and creating a certain tension.

In one sense this theory is suggesting that opposites attract, a theory long held in popular belief. While this may be so, it does not mean that such a close relationship would not also be built upon similarities. As we have seen earlier, this usually seems to be a necessary condition for the development of any closer relationship.

Solomon also makes the point (a point which could well be applied to much if not all of psychology) that a theory of love has to make sense at the personal level as well as in academic circles. It follows from his theory that love is not something that is instant, although sexual attraction might be. It is something that develops and grows over time and profits from work being put into it. He is arguing that the very early theories of love had much to be said for them and that they can be reinvented in ways that make sense in our modern world.

▶ Summary

- Social relationships are at the core of life for human beings.

- Liking depends on physical attractiveness (which is largely culturally determined), physiological arousal, proximity, familiarity and similarity.

- Our ability to form attachments in adult life goes back to our very early initial attachment(s).

- Early (and later) attachments can be secure or insecure and, if insecure, they can be avoidant or anxious-ambivalent. The propensity to insecure attachments in adulthood can be overcome.

- Role models are important in forming relationships.

- Love rests on attachment and liking and is partly concerned with mate selection in evolutionary terms.

- There are many types of love, ranging from the romantic and passionate to love for one's children or parents. Love varies according to intimacy, passion and commitment.

- Love changes throughout marriage and the ingredients for a successful marriage are based on effort and work rather than luck.

- One recent theory of love sees it as the culmination of the search for a complementary part of the self.

▶ Questions and possibilities

- Choose the three people that you like the most or to whom you feel the closest and list their main characteristics. Are they similar to one another? Are their characteristics similar to or different from your own characteristics?

- Have you ever been in a situation in which you have become attracted to someone else after you have known them for some time? Why did this happen?

- Think about your own early attachments. Which type did they fit into? Has a similar pattern played out in your adult life?

- Think of people that you know who represent the various types of adult attachment described in this chapter. In what ways do their relationships differ?

- List the different types of love that you have experienced. Do they all fit into one or other of the categories described by Sternberg? If not, what characterises them?

- If you have or have had a long-term partner, in what ways is he or she like you and unlike you? How important is the pattern of similarities and differences been for the relationship?

- What would you look for in an ideal partner? Why? Are these similar characteristics to those you would seek in an ideal friend?

- To what extent do you believe that women and men are similar in their approach to friendship, liking and long-term relationships such as marriage? Do you think that there would be differences between men and women in this regard from one culture to the next?

- Write your own recipe for a successful long-term relationship.

- Would you ever consider trying to arrange a marriage for your own children? What do you think might be the advantages or disadvantages of this approach to marriage?

- What makes people attractive? Is there an ideal face or body shape? Is there an ideal personality?

- Recently, in the USA, the UK, Australia and New Zealand, there has been a television search for a national 'idol'. What are the characteristics of those who are chosen? Why do people choose them?

- Why were the Spice Girls so popular? Is it really possible to create a style for someone that appeals to most people? What would the characteristics of such a person be? In short, could one create a national 'idol'?

▶ **Note**

1 Much of academic psychology has traditionally followed a very reductionistic, analytic approach in which everything is broken into its elements and studied as such, much as in most sciences. Very often this research has ultimately been driven by studying something that has gone wrong. Positive psychology is concerned more with studying the entire, functioning person in circumstances where things are going right. For example, endeavours in this area look at happiness, self-fulfilment, personal growth, and so on. Clearly, love fits into this category.

CHAPTER SEVEN

Social life

Communicating one to one

Scenes from life

Imagine a young man who is setting out on a long train journey. He doesn't travel much and is vaguely excited by the prospect of going to another city for the day (which he has to do for his job) and for a few hours' uninterrupted sitting in the train, reading and feeling slightly important. His head is even spinning slightly with the thought of meeting someone on the train – well, you never know. He finds an empty carriage and settles into a pleasant window seat.

After a few minutes, the door slides open and one of the most attractive women he has ever seen glides into the carriage. She is beautifully dressed and seems to him to be a fine mixture of elegance, sexiness and general desirability. He makes these judgements from small, slightly surreptitious glances up from his book as she moves across the carriage and sits opposite him in the other corner seat. He cannot believe his good fortune. As she crosses to her seat and sits down, she does not once glance at him and when she was sitting, she calmly rests her hands in her lap and closes her eyes. There is no possibility of him striking up a conversation with her. Throughout the entire journey, the only time she opens her eyes is to get up and leave the carriage for a few moments. She returns in the way that she first entered, not once looking at him, and immediately closes her eyes again.

Now picture a man who arrives home from work at the end of a long, arduous day. Many things have not gone well and his head seems to be bursting with the problems and complexities he has been trying to sort out throughout the day. He is looking forward to being at home, quietly, but feels very tense, wound up with the pressures that have beset him.

He goes in and gives his wife a kiss and greets his two young children, who barely acknowledge him because they are caught up in their game, which seems to consist of tearing from one room to the next making dinosaur noises. He sits down in the living-room, leans back and closes his eyes for a moment, wondering if he has the energy to look for something to take for the tension headache that he can feel beginning to creep up from his neck and shoulders.

He suddenly becomes aware that his wife has been asking him a question. He looks at her. 'Sorry. What did you say?' He vaguely notices a flicker of irritation cross her face, but it does not fully register with him. 'I said that I've had a really difficult day with the children; they seem to have the devil in them today.' 'Oh, have you?' he replies, his head aching more furiously and his mind still going to a conversation he had had just before leaving work. What did that man mean? 'Yes, I don't know what's got into them. And you know that good pair of trousers of mine, George rubbed Play-Do into them today. I don't know how I'm going to get it off.' He looks over at her, but seems to be seeing her through a gauze curtain. She sighs and goes back to the kitchen.

Picture a party, not an uproarious one, just a gentle gathering of people who are quietly standing around drinking and nibbling on some finger food. Music is playing quietly in the background and everyone is dressed fairly formally. It is a meeting arranged for visiting cultural groups from overseas for them to get to know one another and to meet the locals. It is all part of the town's aim to keep up cultural contacts, to be friendly and to be part of the modern world.

In the centre of the room, surrounded by a hum of gentle conversation, a rather swarthy-looking man from Italy is talking to the secretary of the group that has organised the party. They are talking easily enough, each with a drink in hand. But as they speak, so he takes half a step towards her. She drops her eyes and, slowly, in order not to give offence, moves away slightly. He seems not to notice this and after another minute of conversation moves slightly forward again. Once again, after a small pause and an averted gaze, she moves back. And so this goes on, with those around being quite unaware of it. During their 10 minutes or so of conversation, until she breaks away with 'Please excuse me, but I must just have a word with . . .', they have engaged in a curious dance in which he seems to have moved her backwards around the room.

▶ To not communicate is impossible

The importance of interpersonal communication cannot be exaggerated. Human interaction is about communication. Of course, the details of the communication between two people are crucial – how words are said, whether they are said at all, what is going on around and beneath the words, whether or not words are needed, who the interactants are, what they are wearing, whether or not they know each other, what the purpose of the communication might be, and so on. But even more basic than all of this is the necessity of communication.

If two people are in a shared space, then it is impossible for them not to communicate. Take the example with which this chapter began. It might have seemed from the description that there was no communication between the two people on the train. The young man sat there obviously hoping for more communication than there was and the woman apparently ignored him. There was no obvious interaction. But to enter a railway carriage and then sit with eyes closed, to never look at the other occupant even when leaving the carriage briefly, is to communicate a clear message. 'I do not wish to communicate.' This is, perhaps, the simplest, most sparing message that can be sent. To close one's eyes, to turn away, to say nothing are all messages that 'I want no further communication for the moment'.

In other words, although it is possible not to communicate verbally, it is not possible completely to shut off non-verbal messages because this in itself is a non-verbal message. As will be seen later, there is an enormous amount that can be learned about another person and about the possibilities of interaction and any potential relationship from observing non-verbal behaviour.

Superficially, communication between two people may seem to be very straightforward but look a little more deeply and its complexities become obvious. Think of an argument developing between two members of a family. They know each well and they have been through the argument a number of times previously and they know when the other is attempting to hide his or her true feelings. But each of them also knows that the other knows and they both know that they both know. Now, in the midst of these various levels of 'knowing', what does any one utterance or even a single glance mean? There are so many different ways in which a single moment of interaction might be interpreted.

People can also be very tricky in their communications, even though they might be doing so unwittingly. Think, for example, of the mother who says to her son 'I want you to be less obedient, you always do exactly what you are told' or the father who says to his daughter 'I want you to be more spontaneous'. How can they win? If the son is less obedient, he is being obedient, and if he is more obedient, he is disobeying his mother's request. How can the daughter 'try' to be more spontaneous? And if she does and she succeeds, then she is obviously not being spontaneous because 'trying' and spontaneity are by definition incompatible. These are examples of paradoxical communications that give one of the interactants no possible way to behave other than to run away from the situation either by turning inwards or by leaving altogether.

Another way in which such communications have been described is as *double binds*. The person on the receiving end is bound whichever way he or she turns. Another example would come from the mother who asks her son or daughter to give her a kiss but shies away from or stiffens at the bodily contact. The child is being given one message verbally and another non-verbally. They are then in a double bind in that whatever they do is wrong.

Most paradoxical communications clearly lead to troublesome outcomes, but some are amusing to conjure with. Think about this. A school-teacher says to the class that they will be receiving a test one day next week but that the day on which it is held will be a surprise. If you think it through, this is impossible. Let's say it is Thursday and the test has not been held, then it must be on Friday, but then it wouldn't be a surprise. So that cuts out Friday. But then if it is Wednesday and the test has not been held, then it must be on Thursday, but then it would not be a surprise. And so on back through the week, thus proving that the teacher has made an impossibly paradoxical communication to begin with; or has s/he?

▶ How and why we communicate

We cannot not communicate; to communicate is integral to being human. Think of what it is like if you have not spoken to anyone else for days, or even hours. There is a strong drive just to hear another voice, to engage with another person. Singing, whistling and talking to oneself are just not the same. We are a social species and have many reasons for communicating with others. Partly it is to make reference to other things, things that we are doing, that have happened, that will happen. We communicate to express ourselves and to give opinions or to give information and we communicate in order to gain information about the world or about the opinions, attitudes, beliefs and feelings of others. And we communicate because we need to know where we stand in the world, particularly in the eyes of others.

The most obvious way in which we communicate is verbally. We say things to other people, we make reference to things and we try to express ourselves. Although what we say can be very subtle, it is only part of the story. Verbal communication is ringed around with non-verbal communication. What we express non-verbally can amplify, modify, distort, conflict with and generally contextualise what we say. Just think, for example, of the *manner* in which we might say something. It is perfectly possible to say 'No' in such a way that it means 'Yes' and to say 'Yes' in such a way that it means 'No'. The misinterpretations that follow these possibilities can cause extreme confusion, not to say embarrassment. Part of learning to communicate involves learning to be as accurate as possible in receiving as well as sending signals. It is also possible to communicate almost entirely non-verbally. Two lovers can sit together for hours communicating without words. The raised eyebrow of a parent may be sufficient to stop a child from doing something. The catching of someone's eye 'across a crowded room' can lead to all manner of mischief.

▶ Body language

Typically, although our parents teach us to speak and gradually improve our subtlety in the spoken language, they do not do much about our body language.

This is something that we pick up as we go along, gradually learning what various expressions mean and how to use our body language. Mostly, this is not conscious learning, although in some cases it can be. If a checkout operator is told to smile more as well as asking customers how their day has been, their use of body language is being manipulated, albeit simply. A salesperson 'making a pitch' is making judicious use of body language to seem more plausible, more genuine and sincere, more encouraging and persuasive.

The most basic form of body language involves *touching* another person. Even observing from a distance, it is possible to work out a great deal about the relationship between people by noting who touches whom, when, where and how often.

Generally, the closer the relationship, the more frequent the touching. To touch another person always means an increase in intimacy. Think of the first touch between potential lovers, especially if they have been unsure; it is as though a huge barrier has been crossed. Or think of the consternation that can be caused by a 'toucher', someone who tends to touch other people more than is socially comfortable.

Touching, then, is the closing of the *physical distance* between people, however temporarily, to zero. Its importance has long been recognised and so all cultures have developed various touching rituals that tend to occur at the start and finish of encounters. Handshakes, back slaps, social kisses and hugs are the obvious examples in Western culture. The physical distance between people when they interact is extremely important; if customary distances are changed, then discomfort results. In most social settings there is an ideal distance between people; too near or too far creates discomfort.

Go back to the party in one of the examples earlier. The visitor from Italy was moving the female organiser of the party backwards round the room. All that was happening here is that each of them was attempting to stand at his or her comfortable distance for a party. Typically, people in Italy stand closer than people in Northern Europe or the USA or the UK, for example. So he would take a slight step forward to increase his comfort level, she would become slightly disturbed by that and take a small step back, to regain her comfortable distance.

We carry round with us several distances that seem appropriate for the various social settings that we encounter. It is as though there were a series of bubbles around us that we use to gauge the 'right' distance. Think of what people do when they step into a crowded lift. Here the physical distance is much less than is comfortable. If the same dozen people were to go into an empty room, they would space themselves out; they wouldn't huddle at a 'lift' distance. Again, this is a matter of an increase in intimacy. So, typically, they do not look at one another; they keep their distance in this way. They studiously observe the lift numbers changing or gaze at the wall as though lost in lofty contemplation.

Interestingly, it is our *eyes* that are, perhaps, the most important vehicle of non-verbal behaviour. We obviously use our eyes (although the other senses come into play as well) to observe the other person's body language. However, our eyes are also used to express emotion and to give information. The most important thing that we do with the eyes when communicating with others is to look into their eyes. *Eye gaze* and *eye contact*, as they are called, fall into quite reliable patterns. As with touching and other decreases in physical distance, eye contact always means an increase in intimacy. Again, we have conventions about this in order to maximise what is comfortable. Think how awkward it is interacting with someone who seems never to look at you and with someone who looks at you too much. It is as though you want to get closer to the 'non-looker' and further away from the 'looker'.

One of the ways in which eye gaze is used in communication is to regulate the order of events. In a conversation, the person listening tends to look at the other person, usually at their eyes, or in the region of their eyes. Whereas the person speaking tends to look much less. Then when the speaker is about to stop, they tend to look at the listener as though to say 'I am finishing; the floor is yours'. The listener then usually looks away just before beginning to speak.

Nowhere is the heightening of intimacy more apparent than with eye contact. If someone holds your eye longer than is normal, then it will set you wondering about what it means. Is he or she wanting something of me? Is he or she suggesting that we move the relationship on a little? Is it aggressive? Is it challenging? It always seems to mean something.

There is even more. When we interact with someone else, we move our bodies, particularly our limbs. We *gesture* to amplify or modify what we say, but we also sit or stand in particular *postures*. We can seem relaxed or tense, we can mirror the other person's posture or we can work against it. We can sit or stand in a closed-off sort of manner or we can be open and expansive.

All of these aspects of body language tend to be maintained in a sort of balance. The description of what happens in a lift is an example of this. It is as though we have an unconscious mixture of what degree of body language expression we find comfortable and if it changes in one area, then we alter one of its other aspects to bring it back into balance. More interestingly, our body language alters if we attempt to engage in *deception*.

Every day we encounter situations when we judge that it is probably better not to display our true feelings, situations when we might be saying one thing but thinking and feeling another. At such times it is our body language that we bring under control, even if we might be doing so unconsciously. We control our tone of voice, and the way we sit or stand. We control our facial expression in order not to give too much away. We control our gestures and hand movements generally. Or sometimes we do and sometimes we do not. It is this that led to the development of the idea of *non-verbal leakage* by two psychologists, Ekman and Friesen (1969).

The idea is that the various areas of our body have varying potentials for sending non-verbal messages. The greatest potential is from the face, particularly the eyes. The next lies with the hands and arms and finally there are the feet and legs. When trying to determine what another person is thinking and feeling, we tend to pay attention to those areas in the same order; we look at the face more than the hands and the hands more than the feet. Accordingly, when we are attempting to control our body language, we do so in a similar way, paying most attention to the face and eyes, and so on. Because of this our true feelings 'leak out' in the reverse order. So we tend to give ourselves away more by wiggling our feet or having our leg jumping up and down under the table, or by fiddling with our hair or tearing up paper cups. The judicious observer can tell much about the other person from paying attention to these reactions; just do it carefully.

▶ Styles of communication

All these subtle and not so subtle aspects of communication do not occur in isolation. For each of us they cohere into what might be called our communication style. In everyday life we see some people as friendly and others as over-friendly or unfriendly. Others we might see as hostile or bombastic or pompous or overbearing or conciliatory or cold or warm or laid back or intense, and so on. On the one hand, these might be seen as personality characteristics (see Chapter 10), but on the other hand, they might also be seen as styles of communication. For example, the overly friendly person might stand slightly too close, touch slightly too often, and attempt to engage in mutual eye contact too intensely. The cold person might smile little, stand in a rigid way, either not look at all or with a fixed state. The laid-back person might appear constantly relaxed and biddable, easy to talk to, rarely interrupting, and so forth.

Such differences in communication style also exist between cultures. Thus, in some cultures (Pacific Island cultures, for example) it is regarded as impolite to look at the other person's eyes very much. Somebody from Western society meeting a person from one of these cultures and finding them looking at the ground rather than at their face would immediately see this as behaviour that needed accounting for. Do they have something to hide? Are they very shy? Is there something about me that they do not like? In fact, it is none of these things – they are merely behaving in the way appropriate to their culture.

If a person from Southern Europe or Latin America meets someone from Northern Europe or North America, then there is a constant shuffling of body language as each attempts to become comfortable. The Latin-based peoples tend to stand closer, touch more, look more and talk more than their 'Northern' counterparts. It pays, therefore, if one is meeting someone from a different culture to find out whatever one can about that culture's style of interpersonal communication. It can save considerable embarrassment and misunderstanding.

There are also cultural differences in the extent to which body language is openly displayed or, to put this another way, in the subtlety with which it is typically expressed. The obvious example comes when comparing the Orient and the Occident. Typically, to the Western eye, people from South-East Asia tend to have a relatively restricted range of body language, whereas, to the Oriental eye, presumably Westerners might seem overblown in their gestures, facial expressions and general non-verbal behaviour.

Added to this, of course, similar gestures have different meanings in different cultures and the same gesture might have various meanings in different cultures. Signs of disgust, contempt and annoyance, for example, vary from culture to culture. Even something as simple as a head-nod might not always mean agreement.

▶ Forming impressions

While we are communicating with another person, we are constantly engaged in forming impressions of them. What is she like, really? Does she like me or dislike me? Is he a person of integrity? Can I trust him? He seems pretty scruffy; will he be OK as a baby-sitter? She has red hair; will she be fiery? Such impressions are all part of the business of communication. She smiled at me. What does that mean? Was she just smiling, just being friendly? Or is she interested in me? Part of what we do when communicating with another person, even if this communication only involves looking at them as they sleep on a train, is that we make *attributions* to them. We don't come away from an encounter thinking that 'He didn't smile much or have much to say', but rather that 'He is an unfriendly or a cold person'.

Our general tendency is to attribute what we see in another person to them rather than to the environment. So, for example, if someone looks at us far more than would normally be the case and does so on more than one occasion and we see him doing the same to other people, then we are likely to attribute this to some aspect of his basic character. However, if we do not have access to all of this type of information, then we tend to take short-cuts in our thinking and to end with biases that are regularly repeated.

Probably the most common bias is the *person bias*, sometimes called the *fundamental attribution error*, because it is so commonplace, in which if somebody dresses a certain way or behaves a certain way, then we are far more likely to attribute this to their personality than to some outside influence. This bias is particularly evident if we are set to actually evaluate the person rather than that person's role, for example. And we frequently are set in this way in everyday life. So we see a nurse, or a teacher or a policeman or policewoman going about their business and tend to judge them as being particular *types* of people rather than as people being constrained by the roles that they are playing in their work.

Interestingly, given the cultural differences already discussed, there are also cultural differences in the person bias. It is more prevalent in Western than Eastern cultures. This may well be because Eastern cultures are less concerned with people being responsible for their own actions and more concerned with ideas of fate or karma or samsara.

A final bias that is worth mentioning comes about through beliefs about other people leading to self-fulfilling prophecies. For example, if one is told that someone that one is due to meet is, say, very emotionally switched on and a good communicator, then one is likely to behave towards that person as though this is the case and so help to bring about those very characteristics. A good example of this came from a study in which teachers were falsely informed that some of their children had performed better on some tests than they had. The teachers subsequently behaved towards these children in such a way that their performance did improve far more than would have been expected.

What of *first impressions*? Are they important or not? When we meet someone for the first time and we look at the way they are dressed, their body shape, their hair colour, how close together their eyes might be, their skin colour and, particularly, how they communicate with us, what their communication style is, so we form an impression of them, their character, of what they are like. How significant is this impression?

The general answer to this is that first impressions are extremely important. How you behave towards someone on first meeting them, how you communicate, how well you control your body language, can make a large difference to the impression that they form of you. However, it is relatively easy to overcome the effect of first impressions by warning people of their danger. The problem is such warnings are not often given in everyday life. Moreover, they might not be appropriate in the sense that the first impression that we form of someone might well be as accurate as we will ever be, as long as the person, at the time, was behaving roughly as they normally would.

▶ **Impression management and effective communication**

For the most part, the subtleties of one-to-one communication happen automatically and unconsciously. Occasionally, in daily life we might seek to create a particular impression and so consciously control what we say, the way we speak, and the way we sit, stand, gesture, look, and so on. We might, for example, decide that it is best not to show much emotion in a particular setting and we certainly become used to communicating differently in different settings.

People in some occupations have to pay particular attention to their manner of communication and, indeed, have to undergo training in the various skills involved. For example, salespersons, passenger attendants on aircraft and people who serve customers all have to do so with attention to how they communicate. If all hotel managers behaved like John Cleese in *Fawlty Towers*, not many people would stay in hotels.

The important point here is that although interpersonal communication often takes place unconsciously, it can also be seen as a skill or set of skills that can be learned. Or, to put it more dramatically, how we communicate can be used manipulatively. Manipulation is a harsh word to use within a social context, but most people do engage in it to some extent. It would be a rare person who has not set out to deceive at some time and an even rarer person who has not set out to create an impression from time to time. Impression management is ultimately concerned with communication.

Paul Ekman (1969) has written extensively about deception, his ideas deriving from the work already mentioned on non-verbal leakage. Interpersonal deception can become very complex depending on factors such as how important the deception is to the two or more people who are interacting. Some situations seem to demand more deception than others and some personalities are more prone than others to engage in deception. In some circumstances (the complexities of family life come to mind) it may be that both interactants are deceiving, or one may be deceiving and the other not, and either or both may be aware or not of the deceptions. It may also be that we develop implicit pacts about whether or not the deception should continue. All of these intricacies are played out in the subtleties of communication.

Either consciously or unconsciously, then, to some extent, we change our social behaviour and communication style in an attempt to influence what other people might think of us. Take the example of a job interview. A person might well want to appear to be relatively relaxed and calm while feeling very anxious or might want to give the appearance of not being too eager even though desperate for the job, or might want to give the appearance of extreme reliability when they know that their work habits leave much to be desired. All these impressions are managed by how we dress and how we behave when communicating.

Many years ago, Erving Goffman (1967) did much to further understanding of impression management by portraying human beings as actors who adopt various roles. This idea is convincing – we all know that we adopt different styles of communicating in different circumstances, but it does suggest that we all may pass through social life consciously manipulating others. It is entirely possible both to set out to create an impression and to be sincere in the belief that the impression is an accurate reflection of how one really is. To show one's best characteristics or to show them in the best light in our dealings with others is not necessarily acting a false role. It is simply that it is difficult to be at our best all of the time.

Another way of looking at this is that we all have something of the politician in us. In other words, we set out to create certain impressions because we want to bring about certain ends. So, for example, we want to communicate with others in such a way that they will like us or feel positive towards us simply in order to make life proceed smoothly and pleasantly. If we are successful in this and it is matched by a similar success in others, then life *will* proceed more smoothly and pleasantly than it otherwise would. Whether or not this can or should be described as manipulative and, if so, whether or not such manipulation is 'justifiable' are a matter for debate.

As already mentioned, first impressions are important and our intuitive knowledge of this makes it more likely that we will be concerned to impress new acquaintances than those who know us well. The obvious example of this comes with the difference between people who are dating and those who are married. When dating, in general, people are more concerned to create 'a good impression' than they are when married. In marriage (or at least successful marriages) partners are more concerned with having a true impression of each other than a necessarily favourable impression, although the two might not be incompatible.

There are strong *personality* and *cultural* differences in impression management. To take the obvious example, some people are shy and inhibited socially and spend so much of their time worrying about making a poor impression that they learn to avoid social contact. This is almost like a definition of shyness. Although shyness and social inhibition might be regarded as a basic aspect of personality, it is not set for life. If the intricacies of interpersonal communication are regarded as social skills, it is worth bearing in mind that skills can be learned. Some people might be naturally more adept socially than others, but everybody can improve their level of social skill.

One fundamental way in which people vary is with respect to how much they monitor their own social behaviour. For example, we all differ as to how much we pay attention to whether or not we are conforming with the expectations of others, how well we think we have 'carried off' a social occasion, or how much we are concerned with gaining the approval of others. There are some fairly obvious differences between those who are high and low at self-monitoring. For example, 'highs' tend to have more friends than 'lows' but their friendships are more superficial. 'Highs' tend to choose friends for their general attractiveness whereas 'lows' choose those who most readily reflect their own values.

As well as personality differences, there are also cultural differences in the general styles of interpersonal communication. The obvious and in some ways most interesting example of this comes in a comparison between Western and Eastern societies. Western society tends to encourage the individual and there is therefore a greater tendency to act similarly from one situation to the next, in other words, 'to be ourselves'. Eastern cultures are more collectivist in style, part of which is an expectation that behaviour will change according to the requirements or conventions of a particular group.

Leaving aside the matter of cultural differences, group pressure has a significant influence on impression management and communication. We might well behave as others do simply because we learn from them. We might well watch others for clues as to how to behave socially. For example, it is probably sensible to sit quietly when one first attends meetings in a new position, simply to learn what the communication conventions might be. But it is not just a matter of learning the conventions, groups also produce pressure to behave in particular ways simply because they are the group. They have norms to which most of us feel pressure to conform merely in order to be an accepted part of the group.

The famous laboratory studies on group conformity were carried out more than half a century ago by Solomon Asch (1956), but the results remain valid today. They involved participants sitting with a group of others simply carrying out the task of saying aloud to which of three lines a fourth line was equal in length. It was a very easy and obvious task in each case. During the testing, all but one member of the group had been instructed to start making a consistently wrong call, with the 'real' participant always being near the end of the list. Most subjects were swayed by this and themselves made the wrong judgement calls on a number of occasions. Remember, these judgements were obviously and clearly wrong, but, nevertheless, people were sufficiently pressured by the need to conform, to be part of the group, that they also made the wrong call.

When questioned afterwards, the participants who conformed in this way created elaborate rationalisations for why they had, saying, 'Eight people were more likely to be right than one', and so on. And this was just with respect to judging the length of a line. Compare this with the complexities of general interpersonal communication and social behaviour and the huge pressures to conform that might exist therein.

Conformity is part of impression management, as, of course, is non-conformity. Some people might want to create the impression of independence, standing alone, being of integrity and so forth by avidly not conforming to the group.

If you think back to the three examples at the start of this chapter – the young man in the train, the man coming home to his family and the woman at the party – you will see that each of the descriptions could be greatly expanded. They contain all the elements discussed in this chapter, it is just that some of those elements have been picked out and made more salient.

▶ Being socially skilled

Regarding all these facets of one-to-one communication as elements of social skills has already been mentioned. Viewing such communication as a matter of skilled performance leads to a particular way of thinking about it. For example, how would you go about getting another person to talk more, to open up? Breaking this down, you would do certain things such as: talking less yourself, asking the other person open-ended questions rather than questions that could be answered with a single word, talking about things you knew he or she to be interested in, and rewarding anything that they did say with smiles and nods, and so forth.

Timing, pace and rhythm are very important in interpersonal communication. If the timing and rhythm between two people do not match, then it is difficult for them to develop a good relationship. To take the simplest example of this, for a conversation to develop reasonably, then those involved have to speak in turn rather than all together. Think of situations in which everyone is talking at once. If communication has not already disappeared, it soon will. So, if you wish to have certain outcomes, then it is important to learn the skills involved in controlling the pace and timing of an interaction. For example, if your own natural pace is faster than the person with whom you are interacting and you want the interaction to go in a particular way, then you will need to slow yourself down and to be aware of the other person's manner of pausing and speaking.

To see interpersonal communication as a matter of social skill is also to try to analyse what is meant by *establishing rapport*. It is not only therapists who do this, but to some extent it is done by anyone who wants someone else to do something. Unless you are going to coerce or force them, then you have to establish a reasonable relationship with them if you wish to change them in some way, to make them do something from buying a new vacuum cleaner to simply being more pleasant when you see them.

To establish rapport you need to have a clear way of communicating with the other person; there has to be some degree of mutual trust and acceptance – without this there is no starting point; and you have to develop a smooth pattern of communication, pace and timing again being important. So, how do you do this? By adopting a warm, friendly manner, by treating the other person as an equal, by establishing a smooth pattern of interaction, by finding common interests or experiences, by showing the other person a sympathetic interest and by meeting the other person on their own ground (e.g. by using their words and ways of speaking). Overall, it is necessary to keep the other person in play by finding ways in which it is pleasant or rewarding for him or her to be there. And if all of this sounds manipulative, it is because it *is* manipulative. However, it is only spelling out a process that to some extent we all learn and engage in, but usually not as consciously as this, unless our job happens to demand it.

▶ **Summary**

- One-to-one communication is integral to interpersonal life. One cannot not communicate; in other words, it is impossible to shut off non-verbally even if it might be possible not to speak.

- Interpersonal communication is multi-layered, depending on the extent to which everyone involved is aware. It can even take the form of paradoxes that put us in double binds.

- We communicate one to one in order both to express and to gain information, all of which reduces uncertainty and so makes social life easier.

- A crucial part of interpersonal communication is body language or non-verbal communication, consisting of touching, physical separation and space, posture, gesture, facial expression and, in particular, eye gaze.

- Non-verbal behaviours are in balance and if we try to mask them and so deceive others, then they tend to 'leak out' in ways of which we are unaware.

- Each of us develops a personal style of interpersonal communication, although such styles fall into broad clusters and also reflect cultural differences.

- Interpersonal communication tends to begin with impression formation based on initial observations.

- An important aspect of impression formation is the fundamental attribution error which involves ascribing to personality whatever impressions people give, rather than ascribing them to some outside influence.

- Clearly, first impressions are important.

- A great deal of effort is put into impression management in Western society, not always consciously. It varies with both personality and culture and also gives many people a strong push towards conformity.

- One-to-one communication can be seen as a question of learning social skills, something that is dependent on timing and rhythm and which leads to an analysis of such techniques as to how to establish rapport.

▶ **Questions and possibilities**

- Do you agree that it is impossible not to communicate? Can you think of any examples of two people being in each other's presence without communicating?

- Take a recent interaction between you and a close family member and write down a description of what occurred. Now write the description from the viewpoint of one of the other interactants. How much do you think that each of you knew what was going on? How do you think that you knew?

- List all the ways that you can think of in which two people can communicate. Are there differences between the way in which adults and children communicate?

- Go out and observe some non-verbal behaviour, particularly patterns of eye gaze. How important do you think that this body language is? How important is it in the workplace?

- Think about some of the ways in which you have deceived other people or have been deceived by them or have watched others being deceptive. How do you know that deception was occurring? Do you think that it is wrong to deceive others interpersonally? Always? What are the differences between occasions in which social deception is acceptable and those when it is not?

- Think of situations in which you have been very uncomfortable socially. Analyse them in order to pin down exactly what made you uncomfortable. Did you try to hide your discomfort? How did you do that and how successfully?

- How important do you believe first impressions to be? Do you make snap judgements of others? What do you base such judgements on?

- Imagine the people that you work with. When they behave in ways of which you strongly approve or strongly disapprove, do you tend to believe that this is part of their character or that it is because of external forces?

- Do you manage the impression that you try to give? In what way? What are the differences between how you behave at work and at home? Do you communicate in the same way in both settings?

- How strong or weak a conformist are you? Would you stand out against the judgements of others if they all disagreed with you? What do you think makes some people into conformists and others into non-conformists? Is this an aspect of their character or due to some outside influence?

- In what ways do you think that your own social skills could be improved? How would you go about making the improvements?

- Do you know some people who are better than others at establishing rapport? How do they do it?

CHAPTER EIGHT

Social life

Communicating in groups

> ### Scenes from life
>
> *Imagine that you have agreed to take part in a psychological experiment.* You were recruited by a rather formidable-looking middle-aged man of obvious maturity. He was wearing a white coat and you felt that he was clearly someone who was knowledgeable and expert, a person of some authority. You are invited into a psychological laboratory and find yourself surrounded by some surprising and interesting examples of electric and electronic equipment. He asks you to sit in front of some of this equipment and instructs you about the procedure that will be followed.
>
> He explains that there are 10 buttons in front of you, each of which, if pressed, would deliver an electric shock to another person. The shocks range from very mild on button number 1 to reasonably severe on button number 10. Hidden from your sight on the other side of the apparatus is a second person whom you are told will attempt to learn a task. You will be the 'teacher' and will give feedback to the person in the form of an electric shock controlled by your 10 buttons when he makes a mistake. The task is explained fully and the other person begins his task.
>
> At this point, do you think that you would have stayed in the situation and agreed to the task? Imagine that you have agreed and you are apparently dealing with a person who is not a very good learner. He keeps making mistakes, and your only form of communication with him is by pressing the 'shock' buttons. His learning is very poor and you ask the experimenter what you should do. He suggests that you might think of increasing the intensity of the shock that you are giving. But he also says that 'we' will have to take a little care because the man attempting to learn the task does have a bit of a heart condition. Would you accept the suggestion and step up the shock intensity?

What I have described here forms part of a series of experiments carried out many years ago by Stanley Milgram (1974). He found that a surprising number of people (in fact, most that he asked) were prepared to take part in his experiments and to attempt to make someone else 'learn' by giving them electric shocks, sometimes apparently of very high intensity. In one extreme case where the learner apparently had a heart condition, one participant, in the face of poor learning, increased the shock intensity to the highest level and then stopped for a moment after he heard a plaintive cry from the other side of the apparatus. After that there was silence and no response. His reaction was to tentatively start pressing the buttons again.

This procedure, which nowadays would be unacceptable for ethical reasons, is about obedience to authority. In all cases, there was not a real learner behind the screen and no one, in fact, received any electric shocks. The whole setting was rigged. But what it demonstrated very clearly is that many of us do what those in authority suggest that we do. We don't question their authority. Parallels with the extremes of war are only too clear, thinking of Nazi Germany and WWII as the obvious example. This is but one of the many aspects of the influences of communication by the group upon the individual.

Geoff is in his thirties, relatively young to be in a senior management role in his company. He and seven other senior managers form the executive team of the company. They meet once per week to discuss whatever needs to be discussed and to sign off the various matters that come to them. There are occasional moments of friction but mostly the group works comfortably and the company is progressing well; at least the financiers are happy. Geoff is still learning how to be part of the group but is gaining in confidence each week. He has not been promoted beyond his ability and is pleased with his personal development.

Early one morning immediately Geoff has arrived at work, he finds an email calling him and the other executives to an urgent meeting on that same afternoon. The meeting is scheduled to last for the entire afternoon and perhaps into the evening and it will be held in the meeting room of a hotel not far away. There is a crisis. The company's finances are not in such a healthy state as everyone had thought, but, more to the point, the managing director has firm evidence that their main competitor is developing a product that will blow the company away. Their sales are likely to drop so dramatically that they would have to fold.

As Geoff and the others gather in the hotel meeting room, the tension in the air is palpable. Everyone looks strained and anxious. The managing director starts straight in with no preamble, telling of the state of the company and describing their competitor's potential market advantage.

Everyone sits in silence except for the occasional and somewhat tentative question. At no time is any mention made of how the meeting should proceed or what exactly the objectives are. The MD ends with, 'Well, what are we going to do?'

Geoff has never felt so much a part of the group. Everyone starts talking at once and they are all clearly bonded by the common goal. As the talking goes on and more and more suggestions are made, so the group seems to grow in strength and confidence. The MD keeps interrupting with ideas of his own and as the time passes, so the suggestions become more and more extreme, even reaching the point of someone arguing for industrial espionage. Geoff cannot believe what he is hearing as all of the others, including the MD, appear to take this seriously.

Gradually, the arguments in favour of some sort of espionage, even sabotage, are mounted with greater force. The group seems to grow in strength, gaining an almost invulnerable edge as ways and means are considered. At one point Geoff whispers to the person next to him that he doesn't like the turn the meeting is taking and that he feels that he should make some protest. The whisper comes back, 'I wouldn't do that; the MD has made his mind up.' Geoff sits back quietly and stops himself from blurting out his objections. Someone else speaks up with a tentative objection of the 'What if we are caught?' variety, but is quickly squashed by the others.

By 6.15 p.m. the meeting has finished and a plan of full-on industrial espionage has been devised and the possibilities left open for some clandestine sabotage if the person they will employ has the opportunity and the means. Geoff went home feeling as though he had been through a harrowing experience but, nevertheless, feeling even closer to the executive team than he had the previous day.

This has been an example of Groupthink, not unlike that which led to the Cuban missile crisis in the USA in 1961.

▶ Types of group

Almost everyone belongs to many groups. Even the extreme social isolate is a member of a loosely constructed and ill-defined group of social isolates. The members of a group usually share common goals and usually gain some pleasure from group activity. If a group meets regularly for some common purpose, then a structure will develop for the group and people will begin to adopt and assume varying roles and status. Of course, some groups endure for many years, with members joining and leaving regularly. Schools, companies, sports organisations and churches are all examples of enduring groups.

The most obvious groups are based on face-to-face interaction. People meet regularly and share common aims. As well as attempting to realise these aims, the members of such groups will also gain considerable satisfaction from being in the group. Their social needs might well be met, for example. The family in its various forms is probably the most common instance of the face-to-face group, but so are sports clubs, adolescent peer groups, hobby clubs, and so on.

The other type of group does not depend on close contact between the members. There might be a common background, common interest and goals and even a common training and education, but most of the members of the group might never have to meet. A political party might be said to form such a group, or the members of the Church of England or all of the Jewish people in the USA. And, of course, either of these types of group can vary from just involving a handful of people to being very large indeed.

Another way in which the groups to which we all belong might vary is in their formality. Some groups are very formally constructed, their members having very clearly determined roles. The armed forces provide the most extreme example of this, or, perhaps, the main structure within a prison in which the roles of prisoners and guards remain quite distinct for much of the time. Within an informal group, however, the structure and roles might vary considerably. So, within the armed forces, for example, there might spring up large numbers of informal groups based on friendships or common interest, all existing within the highly formalised structure of the major group.

The final distinction to make between the groups to which most of us belong is in terms of size. We join, either by design or by default, both small and large groups. On the one hand, there are families, groups of friends, interest groups and small groups that form in order to run things (such as a school committee or a sports club). On the other hand, there are large reference groups such as the people who live in a neighbourhood or district, those who live in a city or even within a country, those who have an income below or above a certain amount, and so on. The matter of how the members of such groups behave and, in particular, how they communicate varies considerably.

▶ Small groups

Joining

What makes us join one group rather than another, assuming that these are not groups that we have to join because of our work or that come about for other reasons such as marriage and family? There are several reasons that have been identified, depending somewhat on whether one is considering initial joining or continued membership of a group:

■ *Attachment.* As is made clear in Chapter 14, the nature of the initial attachments we make in life is crucial to our later development and social and emotional experiences. These attachments have a strong influence on any later attachments that we might make. So, for example, if an initial attachment has been ambivalent, flicking about between feeling secure and feeling insecure, then such might also be a person's commitment to a group. A person might join an interest group reluctantly, become enthusiastic for a time but constantly be on the alert for social slights or loss of status perceived as brought about by other members of the group. This would lead to a tendency to withdraw. In comparison, a person whose initial attachments were secure might well be attracted in a straightforward way to joining groups and to be reasonably steadfast in membership.

- *Stress*, as seen in Chapter 17, is a very complex topic. However, in small part it relates to the propensity to join a group. Think of sitting in a dentist's waiting-room, considering the prospect of a forthcoming root canal procedure. For many people this would be a relatively stressful time. Other patients are also there, awaiting their treatment. There is a strong likelihood that conversations will be struck up, much more so than if the same people were waiting for a haircut or a bus. Think of travelling in a lift, standing facing the front as usual, firmly avoiding eye gaze with the other passengers. Then the lift becomes stuck between floors and remains so for some time. Conversations begin and a series of unengaged liftees suddenly begin to form a rudimentary group.

- *Contact*. In general, the mere relatively frequent exposure to other people tends to lead to increased liking. Of course, there are exceptions to this, but, in general, the more we have to do with people, the greater the chance that our liking for them will increase and hence the more time we would like to spend with them. This not only helps in the formation of small groups but also in the probability that they will stay as a group. In short, increased contact leads to increased contact.

- *Common interests*. This is probably the most obvious reason for joining a group. People with similar interests tend to come together in the simple pursuit of those interests, the interests varying from hang-gliding to stamp-collecting, from studying the mating habits of insects to reading the scriptures. And then the increased contact will lead to increased liking, and so the group begins to become well established.

- *Personal and social identity*. Much of our daily life is spent in seeking to define ourselves. Who are we? What are we really like? How do others see us? We become concerned with self-esteem (How good are we at things? How well do others think of us?), and with anxiety about our status (Am I doing as well as him or her? Am I doing as well as I should be? Am I wearing the right clothes, driving the right car, living in the right neighbourhood? and so on). Membership of a group helps us to answer these sorts of questions. We find out a little about how others see us and we enjoy particular roles within the group, roles that others recognise. We may gain personal pride from what we do in the group or, alternatively, there might be times when we can forget our individual concerns and almost become depersonalised through allowing the group to take over. (This might well be at potential cost to their individual well-being at a later time.) All these possibilities lead people both to join groups and to maintain their membership of them.

■ *Socialisation.* Socialisation is a process that continues throughout life. It might rest on the early years and our initial attachments and our early experiences such as first going to school, but in a smaller way it occurs whenever we join a group. After joining a group, we tend gradually to become assimilated into it, taking on the group's goals and aspirations and ways of behaving. This is becoming socialised into the group. This process often becomes almost ritualised through a protocol of initiation. In general, the fiercer the initiation procedures or even ceremonies that a prospective group member is subjected to, then the more highly committed he or she will be to continued group membership. This is probably due to the reduction of cognitive dissonance. If I have been put through all that and have managed it successfully, this group must be worthy of membership. This process is seen in its most extreme form in military academies and public schools, but is also seen in much less structured groups such as on a building site, for example. Here 'the lad' might well be sent down to the shop to buy a tin of striped paint or a rubber hammer (for knocking nails in quietly).

The other end of the group socialisation process concerns the leaving of a group. This might simply happen because interest decreases, one's personal aspirations change or the group is no longer satisfying. This is a process of gradually drifting away. But the exit from a group might well be more abrupt than this. One might be rejected, ousted or ostracised, an event that has considerable implications for self-esteem and self-image.

Influence

Once we are the member of a small group, how does this affect what we do? In other words, in what way does the group influence the individual? One significant issue concerns our own individual performance. In many small groups, whatever we do is *observed* by the other members of the group. People vary in their reaction to this. Consider yourself. Do you like people watching when you are doing something or do you prefer to do things unobserved? Do you think that you perform better or worse when you are being observed?

Interestingly, being observed has two quite distinct effects on performance. In some cases, performance is decreased, even to the point of non-existence. The extreme of this is stage-fright, the sudden fear of public performance. There are many instances of well-known actors who, in mid-career, develop stage-fright and simply cannot perform. They might leave the theatre for several years and then return to their career later. The other extreme is that being observed enhances performance, people doing whatever it might be better when they know that others are watching. The general rule seems to be that if one is doing something new or for the first time, then being observed while doing it detracts from performance. On the other hand, being observed while doing some task or engaging in some activity that is well known or well rehearsed tends to enhance performance. So, if you are learning to play a new sport, it is better to begin it alone, but when you become adept at it, then you will probably perform better with an audience.

How does this work? Why does an audience have these two different types of effect? An audience probably arouses motivation above the level it would be when the individual is alone. Up to a point, increased motivation leads to enhanced performance. This is a straightforward relationship. But then status anxiety might cloud the water. People become anxious when they know that they are being evaluated, particularly if they are not especially confident in their abilities. And to be observed is inevitably to be evaluated, or so it seems. Again, as was seen with motivation more generally, a moderate degree of anxiety can facilitate performance. However, the anxiety might increase to such a great extent that it detracts from performance.

The other major way in which the small group influences the individual is through *social norms*. In general, there are four processes that any small group goes through in its early development. Interestingly, these four processes can be made use of quite formally if one is interested in creating and developing a group. The first is *forming*, which, as the name implies, is the earliest stage of group development in which the members of the group come together and begin to discuss the nature of the group, what it is for, why they are there, and so on. Then comes *storming*, during which the group members begin to organise the group. This might include moments of disagreement and argument as individual motivations are sorted out and the personalities of the individuals involved begin to become evident, either for good or for bad. At this stage, group members are jockeying for position and starting to sort out the processes by which the group might proceed.

After storming comes *norming*, a time of establishing the norms of the group. What are the shared beliefs and opinions, what is the overriding goal of the group, what are the behaviours which are considered appropriate and inappropriate for the group? It is not known exactly how the process of norming occurs; sometimes it is overt and sometimes covert. Finally, there is *performing*. Having become established and worked out the norms, the group can now do whatever it is that it wishes to accomplish.

As already mentioned, these four processes occur regularly and naturally in the development of any small group, but can be used directly to bring about the formation of a group, whether it be for a specific task or tasks or for a longer-term commitment. In any event, these four developmental stages each have an effect on the individual members within the group.

Power

An integral part of influence is power or the ability to influence others. There are many ways in which power can be deployed, it not simply being a matter of telling people what to do. And its use is clearly related to leadership (see Chapter 9).

Power may be exercised by *rewarding* people for their compliance. In other words, if a person within a small group does what those in powerful positions expect or desire, then they can be rewarded for so doing. Having power means controlling resources so that rewards can be given. The antithesis of this is coercive power in which group members are *punished* for non-compliance. Again this rests on having control over the resources necessary to be able to punish. For example, if a member of a sports team complies with the training regime and sets the example for others, then any number of rewards can be applied (making the first team, being allowed a day off from training, etc.). Alternatively, if a member of such a group is cavalier about adherence to the training regime, then he or she can be 'benched' for a period of time, made to do extra training before consideration for first-team membership, etc.

Another type of power is described as *legitimate* power. This occurs in more formally constructed small groups in which a person enjoys a statutory or legal position of influence within the group. Such a person may legitimately tell others what to do and can expect compliance. Of course, the style in which the person with power does this can vary enormously, from simply telling others what to do through to asking them gently to comply, even though everyone knows that compliance has to occur.

A more subtle type of power is *referent* power. Here the members of a group identify strongly with a particular person in the group – they *refer* to him or her – and because of this they comply. This is likely to occur in particular with transformational leadership (again, see Chapter 9). Related to this type of power is that which stems from a person having extra *knowledge and information*, this again being related to the power that comes from being the *expert*. Knowledge and expertise indeed bring power. In any small group there are people who do not know quite what to do even though the group has a purpose or goal. Those with the knowledge or expertise naturally become leaders, whether they want to or not. They are followed simply because they know what to do or because they have the information necessary for the group to fulfil its function.

The extremes with which power can be manifest in small groups was shown in a series of experiments carried out in the late 1960s by Stanley Milgram, described in the aptly named *Obedience to Authority*. The typical form of Milgram's experiments (which, it might be interesting to note, would not be possible to run nowadays for ethical reasons) is portrayed in the first few paragraphs of this chapter. The experiments, like many similar investigations, show that if people believe someone to be in authority, then they are likely to obey what that person asks or tells them to do without much demur. This might even be in some fairly extreme circumstances. There have also been similar studies in which people are asked to play the roles of prison guards and prisoners. Very rapidly, people 'get into role' and, if they are guards, start to be guard-like in stereotypical and even cruel ways.

Of course, not everyone is so obedient. Some people are seemingly always reactive against any type of authority or group pressure. Similarly, in many groups there is someone who takes on the role of whistleblower, in spite of group pressure or pressure from authority not to do so. This is simply an extreme example of the large individual differences that there are with respect to how obedient to authority people are. Such differences point to a difficulty with the Milgram type of study, fascinating though its results might be. It is difficult to know whether the results are due to people being obedient to authority or not, conforming to a group or not, or simply being dependent or independent. Possibly, all three of these factors might be involved.

Group performance

By definition, any small group is formed for a purpose. The members of the group have to work together towards some common goal. Key questions then become: How well does the group work? How does the group perform? To some extent, the answer to these questions depends on the task.

Any practical task involves the members of a group working together in a highly co-ordinated way, whether it is playing a team sport or putting together a product on the factory floor. Anything that leads to a drop in motivation or to a reduction in co-ordination of whatever the group are doing will lead to decreased productivity. One form that this takes that has been noticed in recent years is that of one or more members of the group not pulling their weight, being described as *social loafing*. Interestingly, women are far less likely to do this than men, perhaps because they are more attuned to the social and emotional consequences of group membership and teamwork.

If a group is involved in a problem-solving intellectual task, then the efficiency of the group tends to decrease as group size increases. So a group of three or four people will be far more effective at solving some intellectual task than will a group of 13 or 14. In general, if you want to predict how efficient a group will be with this type of task, then look at the second-best member of the group (however second best is defined, presumably in some way to do with the task at hand). This will be the level at which the group tends to perform.

Co-ordination within a group depends largely on the use of whatever information is available. There is often failure to use the available information and this will mean that co-ordination and communication and hence performance will break down. The possible patterns of communications are enormously important to group performance. For example, if someone sits in the centre of a communication network so that he or she is the hub of all incoming and outgoing information, then the group will work very efficiently if there is an urgent task at hand, as in a military operation, for example. That central person will also gain considerable satisfaction from his or her position. Think of the pleasurable power sometimes wielded by a departmental secretary, who, by the nature of her job, sits like a spider in the middle of a communications web.

By contrast, think of a group in which all members can freely communicate with just two other members. If such a group is given a problem to solve in which they all have some pertinent information, then they will tend to be much less efficient in solving the problem than the group with an obvious centre. This is a sort of constrained democracy in which not much gets done but in which the group members quite enjoy the experience. The question, then, concerns how group performance is measured. If efficiency of completing a task or solving a problem is the measure, then a centralised communication system is best. However, if satisfaction with group membership is considered, then a more liberal communication pattern is better.

Another issue that can affect group performance is polarisation. Polarisation is an almost inevitable result of discussion; opinions become pushed to the extreme when other people's viewpoints are heard. For many years, psychologists believed in the existence of a phenomenon known as 'risky shift'. This referred to group decisions tending to be riskier than the average of the decisions made by the members of that group alone. However, more recent and more precisely conducted research has shown this effect does not always occur. Group decision can move either way (that is, riskier or less risky) than the average of the individuals, depending on the nature of the initial average inclinations. In other words, if the individuals in a group have already decided in a relatively less risky direction, then the group as a whole will shift further in this direction. The reasons for this type of polarisation, which even happens with jury decision-making, is that people are influenced by the new information that they hear when the group meets, this being reinforced by the usual normative influence of the group.

There is also the matter of *groupthink*. Here the effect is that the group creates pressure not to express a minority opinion. As more and more members believe that more and more members are thinking alike, so a sense of cohesiveness develops in the group, a shared sense of being united. In other words, individuals suppress their own dissent in the interests of group consensus. Groupthink tends to happen when a cohesive group meets in isolation, without any systematic procedures for evaluation of their decision-making, in particularly stressful situations and with a directive leader.

The problem with groupthink is that it can lead to inappropriate decisions being made. If, for example, the best solution for a problem is to make a boldly imaginative leap in thinking, then the pressures of groupthink are likely to work against this and to suppress any boldness and imagination. Individual members feel invulnerable in that situation and tend to put pressure on dissenters; they rationalise what they are doing, some even becoming 'mind-guards', saying, 'Don't do that, don't think like that', and so on.

It is, of course, possible to be aware of the conditions that lead to groupthink and to guard against its effects. Typical ways of doing this are by warning people of the dangers of groupthink, by appointing someone to play the role of devil's advocate and question all decisions, to have an overview made by an outside expert, and by always setting up a second chance meeting a little later, when any decisions made are reviewed.

Boosting group performance

There are various ways in which the performance of a group can be boosted. One that has received some notoriety in recent years is *brainstorming*. This involves the group members sitting generating ideas about the problem at hand as fast and furiously as they can in a very receptive environment, one in which, for the moment, anything goes. The results of brainstorming sessions have been shown to be not overly effective and, in fact, it is a process that may produce the blocking of ideas. If the aim is to brainstorm a problem, then the best way to go about it is to break a group into smaller groups, ensure that these groups have a varied membership, and then to bring them together later in order to pool ideas.

Another way in which group performance can be boosted is to make sure that the minority opinions are facilitated and enhanced. Openness to minority opinions has been demonstrated to lead to more creative outcomes. This is, perhaps, not surprising since it is likely that there will be relatively few reasonably creative people in a group and so by definition their opinions are likely to be in a minority.

Finally, the most crucial factor in facilitating group performance lies in the style of leadership of the group. This is discussed in detail in the next chapter.

Large groups

Most of us belong to large groups as well as small groups. As mentioned earlier, most of us live in a particular neighbourhood, are of a particular religious or political persuasion, or simply share certain behaviour or opinions or beliefs with a loosely knit group of others. Simply to be of one gender or the other or to be within a particular age range or income category is to be the member of a large group.

Our relationships to such large groups are complex. If we refer to a particular group, then our tendency is to comply with its customs, by and large. This is particularly the case if there are people in the group whom we admire. This is sometimes known as the process of internalisation (of the group's behaviours, practices, customs, attitudes and beliefs.) This is, perhaps, most easily recognised when, from time to time, there are conflicting pressures from different reference groups to which we might belong. For example, there might be conflicting pressures between a business group and a church group, or between an educational group and a sports group, or, for the young, between peers and adults. Such conflicts usually push us in the direction of trying out new beliefs or attitudes to help to resolve the situation.

Prejudice, stereotyping and discrimination

A major characteristic of the members of a large group is the tendency to share attitudes, these being tendencies to think, feel and behave in some consistent way towards the object of that attitude. So, for example, we might feel only positively about all those who engage in competitive sport, mainly because we do so ourselves. Of, if we are city-dwellers, then we might share in a particular set of attitudes towards those who live and work in the country.

Prejudice is a particular type of somewhat pervasive attitude. A prejudiced attitude predisposes us to react in either favourable or (more usually) unfavourable ways towards a group or its members. Unfortunately, it is a type of attitude that is difficult to change. Closely linked to prejudice, almost such that it is an integral part of it, is *stereotyping*. This usually follows a standard pattern. The members of a group are seen as having clearly identified characteristics (green skins, upturned noses and close-set eyes). Members of the group doing the stereotyping agree that a particular green-skinned, upturned-nosed and close-set-eyed person also has other characteristics – laziness and tight-fistedness. And, most importantly, there is a discrepancy between the attributed traits and the actual traits (averagely hard-working and averagely generous).

The final link in this chain is *discrimination*. This is the behavioural or overt side of prejudice and stereotyping in which the member of a particular group is treated in a particular way, simply because they are in that group. This usually takes the form of the person being denied some right or privilege. I am not having that green-skinned person in my golf club; it wasn't set up for green-skinned people, they can form their own club.

Once prejudiced attitudes have been established within a group, then they tend to become institutionalised. They might come about when there are large-scale differences in status or where there is an unequal power relationship between groups. But prejudiced attitudes stay in place because they become normative, that is, the members of the group expect one another to hold those attitudes. Prejudice and discrimination themselves also help the group to cohere through strengthening the patterns of interaction. So, if you are a young soccer supporter in Europe, you might well expect the supporters of the rival team to be pink-haired monsters and will talk to your friends about that and even go looking for all of the pink-haired monsters to get them before they get you. Not to do this, not to conform, would have its costs, even to the extent of putting group membership at risk.

Of course, prejudiced attitudes might well be supported by all manner of individual factors such as the need for status. Thus one might feel more secure if one believes that the members of a stereotyped group are being inferior in status. It is also the case that we tend to dislike someone whom we suspect has different beliefs from our own. Eventually, attitudes towards minority groups become part of the prevailing cultural values. Green-skinned people might eventually be regarded as in all ways inferior and primitive, such that marriage with one of them is unthinkable. Such attitudes help to make inconsistent attitudes into some degree of consistency. Green-skinned persons are clearly persons. But if they are seen to be sub-human by white-skinned persons, then to discriminate against them is not to abuse the idea of equal rights for all people. Green-skinned people are somewhat sub-human, according to the stereotype.

Changing attitudes

Given that attitudes are such an important part of defining membership of a large group, how might they be changed? If one is the member of a particular group, is one necessarily stuck with the prevailing attitudes, prejudiced or not, of that group?

In general, our attitudes are both formed and changed through communication. As has become clear, much of our behaviour within a group, whether it is large or small, is about communication. The major ways in which attitudes can be influenced are by sustained messages that come from a credible source. This is precisely why famous sportspersons, or doctor look-alikes wearing white coats and dangling stethoscopes, are used to front advertisements. If someone 'important', someone to whom we look up, drinks X or eats Y or drives Z, then it must be desirable, trustworthy, beneficial or whatever. In general, the more credible the source of the communication, then the more persuasive it is likely to be.

Another type of persuasive, attitude-changing communication follows what is called a 'fear-fact' sequence. This is sometimes used by politicians to good effect. The members of the group are told something that might reasonably be expected to worry them: 'If you vote for X, then within two years your personal income tax is likely to treble.' Then they are told what they should do in order to reduce whatever fear or worry might have arisen for them: 'Vote for me.' If you keep on driving that sort of car, everyone will lose respect for you and think that you are a loser. Buy this sort of car and your status will go up.

These types of persuasive communications are believed in the end to be self-persuasive. If a particular communication provokes thoughts in the person that are in the direction of supporting the communication, then the person will move towards being influenced by the message. Conversely, if the message provokes anti-thoughts, then the person will move against it. So, the precise wording or style of a persuasive message is very important as also are the characteristics of the intended receiver of the message. For example, one is far more likely to persuade an intelligent audience with a balanced presentation that produces both sides of the argument than with a one-sided case. However, no matter how well contrived and persuasive a communication might be, if the receiver of it is already set to produce counter-arguments, then it is much less likely to succeed. Generally speaking, what is crucial is how much involvement a person has in an issue. Changing attitudes is no easy matter, particularly if they are well entrenched in the way that prejudiced attitudes are.

▶ **Summary**

- Groups vary with respect to whether they are face-to-face or based on much larger, more distant conglomerations, or the extent to which they are formal or informal and with respect to size.

- Reasons for joining small groups are attachment, stress, contact, common interests, personal and social identity and socialisation.

- A major way in which membership of a small group influences individual members is through knowledge that they are under observation. Depending on the precise circumstances, this may push performance either up or down.

- Influence on group members also comes from social norms, there being four phases that groups typically go through: forming, storming, norming and performing.

- Power is an integral part of influence, occurring mainly through the delivery of rewards or punishments. There is also legitimate power and power based on reference, often through the powerful person having greater knowledge and information. Power comes from expertise.

- The extremes of power and influence can be seen through Milgram's seminal studies on obedience to authority.

- Group performance depends on whether the task is practical or intellectual and particularly on the information flows that come from patterns of communication.

- Group performance also depends on the propensity for discussion to lead to polarisation and, in the extreme, on the results of groupthink.

- Group performance can be enhanced by brainstorming and the welcoming of minority opinions.

- Membership of large groups tends to lead to the internalisation of group values.

- The attitudes of members are fundamental to large groups. In this regard, of particular importance are the processes of prejudice, stereotyping and discrimination.

- Attitude change in large groups occurs mainly through communication, particularly if it is from a credible source, but also depending on the information being provided in the most effective sequence and also on the characteristics of the members of the group.

▶ **Questions and possibilities**

- List the small groups and the large groups to which you belong. What characterises these groups? Why are you a member of these groups? How has your membership of these groups affected you?

- Have you experienced the group processes of forming, storming, norming and performing? Which of the four processes do you believe to be the most important?

- Think of groups in which you have been a member. What types of group influence have you observed? In what ways have you been influenced by group membership or by particular people within the group?

- How do you think that you would react in an 'obedience to authority' type of situation? Would your friends and colleagues react differently? What determines differences in reaction in these types of situation?

- Have you ever experienced groupthink? If you have, list the characteristics of the circumstances that brought it about. If you have not experienced it, imagine a situation in your present work environment in which it might happen.

- List the major ways in which your membership of large groups has helped to form your values. When you compare your own values with those of your family and friends, are the differences due to their membership in large groups?

- Think of people that you know who are prejudiced. Do they stereotype others? Do they discriminate? What causes them to hold these attitudes? Is there any way in which you or anyone else could change these prejudices in other people?

- How would you go about trying to influence the attitudes of your family, your children, or the people that you work with? How have your attitudes been influenced by them?

CHAPTER NINE

Social life

Leadership

Scenes from life

The weekly round-up meeting had started and the case managers were making their presentations about the patients. Quickly, the usual petty envies began to emerge between the various professional groups. The occupational therapists crossed swords with the physiotherapists, the social workers looked askance at the psychologists and the psychologists looked askance at everyone, particularly the doctors. The doctors looked down their noses, or so it seemed to the paramedics.

The team leader sat back and let it all wash over her, her thoughts turning as usual to ponder on how easily everyone seemed to forget that they were there for the patients. They also seemed to forget that just 36 hours ago they had all been letting their hair down very amicably at a fortieth birthday celebration. The moment that status reared its head, so the skirmishing for territory began and the nastier side of the team members seemed to jump out.

As usual, she thought that there was nothing she could do except to let it all take its course. If she let them all have their say, then the jockeying for position might stop. She could see that they all felt very insecure and somehow threatened by the lack of clarity but could think of nothing to do about it. Anyway, it is only right that everyone should be allowed to say whatever they want to, isn't it?

On this particular occasion, the general discussion seemed to grow ever-more personal, words like blame, fault and responsibility filling the air. The exchanges became more and more heated and petty. Occasionally, someone would glance over at the team leader as though expecting something to come from her, but nothing did. The situation built up further and further until it struck the leader as sounding like a children's playground, with exactly the same sort of hectoring, sarcasm and bullying. She was finding it more and more irritating but still did not know what to do

---

about it. Why couldn't they grow up? Why did she have to be put in this ridiculous position of trying to control them?

Eventually, the team leader could take it no more. She screamed at the top of her voice, 'SHUT UP! WHY CAN'T YOU ALL SHUT UP?' The room quietened instantly, everyone turning to her with looks ranging from puzzlement through astonishment to shock. She ignored all this and simply told them off, her anger barely controlled, much as a parent who had let things go too far would tell a recalcitrant child.

The next meeting was relatively quiet but within a month the same thing had happened. This is typically the pattern that is repeated by *laissez-faire* leaders. They do nothing and then blow up and the group remains forever dysfunctional. Compare this style with what follows.

A new school principal has just called the staff together for their first meeting under his reign. They do not know quite what to expect. He is relatively young and has come from outside the district. He brings with him a reputation for being a high-flier with energy and the staff await what he has to say with the usual mixture of trepidation (Will he make my easy life more difficult?); cynicism (I've seen them all come and go); interest (It's about time this place had a shake-up); bad nature (What a prat he looks with that rotary badge in his lapel. Who does he think he is?); and good nature (He looks like a pleasant man; it will be interesting to see what he has to say).

'I have looked very carefully through all of your CVs and have seen a very talented group of teachers At some time in your careers, you have all done something really quite out of the ordinary. And I have looked very carefully all round the school. It is full of innovative ideas but there seems to be plenty of space and I am sure that together we could develop a lot more. And I have had some excellent conversations with the Board of Governors. They appear to be very supportive and will let us do whatever we wish, within reason, of course.

'Some of you may well see me as a bit young for the job of principal of such a large and progressive school as this. It is true, I am quite young but I have had quite varied experience and am deeply committed to the type of education that a school like this can provide. Let me tell you a little of my core beliefs about school life and the educational system . . .' And so he went on for some time. And then . . .

'So, if you put all of this together, I think that you can see that I have a very strong vision of where we can take this school. You certainly share enough talent between you to turn this into one of the best schools in the country. And I don't just mean in terms of academic results. I am sure that we can achieve those. But we can also make this into a school where the pupils enjoy themselves, where they want to come each day. A place and time that they will remember with affection. A school that they would want their own children to attend. And the point is that we don't have to do very much to achieve this. We have, and we are, the raw materials to do it.

'Now, I would like us to have a meeting like this every week and I would like you to feel that you can bring to and express with total freedom any ideas that you have for development.'

By the time that a question session was over, the new principal had brought about a mini-conversion in even the cynical and the bad-humoured among his new staff. They were not yet fully convinced but they were at least willing to give him a go. This is an example of a transformational, or charismatic or visionary, leader offering a very different set of possibilities than the *laissez-faire*.

▶ What is leadership?

In the other chapters on social life, the matter of leadership has been mentioned several times. There are very few groups which exist without leaders or in which leaders do not emerge. If a group is to achieve goals, and most groups have goals to achieve, then it needs a focus and the leader enables that focus. There are many ways of describing leadership and most of them will be touched on below. For now it is enough to say that although leadership can take many forms, leaders always influence the behaviour of the other members of the group, to some extent. They are concerned for the group (frequently more so than the other members of the group might be) and they are concerned with the goals of the group.

Of course, all of the members of a group might be concerned for the group and concerned about the group goals, but they will not also be influencing behaviour to the same extent as the leader. It is this combination that makes a leader distinct from other group members.

The obvious ways in which leaders differ is in terms of style. As will become clear, leadership has been described in many ways and the history of this to some extent reflects the history of much of social and personality psychology. To give an example of an obvious difference in leadership style, some leaders are naturally democratic and others are naturally autocratic. Democratic leaders allow group members to participate in decision-making, and policy-making, whereas autocratic leaders give orders without much consultation. The democratic leader shares power and the autocratic leader keeps all of the power for him- or herself.

Generally, democratic leadership is more effective than autocratic, that is, the group goals are more readily met and the group members enjoy group participation more than they do under an autocratic regime. There are exceptions to this, however. Most groups cannot make decisions on a wide range of problems, in which case an autocratic leader can be useful; a leader might stop leading if the group becomes too democratic; situations in which quick decisions need to be made favour autocratic leadership; where there is more risk or uncertainty greater autocracy follows; and in some groups the members simply may not like democratic leadership. This gives the flavour of ways in which leadership may vary and it is easy for most people to see such differences in leaders that they have known.

▶ Traits

Psychologists started putting together ideas on leadership in the 1940s. These ideas were based on the view that leaders are born rather than made. In other words, leadership is a matter of having various traits and these traits are inherited. These traits were thought to be a mixture of the physical (height, strength, speed, and so on); general ability (intelligence, fluency, adaptability, and so on); and personality (extraversion, sociability, and so on).

Ideas such as these dominated the early thinking in armed forces throughout the world. In the British army, for example, officers tended to come from the upper classes, for these were thought to embrace all of the necessary in-bred characteristics that made for good leaders. Of course, in reality they did not, a discrepancy that it has been argued is at the basis of many lost battles and appalling wartime blunders.

As soon as concerted research was carried out, it was seen that any personal factors that showed up in leaders were merely specific to the situation. So a characteristic that made a good leader in one situation might not work in another. For example, extreme extraversion might well be useful in a practical problem-solving situation that involves co-ordinating a group of people who have not previously known one another. Such a trait might not be appropriate for the co-ordination of a group of bibliophiles to search through library materials in order to find a solution to a problem.

Recently, interest has again begun to develop in whether or not there might be some traits that characterise leaders across situations. The traits that are now being found are very different from those of the 1940s. They are: drive, the desire to lead, honesty and integrity, self-confidence (which includes emotional stability), cognitive ability and knowledge of the business of the group. Some people have further argued that verbal fluency and intelligence also stand a leader in good stead in many situations, although there should not be too great a discrepancy in intelligence between the leader and the other members of the group.

▶ Leadership style

Mention has already been made of leadership style. This idea dominated psychological research from the late 1940s until the late 1960s. Now, rather than being concerned with what personal characteristics a leader might have, interest centres on how the leader behaves. In this context, two aspects of behaviour stand out above all others – *consideration* and *initiating structure*. These refer to having consideration for the group members (their goals, aspirations and personal triumphs and failures) and initiating or prompting ways of structuring the group so that it can best achieve its goals.

Of course, a leader can have many functions other than these two but they seem to be the most important. For example, a leader plans, makes policy, has expertise, represents the group, controls the group, purveys rewards and punishments, arbitrates and mediates, acts as an exemplar, acts as a symbol, allows members to forego individual responsibility, is an ideologist, a father or mother figure, and can even be a scapegoat for the group.

All such functions can and do occur from time to time. However, again, the situation is important. Different situations demand different functions from the leader, and, perhaps, different leadership styles, as in the example of democratic and autocratic leadership above. A basic question is: does style influence the outcome in a group and/or do leaders adjust their style in response to what they perceive as the group's performance or the group's satisfaction?

With respect to leadership style, there is also the matter of informal or emergent leadership. In many groups, leaders are placed there by virtue of employment, their right, their status in some other setting, and so on. However, in most groups, leaders also emerge in a more informal way. Groups tend to have both formal and informal leaders. Generally, informal leaders are those who are more active than other members of the group, who have a greater ability at the task in hand and who are more likeable. Rarely, such characteristics all emerge in one person and then a particular type of leadership is likely to develop. More of this later. And, of course, it may be that those same characteristics occur in someone who is placed into a leadership role rather than in one who emerges as a leader.

For now, it is enough to say that it can sometimes happen that emergent or informal leaders might clash with formal leaders. So there might be an influence on group members by someone other than through the direct reporting line, and influential leaders can arise from among one's peers in a group. This can prove to be awkward for some formal leaders, but, of course, can always be used to advantage by the astute leader. For example, as the formal leader of a group it is useful to keep an eye out for the emergence of any informal leaders and to enlist their aid at problematic times. This is far more likely to enhance the group goals than simply warring with the emergent leader.

▶ The contingency approach

As happened in several areas of psychology, from the late 1960s to the early 1980s, the trait approach and the style or situation approach were amalgamated into the contingency approach. Simply put, the idea is that effective leadership is affected by the situation in which the leadership is occurring. Some styles and personal characteristics are effective in some situations and other styles and personal characteristics are effective in other situations. For example, in an emergency, an autocratic style of leadership is more effective than a democratic style. There are no universally appropriate styles.

At this point researchers in leadership became particularly concerned with how leaders affect the motivation of group members – this, after all, is what a leader does in order to achieve the group goals. There are four major ways in which leaders motivate group members. These can either be seen as descriptive or as types of motivation that a potential leader can attempt to adopt.

- *Instrumental or directive.* This type of leader is very systematic and makes it clear exactly what is required of members of the group, how the group and the individual in it will work, and precisely what everyone's role is to be. Clearly, this style characterises groups such as the armed services or even some types of industrial setting.

- *Supportive.* The supportive leader is concerned with the subtleties of the well-being and status of the group members. He or she tends to be, and also is perceived as being, friendly. Groups in the caring professions might exemplify this style, or, indeed, any group that is based loosely on a family type of organisation.

- *Participative.* The participative leader is consultative. In other words, he or she attempts to draw everyone in to all the decisions and processes of the group. This type of leader tends to emerge in any setting in which the situational demands are not too pressing, a good example coming from the way in which departments in establishments of higher education are run.

- *Achievement-oriented.* The achievement-oriented leader is concerned with setting high performance goals and in generating feelings of confidence in the members of the group. This type of leader can arise in almost any setting. This is connected to the discussion of transformational leadership and charisma (see below).

Of course, the ideal leader, viewed from this contingency perspective, would manage to put together all of these ways of motivating group members. Each would be used in its appropriate context. For example, in more urgent situations an instrumental approach would be better than a participative approach. The participative approach would be more useful when the situation was more leisurely. The supportive approach might be particularly important during a time of stress for the group members and pushing for high achievement could be useful when very particular demands are made of the group.

▶ The new leadership

The approaches to leadership described so far all have their uses. None of them could be said to be fully appropriate or fully inappropriate. Each has some insights to offer, such insights all being useful to anyone who is interested in improving their leadership skills. Leadership can certainly be seen as a mixture of skills, and skills can be learned even though some people might have a natural head-start over others.

In recent years these approaches have been replaced by what has come to be called the new leadership. This brings us to the topics of *transformational* and *transactional* leadership and to the interesting matter of *charisma*.

One of the most perceptive ways of distinguishing between types of leadership involves the difference between transformations and transactions. The transactional leader is a development of the instrumental leader, mentioned already. This type of leadership is based on contingent rewards. With this type of leadership, group members are clearly rewarded for their contributions. They are told exactly what they have to do to achieve the desired results. They are told how to do it and precisely what it will bring them in return. This type of leadership frequently involves 'management by exception'. This means that the leader avoids giving directions as long as the old ways, whatever they might be, are working. The leader will only intervene if and when the standards are not being met. Then new transactions will take place. So, with this type of leader, leadership is a matter of a clear transaction between the leader and the followers or group members. It is akin to a business transaction but the medium of exchange is not money but various facets of social life such as status anxiety.

The transformational leader tends to have charisma and, as the name implies, works to transform the group. This is done by instilling pride, faith and respect through a clearly articulated vision. Everyone in the group is treated with respect, there is considerable delegation and trust and an individualised consideration for group members. A transformational leader also provides intellectual stimulation. He or she will generate new ways of looking at problems, will come up with new ideas, and will generally always be rethinking the issues and the group goals and how best to achieve them. Many of the great world leaders have clearly been transformational rather than transactional. Churchill and Gandhi provide obvious examples, as does Mandela and even someone like Adolf Hitler. Of course, Hitler's message was not good but he was able to put it across in an inspirational, charismatic way.

While the differences between these two types of leadership might be obvious and while it might be equally obvious that transformational leadership is better, for the most part, than transactional leadership, the question of charisma remains. What is it? We all know people whom we would describe as having charisma or even as being charismatic. They might be friends or politicians or actors, sportspersons or even the person along the road to whom everyone takes their troubles. They might even be someone whom we simply see across a crowded room.

Popularly, charisma is thought to be an attribute of the person. It is as though we can instantly recognise charisma when we see it; it almost seems to be a larger-than-life quality about a person. A person with charisma stands out and draws others to them. They are not simply attractive in a conventional sense but nevertheless attract attention. People orient to them, talk to them, look to them, and seek their opinion and their good offices in general.

However, charismatic leadership is always to do with the relationship between a leader and the followers. It is a form of exchange that clearly involves power. But this is not a unidirectional exercise of power by the leader; the followers are always involved as well. One cannot be charismatic on one's own. Another way of looking at charismatic leadership is that charisma is *socially* constructed by the leader and the followers simply in order to produce the effects with which charisma is associated.

Some people argue that 'true' leadership or, perhaps, 'good' leadership always involves some form of charisma, in that there has to be a vision of the future. A good leader will always put forward a new principle and value and generally show a way forward for the group. There is a delicate balance here, however, in that the leadership ceases to be effective if the views that the leader is putting forward become close to an obsession. Moreover, leadership that consists *only* of a vision for the future, a sort of preoccupation, becomes vacuous. This has to be tempered by appropriate leadership practices and management. It is no use simply repeating 'I have a dream' if nothing else follows.

It is possible to reorient all that has been said so far to think about *becoming* an effective leader rather than simply describing what an effective leader might be. When thinking about attempting to become an effective leader, it is important to bear in mind the following points.

- Leadership and management are distinct.

- Vision is important.

- Instilling values is crucial.

- There must be good patterns of communication established and also good communication skills.

- Part of effective leadership is finding ways to empower others in the group.

- Leaders have to be trusted and to be seen as having personal integrity. Anything that suggests otherwise will detract from their effectiveness.

- Leaders cannot work alone; others have to be trusted and used.

- Charismatic leadership is heavily dependent on the behaviour and attitudes of the other members of the group. It cannot exist in isolation.

- Charisma, although important to leadership, is not its be-all and end-all. There can be leadership without charisma but leadership with charisma tends to be more effective.

In the end, leaders are only leaders because they are the people in a group that make more of a difference to the group than anyone else. If a person is put into a position of leadership and does not make much difference to the group or help the group to realise its goals, then there will be a natural emergence of other leaders who do afford these outcomes. Such circumstances are common enough and frequently involve one person getting the rewards (including the salary) for what another person is effectively doing.

Some leaders are obviously visionary and charismatic, others, develop because of a crisis and others, rather more dourly, simply control transactions. But in any of these instances, the leader is the person who is making a difference to the group.

▶ A dimensional model – the skills of leadership

One of the most interesting and practically useful approaches to leadership in recent years has come from Lefton and Buzzotta (2004) in which they put forward what they term a dimensional model of leadership (Figure 9.1). The model rests squarely on how leadership comes about through people exercising their people skills, with three main reasons offered in support of it. These are: (1) it systematises the work on leadership that has gone before; (2) it makes sense; and (3) it helps forecast many aspects of leadership. These reasons are clearly well supported by the model but added to them might well be the idea that the model also affords ways of developing leadership skills.

There are four defining points of the model, combinations of which give rise to four typical patterns of leadership. As Figure 9.1 shows, the four points represent the extreme ends of two dimensions – dominance–submission and hostility–warmth:

■ *Dominance* is about controlling and influencing other people. It involves being assertive, taking charge of all circumstances and being oriented to 'getting things done'.

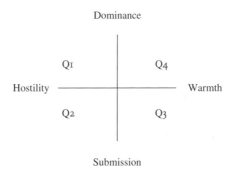

Figure 9.1 The dimensional model of leadership

- *Submission* involves following the lead rather than taking it. The submissive person tends to be passive and reluctant to speak, giving in at any sign of controversy. The totally submissive person is of no influence.

- *Hostility* is about being self-centred. In a group, the hostile person is unresponsive and insensitive, always sceptical about other people's motives and tending to be angry. This anger need not be overt, the hostile person often taking a passive–aggressive stance in the group.

- *Warmth* involves having an obvious concern for others and being open-minded, responsive and sensitive. The warm person is optimistic rather than having the pessimism of the hostile person.

From these two dimensions of what essentially is interpersonal behaviour or style, there emerge four possible patterns of leadership as represented by Q1, Q2, Q3 and Q4 in Figure 9.1. As these patterns are briefly described, it is important to remember that this model is about understanding our own behaviour and that of other people in order to improve interactions within groups. In other words, the patterns of leadership are about behaviour, not character.

Q1 Dominant–hostile

This is *autocratic* leadership, based very much on the principle of 'Do it my way, or else'. This type of leader rules through power and fear. He or she is the single source of power within the group, rarely, if ever, delegating and always micro-managing, that is, allowing no autonomy. Communication tends to be one way, that is, from the leader to everyone else and the leader tends to lead, at least some of the time, by offering inducements ('You stick with me and I'll see you all right'). The members of autocratically led groups receive far more punishments for what they have done 'wrong' than rewards for what they have done 'right'. For this type of leader, results are paramount, the ends always justifying the means.

Q2 Hostile–submissive

This is the *unassertive* leader. This type of leader is pessimistic about people and their beliefs, what they stand for and what their motives and hidden agenda might be. He or she tends to be interested in the maintenance of the status quo rather than in change, mainly being concerned with self-protection, or arse-covering as it is more popularly known. This type of leader does not really lead, whatever measure of leading is taken. He or she is merely a conduit for information from a source above to the group members below. Decisions are rarely made, but usually postponed. This leader's behaviour is made of a list of characteristics of exactly the type that one would want not to see in a reference –

distant; remote; reserved; conservative; traditional. The autocratic leader might give mainly punishments to the group members, but the unassertive leader gives nothing, neither rewards nor punishments.

Q3 Submissive–warm

This is the *easy-going* leader who tends to ignore mistakes in the group members. In a loose, unstructured way, this type of leader tends not to confront difficulties and also tends to be very undemanding. He or she dislikes thinking of him- or herself as the boss and prefers to hang around chatting about irrelevant matters.

Q4 Dominant–warm

The *collaborative* leader demands results and aims at optimal productivity for everyone. He or she sets very tough goals and makes high demands of the followers with respect to their use of their intelligence or their analytic skills. The collaborative leader is toughest of all on him- or herself and is very practical although dealing with every person in the group as unique. This is the type of leader who will seek help with things, but who will also, nevertheless, take responsibility and who can, of course, be called to account for the behaviour in the group.

From these brief descriptions, it should be possible to pick out leaders you have known who fit into one or other of the main styles. It is important to bear in mind, however, that most leaders are probably some amalgam of one or more of the styles. Moreover, it may be that the styles can give you pause for thought about your own personal experiences of leadership. Does your own style fit neatly into one of those quadrants? If so, would you prefer to fit into one of the others, or even to be an aggregate of more than one?

▶ Probing

In their very helpful book, Lefton and Buzzotta (2004) take matters several stages further than is portrayed in this brief description of their model. For example, they maintain that each of us has what they term a distinctive *probing style* just as we probably have a distinctive style of leadership, if we lead at all. Probing involves a series of techniques that allows us to gain information about another person, about what they might know or think or feel. Probing for information is an essential aspect of leadership. It not only allows the exploration of another person's mind, but it also draws the other person into the interaction, in other words, helping to sustain the reactivity of the follower to the leader. At some level, this will be meaningful to the other person, it can help to give vent to emotions that might be interfering with the interactions (or the job at hand) and it encourages the leader to be a listener – to listen before drawing hasty conclusions.

Any probes that you might use in assuming your leadership role will be aimed at achieving one of three ends. The eight types of probe fall within one or other of these categories:

1 Probes that encourage the other person to open up and start the flow of information. There is only one probe in this category – the *open-ended* probe. For example, 'Tell me what you think about the people that you work with.'

2 Probes that encourage the person to keep talking, that is, to continue the flow of information. These are:

   (a) *Pauses*, that is, pausing without saying anything, thus putting considerable pressure on the other person to break the silence.

   (b) *Reflective statements*, for example, 'So you think that she said that because she was envious of you?'

   (c) *Neutral probes*, for example, 'Oh yes, tell me more.'

   (d) *Brief assertions*, such as 'You quite like her, then.'

3 Probes that help you either confirm or check the understanding that you have gained. These are:

   (a) *Closed-ended questions*, for example, 'Are you saying that you like her?'

   (b) *Leading questions*, for example, 'You like her, don't you?'

As is clear from other chapters, there is far more to interpersonal communication than this type of probing. However, it is a natural part of what we do when in situations of leadership and so it helps to be able to think about it systematically. It is also of great assistance to consider which of the four styles of leadership your own most closely approximates. Then the next step is to consider if this could be changed for the better and, if so, how? For example, it is clear that the collaborative style of leadership is to be preferred in most situations and that in some more extreme or more dire circumstances the autocratic style might be useful. However, the easy-going and the unassertive styles are ineffective in that they do little towards achieving group goals, even though the easy-going style might generate a few warm fuzzies.

▶ Conclusion

The development of an understanding of leadership has followed a similar course to knowledge about personality. In summary, the progression has been from thinking of leadership as determined from personal (largely inherited) factors, to environmental factors, to a mixture of both. Then, in more recent years, the complexities of the various types of leadership have been elucidated more clearly, building on the information gathered from those previous perspectives.

Perhaps the most important matter to be borne in mind when considering leadership is that although not everyone is a 'natural' leader and although even those who are 'natural' leaders might not be so in all situations, it is perfectly possible to improve one's skills at leadership. Many people are comfortable in followers' roles and do not aspire to leadership. However, for those that do so aspire, it is a relatively straightforward matter to become increasingly adept. It may well be that you find that you can assume some styles of leadership more easily than others or that you are better able to exercise leadership in some situations rather than others. Like many other aspects of our psychological make-up, our leadership abilities are not fixed in stone.

▶ Summary

- Leaders are leaders because they influence the group and are concerned for the group members and their goals.

- Leaders differ in style, one important difference being between the autocratic and the democratic style.

- Early ideas on leadership viewed it as the result of traits (mainly inherited), but such traits were shown not to hold up across situations.

- Two salient aspects of leadership style are consideration for group members and initiating group structure.

- There are important distinctions between formal and informal leadership and the manner in which leaders emerge in groups.

- Leadership is clearly dependent on the situation, a finding that gave rise to the contingency approach to leadership.

- Ideas up until the 1980s suggested that there are four major types of leadership – instrumental, supportive, participative and achievement-oriented.

- The new leadership distinguishes between transformational and transactional leadership.

- Charisma characterises transformational leadership and is somewhat difficult to define.

- The dimensional model of leadership views it as dependent on two orthogonal dimensions – dominance–submission and hostility–warmth.

- The dimensional model results in four types of leadership – autocratic, unassertive, easy-going and collaborative, of which the latter is by far the most effective.

- To increase their own effectiveness, leaders can use various types of probe to gain information about the group and its members.

- Leadership abilities are not fixed but can be improved if that is what a person wishes.

▶ Questions and possibilities

- List some of the leaders you have known personally. What are their characteristics? What has made them effective (or non-effective)?

- Are you a leader? If so, do you lead in all situations? If you lead in some situations and not others, what is the difference between them?

- Have you observed people emerge as leaders rather than being given a leadership role? What are their characteristics? What makes them different from those who do not merge as leaders?

- What are the differences between Churchill and Hitler as leaders? What are the differences between Saddam Hussein and Mahatma Gandhi as leaders? Are there any regular differences between right-wing and left-wing political leaders?

- Think of people that you know who have never been leaders. What characterises them? Why don't they ever lead?

- If you wanted to assume a position of greater leadership in your job, how would you go about it? What would you attempt to change about yourself?

- Why do you think that transformational leaders are more effective than transactional leaders?

- Think of someone you know who is charismatic (it may even be you). What makes that person charismatic? Do you think that charisma can be acquired?

- Sometimes, some people are rather cruelly described as anti-charismatic. What is it about them?

- Think about the ways in which you probe others when you are in conversation. Could you be more effective at doing this? How?

- How would you go about training your own children to become leaders?

- Do you think that some people simply cannot help taking leadership roles? If so, what is it about them that makes this happen?

CHAPTER TEN

Inner life

Personality

Scenes from life

John and Jean are brother and sister. They get on very well and even though one is 19 and the other 18, they spend a fair amount of time together. They both attend the same university, Jean studying History and John studying French Literature. Several times a week, they meet for coffee or lunch and generally catch up with how things are going for each of them. But they are very different from each other.

Jean is outgoing and loves anything new. It is not as if she cannot settle to routine – she can, but nevertheless there is nothing she likes more than a new experience, social, physical or intellectual. When she is bored, she seeks out new things to do. Already she has been on several overseas trips and has tried her hand at numerous activities. She worries about none of this, but remains equitable and balanced all the time. She sleeps well, doesn't have a hang-up about her weight or her appearance and, generally speaking, is thought by most people to be reliably good company, an interesting person with whom to spend time.

By contrast, John is moody. He likes a fixed routine in his life, with as much as possible being certain. He becomes highly anxious when things get out of kilter or seem unpredictable. He nods politely to many people but has few friends, unlike his sister who has many. The friends he makes tend to last for only a limited time. They never know quite where they are with him because he frequently says so little or makes conversation that is full of innuendo rather than direct. He sleeps poorly and often wakes in the night covered in sweat and then worries about not getting back to sleep and how tired he might be on the next day. Unlike Jean, he has never been overseas and although he thinks that he should go, he never quite gets round to it.

Jean and John are sitting having a good conversation over coffee, with John for once being quite animated; he feels very secure with Jean. One of Jean's friends comes up to them, a man than John knows a little as well, and invites them both to a retro party (everyone is to dress in 1960s style) in a few days. Jean quickly accepts, already thinking of what she will make or scrounge to wear. In the heat of the moment, John accepts as well and even discusses it all with Jean, starting to think of what he might wear.

During the few days before the party, Jean barely gives it a thought, simply finding the clothes to wear and then forgetting about it until the night. The same evening of the invitation, John starts to worry; he worries about his clothes, who else will be there, whether he will have anything to say to anyone, whether anyone will speak to him, whether he should have accepted; what he will feel like afterwards; whether Jean will think less of him if he pulls out; and so it goes on.

They both go to the party. Jean has a fairly good time – it was not the best party she has ever been to, but she had some good fun and even had one or two memorable conversations. She very much enjoyed seeing one or two people make fools of themselves. Afterwards, she barely thought of the party again. John had a completely dreary time, anxious throughout. He spoke to very few people, felt out of place, even though his 1960s clothes were authentic. He smoked and drank too much, mostly by himself. The few conversations he had preyed on his mind for several days afterwards mainly in terms of what he might have said but did not, or that he might have said something better. He barely slept at all that night even though he left the party early.

Richard is 30 and works in a car sales yard. Or at least he has done for a few months, but he is thinking about moving on. There is not enough excitement in the job for him and he seems to be getting off-sides with many of the people he works with. He lives alone, having had a series of disastrous relationships with women, many of whom have left him because of his unpredictable violence. Most of them feel lucky to have escaped. He has had nothing to do with his parents for years, even though they are still alive. They don't mind the lack of contact because they had always found him a difficult child and an even more difficult adolescent. He stole and lied, cheated at school and was cruel to animals.

He has quite enjoyed the car sales job (even though it is time to move on) because he has usually managed to take home a good car on most evenings. He has used it to impress friends and to pick up women. Of course, he passes it off as his own. He has also managed to find a way into the petty cash at work and has quietly managed to keep himself going in daily expenses rifled in this way.

Not surprisingly, Richard has been before the courts on a few occasions although he has not yet been caught for anything major. On some of these occasions, he has had to see a social worker and in one case a clinical psychologist. They have all attempted to talk to him about what they and the rest of society see as his problems, or more properly have him talk to them about what he does and what he thinks and feels. But he finds this extraordinarily difficult, not really understanding what they are getting at. In fact, all he could think of was what a waste of time – he could see no possibility of gaining anything for himself out of what was going on. In one case he did try to chat up the social worker, but even he was able to see that she wasn't interested, or at least, if she was, she wasn't letting on.

The night before, he was idling around at work, wondering when to disappear for good; he had been in an accident. So far, he had managed to hide the damage to the front of the car but wondered how long it would be before someone noticed. Not paying attention after a few drinks, he had suddenly found a cyclist in his way and could not brake in time. The damned old fool's bike had broken one of the headlights and dented the front wing. He had checked after he had arrived at his flat, not having stopped to see at the time. His only thought was to accelerate away before the police arrived. He had no idea what had happened to the cyclist.

Think about these questions:

- To what extent do you see your own behaviour as being under your own control or determined by your circumstances or the people around you?

- You know that you behave differently when you are at home or when you are out at a party, when you are in church or sitting in a library or when you are playing sport. What is your true personality?

- Have you changed much since you were a child? In what way? How did the changes come about? Are there some things abut you that haven't changed at all?

- How good are you at describing other people? Can you judge character? How accurate are you? Do you project your own personal issues onto the person you are thinking about?

- Are you predictable? To what extent do you change unpredictably?

- Is there an inner core to you that remains unchanging?

- What would you describe as your *style* of personality?

These are some of the basic everyday questions that have led psychologists to be interested in personality. Each of us is unique and there are patterns to our behaviour as individuals. Much of psychology is concerned with similarities between people, but personality is about individual differences, what it is that makes us unique. What makes one person mentally ill and another not, even though they are from the same family and from the same environment? What makes Jean, in the example above, a calm extravert and her brother John an anxious introvert? What makes a young woman highly motivated to have a high-flying career and her sister settle down at a young age to a life of domesticity? Why are some people like Richard, in the second example above, a sociopathic or anti-social personality?

▶ **Definition**

What, then, *is* personality? In the everyday sense of the word, personality is something that we all possess to some degree, or to put it more extremely, something that we either have or do not have. 'Well, she's certainly got personality.' 'He's got no personality at all.' By contrast, in psychology, the word denotes an area of study that is concerned with the differences between people. This is a huge topic and so, not surprisingly, there have been very many definitions of personality put forward. They vary from the very general to the highly inclusive. Here are two recent examples that demonstrate the two types:

> Those characteristics of the person or of people generally that account for consistent patterns of behaviour. (Pervin, 1989)

> Personality is the set of psychological traits and mechanisms within the individual that are organised and relatively enduring and that influence his or her interactions with, and adaptations to, the environment (including the intrapsychic, physical and social environments). (Larsen & Buss, 2002)

It is clear that we are here dealing with a person's make-up, whatever characteristics they have that make them what they are. It seems equally clear that although each of us is unique, as humans, we have general characteristics that set us apart from other species and some of the complexities involved in these characteristics are buried quite deeply and have causes that are frequently difficult to pin down.

Pervin (1989), one of the pre-eminent personality researchers, puts it well when he suggests that the study of personality seeks to answer:

- *What* are people is like *what* are their characteristics?

- *How* do people become as they are? In particular, the question here is how do nature and nurture (heredity and environment) play their part?

- *Why* do people do what they do? This question about motivation (see Chapters 4 and 5) is probably the most difficult of all.

So, if you know that a friend or member of your family is more anxious than most people, you might want to find out if the anxiety is typical of that person.

How it came about, why it is being experienced now, and how and why the person behaves as he or she does when they are anxious.

Fundamentals of life

Personality, then, is concerned with some of the big questions about the human condition. A prime example is the topic of human nature. What is it that makes us human? Do we have instincts? Do we have free will? Do we have genuine choices in what we do socially?

To what extent is what we are dependent on what we inherit? It should be said that at present there are no final answers to this question. Certainly, we differ from one another in temperament, some basic characteristics that are there from birth and that seem to endure. Many parents know that their children are quite different from one another from the start, for example, in how active they are, or how afraid they are in new situations or how easily they can be soothed or even in how much they smile and laugh. But there is far more to personality than temperament and there are huge complexities in the links between the influence of environment and genes. Think of the many examples you know of very different people who have grown up in the same families.

To ask another fundamental question: are you you or are you the situation? In other words, do you have your personality because of traits or characteristics that are somehow within you or because of the influences of your environment? Over the years, various theorists have taken all possible standpoints on this question, but the received wisdom nowadays (as in most areas of psychology) is that the answer lies in a very intricate mixture of both sources of influence.

There are many more such questions, but probably the most important of them is about integration. It is basic to psychology to break down or analyse human functioning or behaviour into its parts, but personality is concerned with what all the parts are like when they are put together. How do we become integrated? When considering the 'whole' person, does something extra merge that is somehow more than the sum of the parts? Relevant here is the idea of *self*. Our own notions of our *selves* are important to the way in which we are integrated as entire persons. This is discussed in the next chapter.

▶ Ways of looking at personality

As might be expected in an area as huge as personality, there have been many varied ways of looking at it. What follows is a very brief introduction to a few of the major types of theory of personality. Each of them emphasises something in particular and each of them is 'right' – in its own way. Each provides something significant to consider about personality and would be interesting to apply to people that you know as you think about them.

Traits

One of the most enduring and important aspects of personality is the notion of trait. This is simply the name for the characteristics that make us unique or different from one another. They are stable (more or less) and can come from either our genes or environment or, more likely, from a mixture of the two. We are either born with a set of traits or we come to establish a set of traits through our interactions with the environment.

The most influential way of looking at personality traits rests on the belief that everyone has the same set of traits and that we differ from one another only in the extent to which we show the various traits. Then the question becomes: how many such fundamental traits are there? The answer ranges from three to 23, but the most widely held view currently is that there are five – called, appropriately enough, the Big Five. The traits are:

1 Neuroticism or emotional stability – calm, relaxed and stable versus moody, anxious and insecure.

2 Extraversion or surgency – talkative, forward, outspoken versus shy, quiet, bashful, inhibited.

3 Openness (intellectual/imaginative) – creative, intellectual versus uncreative, unimaginative.

4 Agreeableness – sympathetic, kind, warm, sincere versus unsympathetic, harsh, unkind.

5 Conscientiousness – organised, neat, meticulous versus disorganised, sloppy, impractical, careless.

It might be interesting to think of the degree to which members of your family or your friends could be characterised in terms of these five traits, and the extent to which this gives a full picture of them. If it doesn't, then what is missing? It is worth pointing out, by the way, that although the Big Five have been quite widely accepted, this is only within the English-speaking world (largely the American English-speaking world). Whether they apply to the same degree in Eastern cultures, for example, remains to be seen.

If we think of traits as somehow basic to personality, then an important question concerns how consistent such traits are across a person's lifespan. Do they last throughout life or do they change (or can we force them to change)? Can I change myself from a disagreeable, closed, moody, careless, anxious creature into an agreeable, open, outgoing, conscientious, relaxed player in the game of life?

This type of question has led to a long controversy among some personality theorists about the degree to which traits are dependent on, or modifiable by, the environment. The usual view nowadays is that of interaction. In other words, the relationships between traits and behaviour or among traits depend on the type of situation that we might be in. So, for example, you might be very agreeable when you are with your friends but much less so when you are with members of your family. You might be highly conscientious when working with other people but relatively sloppy when working alone. You might be outgoing and open to new experiences when with people that you know well but shy, diffident and unimaginative when with strangers.

The psychoanalytic tradition

The significance of personality was first brought to general attention by Freud (1933), who had a huge influence on Western thought from the turn of the nineteenth century. Interestingly, his influence on academic psychology has been much less obvious although it is clearly there beneath the surface, perhaps appropriately enough since much of what Freud pointed to in the human condition goes on beneath the surface.

Freud was concerned with both the structure of personality and the dynamic processes underlying it. So he developed the idea of psychic energy, as well as the significance of conflict between any sources of energy within the system, the most basic of which are biological. In general, Freud argued that our personalities are shaped by biological and psychological forces over which we have little or no control. Some of these forces are *unconscious* and hence, by definition, beyond our conscious knowledge and control.

Briefly, Freud suggested that personality is made up of three interconnected energy systems: the id, the ego and the superego. He characterised the id as being primitive, biological, instinctive and unconscious, and dominated by sexual and aggressive impulses, wishes and fantasies. The id drives us towards immediate gratification of any of our urges, for example, of sexual desires that would be all but impossible in real life. So, at night we sometimes have lurid dreams, we day-dream to fulfil some primitive wishes, we make slips of the tongue that 'give the game away', and so on. Freud believed that the powerful energy that derives from the id lies behind creativity.

The ego connects us to the real world, rather than the world as we might like it to be. It has a sort of executive function for the personality, mediating between the urges of the id and the practical demands of the world at large. It is mainly conscious and is what in everyday terms would be called rational. In its executive role, it also mediates between the id and the superego.

The superego can be seen as the opposite of the id. It is the part of the personality (or mind) in which the values of society are internalised. This is the part of us that is made up of 'shoulds' and 'oughts', in other words, being concerned with how we are behaving morally. It is composed of two parts:

1 the conscience – this comes about from experiences for which we have been punished – we do something 'wrong', are punished for it and then feel guilty when the id pushes us to do it again.

2 the ego ideal – this comes about from experiences for which we have been rewarded – we do something that is 'right' or approved of, are rewarded for it and then feel good if we have the impulse to do it, or something like it, again.

In general, then, the conscience focuses on what we shouldn't do and the ego ideal on what we should do. Like the id, these forces are mainly unconscious, as Freud described them.

Huge amounts have been written about this proposed structure of personality, and the idea of unconscious forces driving us to do things of which we might be unaware has become integrated into Western thought even though it plays a small part in more recent and more formal ways of looking at personality. This is also the case with Freud's analysis of the dynamic development of personality.

Apart from built-in biological urges of the id, he saw personality as being laid down within the first five or six years of life. It begins from birth to two years with the *oral* phase, where everything centres on sucking, spitting, biting, and so on, all of which are associated in various ways with pleasure and comfort. This is followed by the *anal* phase (from about two to four years) in which pleasure centres on urination and defecation. Then from five to six years, there is the *phallic* phase in which the main source of pleasure comes from the genitals. It is at this time that the famous Oedipus and Electra complexes come into being, according to Freud. Boys love their mothers but fear their powerful fathers. Girls desire their fathers but worry about the anger of their mothers. All unconsciously, of course.

Freud argued that it is possible to become fixated at any of these stages, depending on the particular experiences that a person might have at the time. This might then lead to the development of particular types of personality characteristic. For example, fixation in various aspects of the oral phase might lead to an adult who eats, drinks, smokes or talks to excess, who might be cheerful, dependent or needy, or cynical and cruel. Anal fixation might lead to a neat meticulous obsessive adult (whose parents praised him or her too much when toilet training and so lead to unconscious worry about giving things up) or to a moody, sarcastic, cynical adult. Fixation at the phallic stage might lead to a self-preoccupied, vain, self-absorbed adult. And so on.

There is no doubt that Freud's ideas have been very influential and that some of the matters just described have become almost as much a part of everyday Western thought as Shakespeare's ways of expressing things. However, the problem comes with their testability in a scientific sense. This is not easy to do and many of the concepts are difficult to pin down in their ambiguity.

Social and humanistic theories

These two types of theory rely very much on concepts of the self in its various guises (e.g. self-efficacy, self-esteem, the ideal self, self-actualisation) and so will be considered in more detail in the next chapter. In general, both types of theory of personality are concerned with growth and development of the self, either through social learning or through our own analysis of our phenomenological experiences.

▶ When personality goes wrong

Can personality go wrong? After all, a person's personality is their personality, rather than being right or wrong; it just *is*. While this might be true in one sense, in another sense, the idea of abnormality is again an accepted part of Western culture. How abnormality is defined is dealt with in Chapter 16, but for now it is enough to say that the formal taxonomies of abnormality (such as those given by the DSM-IV by the American Psychological Association 1994) include lists of personality disorders. In this way, personality is thought of as going wrong simply in that it differs so much from the usual patterns of personality in the person's culture.

The DSM-IV lists ten types of personality disorder. As they are described briefly below, try to think of someone you know or have known that might tend in these directions. After having read the descriptions, again think of the people you have known who might fit them and think about what they typically do that makes you think that they fit the category. They will be discussed in more detail in Chapter 16.

1 *Anti-social* – impulsive behaviour with little or no regard for others and no respect for the norms of social behaviour.

2 *Borderline* – instability, of mood, relationships, and even of the idea of self; impulsive and self-destructive.

3 *Histrionic* – constant need for attention and approval; dramatic behaviour, dependence and being seductive.

4 *Narcissistic* – grandiosity, exploitativeness, arrogance, obliviousness to others.

5 *Paranoid* – constant, pervasive and unwarranted mistrust of others.

6 *Schizoid* – emotional coldness, no interest in relationships.

7 *Schizotypal* – constantly inhibited or inappropriate socio-emotional behaviour, odd cognitions and speech.

8 *Avoidant* – constant worry over criticisms leads to avoidance of all interactions.

9 *Dependent* – selflessness, neediness, fear of rejection.

10 *Obsessive-compulsive* – rigidity in behaviour and relationships, extreme perfectionism.

It is probably fair to say that we all experience many of these characteristics in minor form, from time to time. So it is important to remember that to be described as disordered is extreme. More particularly, they are pervasive; they are there constantly and have a huge impact on the life of the person who is experiencing them or on those around them. Another way of looking at these 'disorders' is to see each of them on a continuum ranging from normality at one end to severe or extreme disability at the other. So, while it might be normal to feel a bit paranoid at times or to sometimes feel moody and needy or to show an occasional lack of respect for others, if these impulses become extreme and pervasive, you or others will suffer.

There is insufficient space to consider each of the personality disorders in detail, so just three will be considered as examples – the first two tend to be among the most awkward and extreme to deal with.

To return to Freud's ideas, those who have an *anti-social* personality disorder (also known as sociopaths or psychopaths) essentially appear to have no con-science; they appear only to consider their own desires, paying no attention to those of anybody else. They seem to be driven entirely by the urges of their id with none of the checks and balances on this that rein most of us in most of the time. They might cause suffering but appear to experience nothing much in the way of guilt or remorse about this.

They tend to be adept liars, to seek sensation in the extreme form without much thought of harm or danger and punishment does not work for them as a deterrent. They can be attractive, charming and intelligent, and so can be good at manipulating other people. The more accomplished anti-social personalities might well be found, then, among the ranks of the con artists.

The sociopath might be good at getting a new job but very poor at keeping it because their true restless, impulsive nature quickly comes to the fore, so they commit crimes of some sort. They might then con themselves out of punishment by appearing to be contrite and remorseful and then immediately go down a similar route. As well as a lack of shame, they also lack empathy – they simply cannot put themselves in the position of someone else. This leads to an extreme ruthlessness in their dealings with others. Interestingly, those with an extreme anti-social personality disorder can appear in any walk of life, from a murderer, on the one hand, to a successful member of the corporate or political world, on the other.

One final point to bear in mind when thinking of the anti-social personality concerns the social context. There are some contexts in which to be impulsive and aggressive and deal without much thought of others to the immediacies of life is not inappropriate. For example, if one grew up in a war-ravaged city or was born into the high-crime area of a city such as Los Angeles, then such an approach to life might be a recognised way to survive. In one sense, such an approach is still anti-social, but in another it is scarcely abnormal or inappro-priate; the social context matters.

The *borderline* personality disorder is perhaps the most difficult and in some ways the most interesting of them all. It does not mean that the person has a personality that borders on the abnormal. Rather, it refers to instability. People with this disorder become suddenly angry or anxious or depressed with no apparent reason. They vary between extreme self-doubt and self-importance, from idealising other people to despising them. They become extremely dependent on other people, particularly new friends or a new therapist but simultaneously seem to be looking hyper-vigilantly for ways in which they will be abandoned or rejected.

There might also be a tendency to self-mutilation (burning or cutting) or even suicide. In the extreme, a 'borderline' person might become dissociated, losing track of time, feeling unreal, even forgetting who they are. As is obvious, any relationships for such a person will be, at the least, problematic and, at the most, extremely tempestuous. The diagnosis also, in some ways, can make matters worse, simply because the person with a borderline personality disorder is so difficult for a therapist to deal with. Their behaviours often seem wilful and so it is hard for any therapist to withhold judgement or attach blame to the person, both of which are essential to a therapeutic approach.

Interestingly, it is the psychoanalytic tradition that has provided some of the more useful insights into the borderline condition. For example, it is possible that they have parents who derive a great deal of fulfilment from their child's dependence on them, this leading the developing child to difficulties in distinguishing self from others. This would make them hypersensitive to the opinions of others (it is as though it is their self-opinion), so if they perceive rejection, they might start also to reject (and even begin to harm) themselves.

For the same reasons, they tend to see themselves and others in a very dualistic way as either 'all good' or 'all bad' and veer from one to the other view with no consistency. A fine portrayal of the anti-social personality is the character Alex in the movie *Fatal Attraction*. In fact, fiction in general, whether in the form of movies or novels, frequently gives accurate characterisations of the various personality disorders. See, for example, Patricia Highsmith's 'Ripley' series for the anti-social personality.

The *narcissistic* personality is entirely self-centred, needs to be constantly admired and has little or no insight into other people's feelings. In this sense, this condition is similar to the anti-social personality. They not only have a strong sense of their own superiority but also a powerful sense of entitlement – they expect things to come their way, as of right. Often, then, they choose friends who are clearly weaker and less able than themselves from whom they can expect the adulation that they need.

There is an essential paradox to the narcissistic personality – although they seem to be completely self-aggrandising, their self-image is very vulnerable. They need to be recognised, to be greeted by everyone, to be warmly welcomed everywhere, and, of course, most of the time this does not happen. They therefore often reject or disdain other people because those people are not giving them the praise and recognition that they regard as their due.

If this is linked with their lack of concern for others, it makes them relatively difficult and unpleasant people to be with. The main pronouns they use are 'I' and 'me' and they have very little concern for the other person in any relationship they might have. This also makes them likely to be envious of the successes of others, believing that such successes should be theirs and theirs alone. With the narcissistic personality disorder it is useful to see such disorders in terms of dimensions. Most of us have times of self-absorption or times when we envy others their success or times when we seem to be overly concerned with 'I' and 'me'. However, think of what it would be like to be in that state all of the time and in the extreme.

▶ Personality and culture

Much of what has been written so far in this chapter might give the impression that personality is fixed, or close to it. Having been laid down genetically or formed very early in life, there is not much that we can do about personality thereafter. In fact, the extent to which personality is changeable is a moot point. To take recognisable everyday examples, the propensity to be relatively prone to anxiety or to be relatively extraverted seems to be there from the start in some individuals. However, even the most anxious and the most extraverted among us are not anxious or extraverted in every situation. And we know from personal experience that we can learn to be calm where we have not been calm before and to be outgoing in circumstances in which we have previously been relatively introverted. To some extent, personality must be malleable.

Such malleability is also demonstrated by what clearly are the influences of culture on personality. What is called *evoked culture* comes from particular environments tending to create particular sets of responses that occur so commonly as to be to do with personality. For example, being co-operative or competitive tends to be a basic aspect of personality. However, some environments generate co-operation and some generate competition in most people. An instance of this comes from something as basic as the availability of food. Plentiful food leads to greater co-operation and food scarcity leads to competition. If such conditions go on for some time, then the style of behaviour becomes regular enough to be regarded as a facet of personality. In fact, it is slightly more complex than this in that co-operation occurs mainly when there is high variability in food supply.

Similar cultural differences have long been documented in the degree to which aggression typifies a culture, aggression again usually being seen as a basic dimension of personality. Some cultures appear to be based on a strong code of honour in which an insult is viewed very negatively and must be met with public confrontation, often physical. Again, availability of resources, such as food, seems to be a determining factor here. With food stores to defend, obvious physical confrontation might well act as a deterrent.

The aspects of culture that affect personality discussed so far might best be described as built in or at least inevitable, given the circumstances of the environment. However, the other aspect of culture that influences personality is termed *transmitted culture*. Transmitted culture is made up the beliefs, attitudes, values, opinions, morals, and so on, that are transmitted from one person to another. These all exist in people's minds rather than in the natural environment. For example, what is regarded as right and wrong varies considerably from culture to culture and even between sub-cultures, between the socio-economic classes in Western society, for example. Some people believe that it is wrong to eat meat, others that it is wrong to eat some meats. Some people believe that it is right to go to church on Sundays and some on Saturdays and some not at all. Some people believe that women should always cover most of their bodies and others don't. Some people believe that hair should never be cut and others that it should all be shaved. And so on.

Culture, then, can be transmitted from person to person and can become so entrenched as to become part of a person's personality. A prime example of cultural influences on personality comes with the idea of the self, which varies considerably from culture to culture. This will be discussed in the next chapter. In this context it is interesting to consider whether or not there exist what might be called cultural universals. There are a few somewhat surprising candidates for possible cultural universals. Before these are mentioned, it might be worth thinking about what they might be. What aspects of cultural influences on personality do you think could be universal, that is, world-wide?

The first cultural universal appears to be the way that men and women are regarded. The list of adjectives that are applied to men in all cultures that have been studied are those to do with being active, aggressive, boastful, loud, reckless, tough, conceited, opportunistic, and so on. The equivalent list for women includes cautious, affectionate, changeable, emotional, modest, sensitive, soft-hearted, and so on. It is a very clear picture. These might be real, accurate descriptions or they might reflect stereotypes.

Similarly, there is strong evidence for universals in emotional expression and in the typical types of words that people use to describe the personality of others. There is even some evidence that four of the five personality traits in the Big Five are universal – neuroticism, extraversion, agreeableness and conscientiousness.

Of course, whether or not the whole idea of personality is a Western construction can be debated. Western culture tends to be individualist and to stress independence and separation from the group. In fact, this is so much so that it is hard for a Westerner to think that it might be possible not to be like this. Some Eastern cultures, by contrast, stress collectivism and interdependence, contextualising the person within the group. This means that personality as we know it in the West is probably a much clearer concept than it might be in the East, where individuals tend to merge.

The final aspect of personality change that can be mentioned does not concern broad influences such as culture but much narrower influences such as that of one individual on another. Parents can certainly influence the developing personalities of their children, but so, presumably, can therapists and counsellors. The aim of some therapy might be to bring about some short-term changes in behaviour or ways of thinking. But sometimes therapy is aimed at much deeper change, a change in a person's general approach to life, a general way of being. This, then, would amount to a change in personality.

If personality can be changed by a blow to the head, by electroconvulsive shock, or by any extreme environmental circumstance, then it can surely be changed in subtle ways by one person's influence on another. Perhaps just as importantly, if personality can be changed by one person's influence on another, then it can also be changed by the person himself or herself. We are not necessarily stuck with our personalities in the ways we might imagine ourselves to be.

▶ **Conclusion**

Personality is one of those parts of the human condition that is obvious in everyday life. Each of us is unique and it is the study of personality that stresses this uniqueness, whereas much of the remainder of psychology emphasises similarities between people. Some parts of personality appear to be built in and others appear to be learned. Certainly, personality is also influenced by culture, either through environmental necessity or through beliefs, values, opinions and judgements.

Whichever way that personality is looked at or theorised about, it is clear that it does not exist in a vacuum. A person may be made up of an id, an ego and a superego, or of an actualising self (see next chapter), or of a series of learned social behaviours, or of a set of traits. Whichever of these it might be occurs within a context or a series of situations or experiences, no two of which are the same. So the best way to look at personality in general, or at someone's personality in particular, is through the eyes of interaction. People cannot exist without their environment, each influencing the other. It is therefore best to make sense of personality as it exists in its particular environment. Personality cannot exist in isolation.

▶ **Summary**

- Personality is about the differences between people, their uniqueness. It is also what distinguishes us from the members of other animal species.

- Personality is concerned with the what, how and why questions about people.

- Personality is not to do with the separate aspects of people but what emerges when all of the parts are put together.

- The most significant current way of looking at personality is seeing it as made up of various traits. Each of us has a set of traits which differs from those of everyone else.

- At present, the most influential view about traits is the model of the Big Five: extraversion, neuroticism, agreeableness, conscientiousness and openness.

- It is important not to look at traits in isolation but to consider the interaction between traits and the environment.

- The psychoanalytic, Freudian tradition looks at personality as involving internal dynamic energy systems, the id, the ego and the superego, and views these as developing through the experiences of the first six years of life.

- There are ten major ways in which the personality can go wrong or be seen as disordered. The most extreme of these are the anti-social personality (or sociopath) and the borderline personality. Personality disorders such as these can either be seen as discrete categories or as dimensions (like traits) on which people vary.

- Personality is not fixed but can be influenced by culture (evoked or transmitted) or by individuals, from parents to their children or therapists to their patients, for example.

▶ Questions and possibilities

- Think of the strongest and weakest personalities that you know. What makes them strong and weak?

- List your fundamental beliefs, attitudes and opinions, particularly about ethical or moral judgements. Are they the same as those of your family and friends? How do they differ? What has brought them about? Do you see them as basic to your personality?

- Think of people that you know or have known that you suspect might be personality disordered. What is it about them that makes you think this? What do they do?

- Score your family and friends from one to ten (one being low) on the Big Five traits. What is it about them that has allowed you to arrive at the scores?

- Score yourself on the Big Five. Do you think that your evaluation is more or less accurate than one that would be made about you by your family or friends?

- What have been the cultural influences on your personality? If you consider some of the people you work with, have they had different cultural influences on their personality than yours? How has it made them different?

- Would you change your personality if you could? If not, why not? If you would, then why don't you?

- What does it actually mean to say that someone has more personality than someone else?

- How would studying someone's personality help you to work with them better or to live with them more amicably?

CHAPTER ELEVEN

Inner life

The self

Scenes from life

Bob and Tom were good friends. Both aged 26, they had been at university together and now shared a flat. They both had reasonable jobs and had forged a life for themselves with the usual aims and aspirations, vague thoughts of what the future might bring, some reflection on the past and varying degrees of engaging with the day-to-day ups and downs of life. On the day that they were both invited to a party, neither of them was in a relationship.

Bob approached the party with considerable enthusiasm. It was coming at the end of a period which had been a little dry socially and he was keen to meet new people and particularly interested in the possibility of meeting someone attractive with whom there might be at least a flirtation, if not something more. Tom, on the other hand, felt that he should go to the party but was going with some trepidation, concerned that he might become involved in conversations that he could not handle well. He thought long and hard about how best to control how much he had to drink, just in case he might make a fool of himself. In short, Bob was looking forward to the party with some confidence of possible social success and Tom feared the possibilities of social failure.

They went to the party together and the moment they walked into the room, which was already quite crowded, each saw someone to whom they were immediately attracted. Bob's eyes lit up and he had instant fantasies about how the evening would go, how it might extend into the weekend and a possible relationship that could come about. All he needed to do was go and make contact and see how things developed. He clapped Tom on the back and set off across the room with a smile already in place.

By contrast, Tom started to think that here was another occasion on which he would fail. He felt that he should have paid more attention to his appearance and that everyone, particularly the young woman whom he had

---

seen across the room, would think that he was drab and uninteresting. He had mawkish fantasies of getting a drink and of nobody actually speaking to him throughout the evening. He cast another quick glance across the room at the young woman and was unsure whether she had been looking at him or not. Thinking that she probably hadn't even noticed him, he moved slowly round the edge of the room, excusing himself with a mumble as he went in search of the drinks table.

And so the evening progressed. Bob found that he was quite rapidly swept up into a very amusing group and standing next to the young woman he had seen. He gained in confidence as the party went on and was clearly getting on well with the person he was seeing increasingly as a potential partner, at least for a while. He had a splendid evening and he arranged to see Sheila the next day. She seemed to be as keen as he was to see how things went over the weekend.

Tom spent most of the evening nursing a drink and found it very hard even to look round at other people. He simply could not bring himself to initiate a conversation with anyone. In the event, no one attempted to start a conversation with him. His worst fears were being realised and the party turned out to be just as bad as he had imagined. He had no idea what happened to the young woman he had seen and never even found out her name. He left early, regretting having gone at all, and went morosely home to bed, alone.

Think about the differences between Bob and Tom and their experiences at the party. At face value, their circumstances were very similar, but their view of themselves was very different. Bob's self-esteem was high, his self-confidence firmly in place and so his experience at the party reflected this. Tom's self-esteem was low; he knew that he would have unsatisfactory encounters and that is exactly what happened. He had little self-confidence and this was obvious for anyone to see. His prophecies came true largely because his own views of himself brought them about.

Gill meditated every day, twice if she could manage it, early in the morning and early in the evening. She always sat in the same place on a cushion in a cross-legged position. Her back was upright, her eyes closed and her hands loosely folded in her lap. Typically, her thoughts while meditating would be something like this:

'Now, I'll start by taking three deep breaths and centre myself in my body. Oh, I hope that I have a good meditation this morning. Now, my breaths. Concentrate on my breaths. Perhaps I'll begin by counting.' Then she would concentrate on her breathing for some minutes with no thoughts intruding. Then, 'I wonder what I should wear today; what did I wear yesterday? What's the weather going to be like? No, my breathing' . . . 'What have I got to do today? Think about breathing; back to counting' . . . 'Is it better to concentrate on my diaphragm or the breath as it enters my nose? Different people say different things. No, breathing' . . . (On this occasion, some minutes passed with no thoughts interrupting, Gill simply observing her own breathing.) Then, suddenly, 'I wonder why Charles said what he did yesterday? If I see him today, what should I say?' Then Gill had a long series of images of her relationship with Charles over the past few months and started to wonder what the future would hold. Then, 'Oh no, I've forgotten about my breathing again. There's no point in sitting and meditating and just thinking about other things. This will get me nowhere, but there again, meditation is not supposed to *get* me anywhere. Yes, but that's getting in the way of observing my breathing as well. Why can't I just get on with it? Perhaps there is something wrong with me and I'll never get the hang of it properly. But there's nothing to get the hang of. It is just observing. Come on, just do it. That's it, I'm starting to do it now. No I'm not, I can't be if I'm thinking that I am.' And then she spent some time again simply observing her breathing with no thoughts intruding.

At the times when Gill was simply observing her breathing with no thoughts coming into her mind, where was her *self*?

The self is a fascinating concept. We take it for granted. It is part of our language – myself, yourself, himself, herself, even *itself* (which is a strange idea – can an 'it' have a self?). In Western society most people assume, without thought, that they have selves, but if you ask them what these selves are and where they might be, the answers are hard to come by. Where is your self? What form does it take? Is it something that you can point to? Does it exist outside your body? Is it something that you have learned or acquired or were you born with it? What happens to it when you are asleep or unconscious or even dead? Can you ever get to know other selves? Do you have more than one self? And so on.

If you were to be asked to define your self, what would you say? You might speak in terms of what you do for a living; many people do. You might list your likes and dislikes, your political or social opinions. You might talk about your education or your background or how much you earn. In the midst of thinking about this, you might also wonder if your self exists independently of you. Or is the self what defines you, your 'you-ness'?

In Western society (there will be brief discussion of alternative Eastern views later) the way in which people have learned to think about the self divides it into three main aspects. There is the *self-concept* which changes considerably early in life and then settles. When it is settled, it is used to evaluate the world, providing a sort of lens through which to view everything that is not-self. *Self-esteem* refers to how you feel about your self and *social identity* refers to the presentation of your self that you make to the world. In our type of culture, knowingly or not, we manage self-impressions all the time. Also linked to self-esteem and social identity is *self-efficacy,* which is concerned with a sense of our own ability.

▶ Self-concept

The task that an infant faces is to learn to distinguish him or her self from the rest of the world. At first, there appears to be no such distinction. This is interesting for it suggests that the idea of a distinctive self is something that has to be learned. For example, it is not much before the age of two that a child can recognise him or her self in a photograph.

Once the child has learned that there is a self that is distinguishable from everything else, then the self begins to develop further. Sex and age become important ways of distinguishing the self from other selves, being older or younger, male or female. So, early on we begin to define the self in these terms. In passing, it is important to note (see Chapter 2 on the development of the socially constructed emotions such as pride, shame and guilt) that the idea that there are other selves than one's own also has to develop. To realise that oneself is distinct from everything else is simply a precursor to realising that there are other selves that are also distinct from everything else but in their own particular ways.

After age and sex, then the self begins to be concerned with making comparisons with the talents and skills that others have, physically and intellectually. Finally, there develops an inner, private view of the world, the self and, indeed, of everything that comes into consciousness. This is a view that no one else knows, from the security of which it is possible to take another person's perspective.

This is merely a beginning. After a sense of self or a self-concept is formed, so *various* selves begin to develop. This is not as flaky as it might sound. We might start to develop images of possible selves that we could be or could achieve. We might see a succeeding self or a failing self, we might see a leader or a follower, and we might see ourselves as a boss or as a worker, a criminal or Salvationist. We will almost certainly develop a sense of an *ideal* self. This is a view of our self as we would really like it to be rather than how it actually is. And most of us, although perhaps not all, will develop a sense of an *ought* self. This is a self that is made up of what we believe that society wants from us, a self that upholds the moral and legal standards of society. This might or might not be in line with the ideal self.

As adults, we have a very complex image of ourselves or, perhaps, our various selves. It is hard to separate this image from an evaluation of it. Do you like what you know of your self? Is it a self with which you are satisfied? Is there a large or a small gap between your self and your ideal self? Is it a very private self or are you happy to make your self public? Interestingly, these are the type of question that it would make less sense to ask in various Eastern cultures.

▶ Self-esteem

The evaluation of the self by the self as to whether it is seen as good or bad, whether it is liked or disliked, is ultimately a matter of self-esteem. Of course, given that we have multiple selves, our evaluation of self might well differ from area to area. The three major areas in which people tend to evaluate the self are: appearance, general performance and social interactions. How well do you think that you look? How well do you believe that you do the things that you do? How socially skilled are you? We tend to make comparisons between our selves and others in each of these areas.

You might, for example, feel reasonably satisfied with the way in which you do your job and the way in which you help to bring up your children but be constantly irked by your hair never seeming to go as you want it to, or by being too short or too tall, or too thin or too fat. You might wish that you had a straight nose rather than a crooked one or have long fingers rather than stubby ones. You might be annoyed that the nails on your two hands do not quite match or that your eyes are brown rather than blue.

On the other hand, you might be reasonably satisfied with your appearance but concerned that you keep messing things up socially. You might think that whenever you open your mouth you say something that you later regret or that you can never think fast enough to make the cogent, witty reply. Or you might be satisfied with both your appearance and your social skills but wish you could be more physical than you are, more adept at sports, or that you could be musical or that you could be intellectual or financially astute. Or, worst of all, you might think that you are inadequate in all three areas, in which case you can only be described as having very low self-esteem. As was seen in the example at the start of the chapter, this is then likely to become self-fulfilling. If your self-esteem is low, then you are likely not to achieve well or not succeed, partly *because* your self-esteem is low.

Two very different approaches to life depend on whether a person goes about seeking success or fearing failure. The extent of the balance between these two rests on self-esteem. Take, for example, the possibility of applying for a job where there is a high risk of not getting it, or taking an examination where there is a high risk of failure, or engaging in some sport where there is a high risk of not succeeding. Generally, people with low self-esteem fear failure more than they seek success and therefore protect themselves from possible failure. They are therefore less likely to apply for a job, take an exam or compete in sport. They might even handicap themselves in order to set up a failure before they even begin. They will not even try to do something in spite of knowing, at one level, that they might succeed at it.

There are very large individual differences in self-esteem, most of which stem from experiences in childhood. A secure, unambivalent upbringing in which the child is encouraged in all endeavours, irrespective of success, is likely to lead to a well-developed self-esteem. A critical, ambiguous, inconsistent upbringing is more likely to lead to a fear of failure. Also, over-riding these issues are individual differences in the degree to which people are concerned with social evaluation. It is far more important to some people than to others and it may be that those to whom it is more important might be more likely to fear failure than those to whom it is less important.

▶ **Social identity**

Putting together self-concept and self-esteem leads to the development of social identity. Some things about our social identity are relatively constant. The obvious examples of this are gender, education, occupation and language, although even these can change. Also there are some enduring characteristics of behaviour or personality. Put all of this together and this is what makes a person unique.

Throughout life everyone experiences various crises of identity. There are two major types of crisis. The first is referred to as deficit in which previously held values are rejected, leaving the person in the position where he or she cannot make decisions. For example, a lapsed Catholic may well flounder with respect to certain life decisions where previously there was a clear road to follow.

The other main type of crisis comes through conflict between various aspects of one's social identity. For example, there might be times where one is attempting to fulfil two goals that are inevitably opposed, to be co-operative and competitive, for instance. Another example might come from wanting to be assimilated into a group but nevertheless wishing to retain sufficient difference to retain a distinct identity.

These types of crisis in social identity tend to occur at times of social change, the major ones being adolescence, marriage, parenthood and retirement. In each case there is great social upheaval and one's social identity is being forced to change. Whether this takes the form of a deficit or a conflict, it is problematic. Typically, a time of floundering about is followed by some resolution and acceptance of a new social identity, as an adult, a married person, a parent or as someone who is no longer a member of the work-force. Of course, such crises of social identity can also occur with lesser events in one's life, such as getting a new job, winning some money, seeing the children leave home, having one's parents die, and so on.

Culture

The matter of social identity becomes particularly important when cultural differences are considered. In almost any culture there are times when the individual has to be independent and times when the culture needs interdependence in order to cohere. However, this is where the major difference appears between Western and Eastern cultures. The predominant social identity that is encouraged in the West is independence, whereas, in general, in the East interdependence is stressed. This is individualism versus collectivism.

This difference in social identity is also reflected in huge differences in self-concept. For example, if you are asked to describe yourself, would you be more likely to talk about inner abstract characteristics (such as, I am reasonably bright, very conscientious, quite lazy but very trustworthy) or to talk about social roles (such as, I am Mildred's son, Charles's brother and Sarah's husband and I am a good father to my children)? Typically, those in the West refer to inner abstract concepts and in the East to social roles, exemplifying the individual versus the collectivist approach. The general point is that people in different cultures and sub-cultures have different types of self-concept and different types of social identity. These differences are neither good nor bad but simply reflect different histories.

▶ Self-efficacy

We all have a sense of our own abilities, both generally and about specific and, perhaps, very detailed matters. This sense gives us a belief about how effective we are. And it is true to say that the higher your self-efficacy, then the better you are likely to do in general or with respect to the particular matters at hand. Again, it is upbringing that is crucial to the degree of self-efficacy that an individual experiences. Upbringing that emphasises success rather than failure is more likely to lead to a greater sense of self-efficacy.

In its turn, a good sense of self-efficacy helps to cause an increased level of performance not because it makes the person directly better at whatever it is, but simply because it leads to greater perseverance or persistence. The greater one perseveres at something, then the more likely one is to be successful or the more successful one is likely to be. This is another example of the self-fulfilling prophecy. However, it is worth bearing in mind the obvious point that self-efficacy is not the only ingredient in success. Someone with little talent but a high degree of self-efficacy might perform at their very best level but this still might not be at the level of someone with more ability but lower self-efficacy.

To put these ideas in another (and more popular) way, they demonstrate the power of positive thinking. An optimistic attitude involving the belief that one is able to do well and will do well leads to a better ability to cope with any stressors that might arise and to sort out any problems and meet any challenges. This is more likely to lead to success than a relatively pessimistic attitude. The sense of optimism must, however, be tempered by realism. There is a difference between having a well-founded belief in one's own abilities and a Pollyanna-like naïve belief that everything always turns out for the best even in the face of contrary evidence.

Although self-efficacy is a compelling aspect of the self, it is important to consider how it might be looked at more precisely. How, for example, is it possible to judge or measure someone's self-efficacy? One way of doing this is to compare a person's accomplishments with their desired accomplishments, or, putting this another way, to compare any discrepancies between their actual selves and their ideal selves. The results of an exercise of this sort will depend very much on whether what is being considered is important to the person. For example, if being physically fit is not important to you, then being unfit will not lower your sense of self-efficacy.

There are also large individual differences in the degree to which people are tuned into these various concepts of the self, or in the degree to which they are self-aware or self-concerned. People obviously differ with respect to how self-centred or self-absorbed they are, but the issue here does not concern these somewhat value-laden areas, but more that of self-consciousness. By this is meant not self-consciousness in the form of potential embarrassment, but the degree to which people are aware of their own feelings and beliefs, the degree to which they are concerned about other people's views of them, their degree of social anxiety, and so on.

Generally, high self-monitors can control their social behaviour (and hence their social identity) very easily, changing their behaviour to fit the circumstances. People such as politicians, who spend much of their time in the public eye, are particularly adept at this. By contrast, low self-monitors tend to be relatively more consistent (that is, less changeable) in their social behaviour, that is, they do not change their behaviour (or their social identity) with the circumstances.

▶ Changing and developing concepts of self and identity

As is probably obvious by now, the self, although part of everyday life and speech, is a very unwieldy concept. Does it really exist or is it an almost fictitious social and cultural construction? If it does exist, then can it develop and change? What happens to it on those occasions when it seems not to be there?

Various psychologists, particularly those concerned with clinical matters, have made the idea of self central to their notions of the human condition. The most notable of these is Carl Rogers (1961) who put forward a theory of personality based on the self, a theory which had important ramifications for the style of psychotherapy that he developed. Central to his views is that a major aim of our lives is to preserve the sense of self in whatever we do in order to grow towards self-actualisation, a topic that was discussed in detail in Chapter 5. Of course, some of those who come from Eastern cultures would argue that the aim is to lose the self rather than to preserve it.

Rogers suggested that the idea of a self-actualised personality implies a steady growth and movement of the self. So, a person who is self-actualised or self-actualising has five main characteristics.

1 They are steadily growing and evolving.

2 They are open to experience and not defensive – they see new things as opportunities rather than problems.

3 They trust themselves, seeking guidance but making their own decisions.

4 They have harmonious relations with others without needing to be liked by everyone.

5 They live fully in the present, neither dwelling on the past nor looking to the future. This does not mean a lack of planning, but once any plans have been made, then the self-actualising person stays in the present.

Although these ideas are very much about the development of the self through to self-actualisation, the notion of living in the present almost suggests the annihilation of self, albeit temporarily. If one is entirely absorbed by the present (which does not, by the way, mean pursuing a hedonistic life), then the self has disappeared. The moment that we look at ourselves being absorbed by the present, then the self is back again. More of this in a later chapter.

Rogers also stresses that everyone has a basic need for positive regard. We all desire love, belonging and acceptance although the self-actualised person realises that this is not possible from everyone. The only time that completely non-judgemental positive regard is experienced is probably in therapy. It is virtually impossible to achieve in everyday life, however much it might be sought. However, it *is* sought and to the extent that it is not found, so various stresses and possible maladjustment may occur.

The self, then, is not static; it changes and develops over time. The aspects of it that are long-lasting are sometimes described as core beliefs. These are basic beliefs that each of us has that represent our fundamental view of the world and which colour our perceptions and our behaviours throughout most, if not all, of our lives. For example, I might believe that people are essentially trustworthy whereas my neighbour might believe that people are essentially not to be trusted. This will alter the way we deal with everyone that we meet and will colour all our interactions.

You might believe that the only way to do a job, any job, is perfectly. In other words, you might have an implicit perfectionist bias. Again, this will influence almost everything that you do and may well mean that you achieve less than the next person, simply because you think that anything that you do is not quite good enough, so you have to spend more time on it.

To use an everyday example, you might be the sort of person that always sees the glass as being half-full, while your partner always sees the glass as being half-empty (essentially optimism versus pessimism). If so, you will have some sorting out to do from time to time in your relationship. You might be the sort of person who sees any change in circumstances as a challenge, while your sister sees any change as a threat. Such core beliefs are the essence of self and always provide a guiding force in life. Sometimes they can be very useful and at other times might be maladaptive and lead us into various traps in life. The example of perfectionism is one obvious trap. To do everything perfectly might sound admirable but it is less than admirable if it means that nothing is ever accomplished.

Core beliefs can change and the self can also change and develop and does so throughout life, to some extent. More immediately, most people have experienced temporary changes to the self that come through altered states of consciousness. Examples of this occur naturally in everyday life. One's self is slightly different if one is very fatigued than if one has just had a refreshing holiday. Heavy fatigue that might come from long hours of extra work alter mood, perceptions, motivations, abilities and, hence, the self.

Similar alterations to the self come from the use of alcohol and other drugs. To make a temporary change to the self is precisely why people drink and take drugs. Even the somewhat euphemistic idea of social drinking falls within this sphere. Alcohol is a cortical inhibitor and one of the main functions of the cortex is to inhibit the lower and somewhat more emotional parts of the brain. If alcohol inhibits the cortex, this frees the cortex from inhibiting the other parts of the brain, which, in general terms, means that the person's general behaviour is less inhibited. So, social drinking means a mild form of temporarily changing the self to be freer in spirit and less careful. Interestingly, those people who are less inhibited socially tend to drink less alcohol – in this sense, they do not need it.

Similarly, if you read descriptions of people's experiences when taking any other drugs, ranging from marijuana to heroin or cocaine, or if you have experienced these drugs yourself, you will know of the changes that take place to the self. Very often people who take drugs seem to be wishing to forget their usual selves and to replace them with something that is more palatable, at least for a short while.

Perhaps the most obvious temporary changes to the self occur during sleep. What happens to the self when we lose consciousness in sleep? Everyone dreams every night, although they might not always remember their dreams. Is it the same self in one's dreams as in one's waking life? Simultaneously it seems to be the same self and yet it can suddenly seem different. It can be a self that is capable of new things (such as flying) or new accomplishments, a self socially more adept or socially hopeless, and so on. So, the self might be changed when we are dreaming but there is still some core part of it that remains the same.

One of the most interesting changes to the self occurs during meditation, as was described in the example at the start of this chapter. The aim of some types of meditation (insight, vipassana and other Buddhist derivatives) is to do away with the self altogether. During this, one sits in a comfortable posture and concentrates on the breathing. This means simply following the in-breath and the out-breath as they occur, either as the air passes through the nose or from the rise and fall of the diaphragm.

When practising this form of meditation, at first it is extremely difficult to concentrate on observing the breath in this way for more than about four breaths. This might sound ridiculous, but it isn't. Try it and see. Thoughts, feelings, sound, smells come crashing in. It is particularly thoughts that intrude, as they did for Gill. Pushing the thoughts away is, in one sense, having another thought, so that is not concentrating on the breathing either.

This is not the place to go into the intricacies of Buddhist philosophy and psychology. It is enough to say that it is the aim of the practice of meditation to set aside the self (or the ego) with all its learned or conditioned aspects. In other words, to set aside the constant preoccupation that most people have with the past or the future. Our selves are made up of thinking about what has already happened or what we believe is going to happen, all tempered by our core beliefs. In Buddhist terms, these thoughts about the past and the future are based on attachments that have come about through conditioning and it is the aim of meditation practices to give up all attachments.

The goal is to stay as much as possible in the moment, engaging with the here and now of the world as it surrounds us and is being experienced. Observing a process such as breathing that goes on steadily within one's body is merely a simple way of beginning to do this. While meditation is an important topic in its own right, for now the only issue is what happens to the self during meditation. It is not that the self is changed in some way, but rather that it seems to disappear altogether. If one's senses are fully engaged with the present moment, then there is no longer any self observing this, and essentially the self is an observer of and commentator on life. Much of life might be easier without such observation and commentary.

▶ Making changes to self-esteem and self-confidence

Although the self is relatively stable in some ways, it is also obviously capable of change, as we have seen. The question then becomes, are there ways of effecting changes to the self that can in some sense improve it? The move towards self-actualisation is one way of doing this, as might be the move towards the setting aside of self through meditation. However, in our daily lives we are stuck with whatever level of self-esteem or self-confidence we have. Are there ways of improving or promoting these?

Some of the ways of making such improvements have already been hinted at. For example, it is important to tell oneself that one does not always have to be perfect – this is easier for some of us to do than others. If you are being unrealistic, then recognise it, as well as recognising that those around you do not necessarily value you more for doing things perfectly. They might just want to get things done quickly. It might therefore be important to lower your standards sometimes by telling yourself that not everything has to be 100 per cent all of the time.

People who are perfectionists tend also to be procrastinators. Things are put off because they are not yet perfect or cannot be done perfectly. Cutting out procrastination can lift self-esteem. This is done by planning, by careful time management, by not taking on too much, and by learning to deal with the anxiety of not everything being perfect.

One of the many things that batters away at self-esteem is *criticism*. People differ markedly with respect to how they handle criticism; some immediately take it to heart and others seem to be able to bat it away. There are a number of points to bear in mind when you are criticised, all of which will help to ward off a dent to your self-esteem.

If you have done something at work or at home or wherever and someone has criticised you for it, and they are clearly correct, this is not a comment about your character. Everybody makes mistakes; everybody can improve on their performance from time to time. A criticism is usually only about a specific thing rather than an attack on one's very self. Your value, your self-esteem is not simply based on things that you do, but on all of your various qualities such as generosity, sense of humour, good nature or whatever. Everybody is criticisable on some occasions and if it is you, on this occasion, then it is worth thinking about how you might improve whatever you did when you next have the opportunity. Criticism can easily be turned into constructive feedback.

Also, one does not have to straightforwardly accept criticism. It might be unjustified, so make up your own mind about whether or not the criticism is warranted. If it isn't, then reject it. Also, it is simply not possible to have the approval of everyone for everything that you do. It is therefore important to pick and choose what you believe to be important and also if you have been criticised for something that is important to you, then to not exaggerate it. What is the point? Life is too short.

The extreme of criticism is *rejection*. Rejection is a fact of social life. Not everyone can be accepted by everyone else all of the time, so it is inevitable that we will all be rejected at some time. Again, when this happens it is important for your self-esteem not to blow it out of proportion. It is very unlikely that you are being rejected by everyone; it is very unlikely that you are being rejected for much of the time; and it may well be that it is only part of you rather than the whole of you that is being rejected. As part of dealing with rejection it is important, in turn, to reject. Saying 'No' needs to be learned and it is hard to accept a 'No' if one has not learned to give a 'No'.

The self-esteem and confidence of many people drop when a relationship ends. This is not surprising; it is an extreme form of rejection. However, it is not helpful to move from that experience into thinking that one must have an on-going relationship to be a worthwhile person. It helps self-esteem but it is not a necessary component of it.

A good relationship of any sort is very worthwhile but it is not a basic necessity of life such as air, food and water. You do not need to be in a close relationship although you might well desire to be in one. Also, it is worth bearing in mind that being alone, or learning to be alone, is in itself a worthwhile endeavour and is very different from feeling lonely. It is possible to feel lonely in a crowd or in the midst of a family but it is also possible to very much enjoy time alone.

Some basic ideas about how to improve self-esteem and self-confidence have come from cognitive therapy. In a book called *Beating the Blues*, Thase and Lang (2004) describe a four-step process:

1 Accept yourself for what you are. This does not mean not trying to be a better person or to do things better today than yesterday, but rather accepting that you are not perfect and never will be perfect. You might be capable of improvement but in general you are not too bad as you are.

2 The way we think about ourselves can put dents in our self-esteem. Many people have many automatic negative thoughts about themselves that they rehearse time and time again. Things like: 'I shouldn't have done this, I'm always spending too much money'; 'What a terrible driver I am, I almost

caused an accident then'; 'I've messed up this (meal, job in the garden, tidying up, essay, etc.) again; everyone will think I am useless; I am useless.' So, it is important to challenge any thoughts of this sort, to see what is underlying them, whether or not there is truth in it and, if so, whether or not it is important and why it bothers you. Then, replace the negative thoughts with positive ones. 'Well, I actually save some money by buying this' (that's a common one); 'At least I noticed that other car and actually avoided an accident'; 'I might have made a bit of a botch of this but I know that I have and I've learned from it and won't do it again.'

3 It might sound trite, but self-esteem is improved by considering positive points about oneself. It is easy enough when in a low mood to think only negative thoughts and to quietly watch one's self-esteem slip lower and lower. It takes some effort but it is worth finding the positives such as: 'I'm a good, caring person even though I've made a mistake'; 'I might have failed in this application for a job but I've made some good achievements'; 'I might have looked a mess tonight but I often look pretty good and people compliment me'; 'She might have rejected me but I have some great friends and a loving family.'

4 Possibly the most important facet of maintaining self-esteem comes from treating oneself with the same type of respect that one would accord to others. One way of doing this is to regard yourself as your best friend and to treat yourself accordingly. Don't beat yourself up over mistakes; you wouldn't do it to a friend.

▶ **Summary**

- In the Western world the self is an integral part of our culture, even being reflected in our language. It is less important in Eastern cultures.

- The self is made up of a concept of the self (itself made up of beliefs, attitudes, values and opinions), self-esteem and social identity, in all of which there is a great deal of individual variation.

- Our self-concept develops from an early differentiation of the self from the rest of the world and then gradually become more sophisticated leading to various possible selves, including an ideal self.

- Self-esteem (linked to self-confidence) is concerned with how well we think of ourselves mainly in the areas of appearance, general performance and social relationships and skills.

- Social identity is made up of relatively static and relatively changing aspects. It develops throughout life via various crises involving either deficits or conflicts. These tend to occur at times of change such as through adolescence or having a permanent partner or retiring.

- There are large differences between the independent individualism of Western culture and the interdependent collectivism of Eastern culture.

- Self-efficacy concerns our beliefs about how well we can do things. It is based on upbringing and is self-fulfilling in that a strong sense of self-efficacy will lead to greater perseverance which in turn will increase the chances of success.

- People differ with respect to their degree of self-consciousness, that is, the degree to which they monitor their own selves.

- The self changes and develops not only through an inbuilt tendency towards self-actualisation, but also temporarily through fatigue, alcohol, drugs, sleep and even might tend to disappear altogether through meditation.

- It is possible to work at raising one's own self-esteem through working on one's belief systems, particularly about perfectionism, considering both approval and criticism/rejection and by working through a four-step process mainly involving changing negative into positive self-thoughts.

▶ Questions and possibilities

- What is your self-concept? Write down a description of your self and compare it with a description of your partner's self or the self of anyone that you know well.

- How many different selves do you have? Do you use different selves in different circumstances, at work and at home, for example?

- Do you have some fundamental beliefs about yourself and the world that guide your take on life? What are they? Are they all useful or do some of them lead you into traps?

- Describe your self-esteem. Is it high or low? Does it stay constant? What sort of thing tends to knock it? What do you do to improve it?

- List all the negative self-thoughts that you have and then keep asking questions about where they come from, whether they are valid and what it is that is really driving them.

- List all your positive qualities, attributes and achievements and set them against your negative self-thoughts. What conclusions might you draw?

- How would you describe your social identity? Does it change from time to time and from place to place? Have you been through any crises of social identity? What did you learn from them? Do you think that such crises are avoidable?

- How committed are you to the social identity that is integral to your culture? How easily could you transform it?

■ Compare your accomplishments with what you would like them to be. Do you think that this is a good measure of your self-efficacy?

■ Try to meditate if you have not done so before. Simply find a comfortable sitting position and concentrate (although not fiercely) on observing your own breathing. See how many breaths you can observe before a thought comes rushing in, even if it is 'What am I doing this stupid exercise for?' If you can manage to observe only your breath for a while, what do you think happened to your self in that time?

CHAPTER TWELVE

Intellectual life

Learning

The snippets that follow feature different aspects of conditioning in reasonably common situations. Each of them involves one person dealing with another (or, in the first case, dealing with a dog). Put yourself into the situations and imagine what you would do, or would do differently, and why.

Scenes from life

Sam is a dog, a friendly enough almost pure Labrador, black and bouncy. He is very good with children and seems not to have an aggressive tooth in his mouth. Apart from over-exuberance, he can be trusted with people. But his exuberance causes problems. For instance, whenever the doorbell rings, he starts barking loudly and jumping at the door of whatever room he is in in order to get out and to the front door. None of this is aggressive.

Typically, whoever is with Sam when this happens tells him to settle down, to be quiet, and eventually to shut up. None of this ever has any effect, if anything, making matters worse. Sometimes a member of the family will get Sam by the collar and pull him away from the door. But he continues to bark and simply strains at the collar. It usually ends with one person going to the front door and someone else attempting to distract Sam by giving him a biscuit. The idea, reasonably enough in one sense, is that a dog cannot eat and bark simultaneously and Sam is always interested in extra food. He shuts up for as long as it takes to wolf down the biscuit and then he is off again.

Sam is a 4-year-old boy, just an ordinary lad of reasonably even temper, averagely bright and gets on with people much as any other 4-year-old boy might. He is out shopping with his mother who stops when she see an old friend. They have not seen each other for some while and they have a great deal to talk about. So they stand in a relatively quiet part of the street and chat.

For a few minutes, Sam is perfectly content, looking round at the people and watching the cars – he likes cars a great deal. After a while, though, he sees something that he wants to show his mother.

'Mum, Mummy, look.'

'Just a minute, dear.'

She effectively ignores Sam. He says nothing, but in another minute or two he tries again to get her attention. The reply is: 'Sam, not now, I'm talking.'

'But Mum . . .'

'Sam . . .' She shakes his arm slightly. 'Can't you see I'm talking? I've got all day to talk to you.'

Sam is becoming more and more agitated,

'Mum, Mummy, look, look, look at that car.'

There isn't an actual car that Sam wants her to see, but he speaks as though there is.

'Oh, do be quiet, Sam. Don't be rude. I'm talking.'

'Mum, Mum.'

Sam is nearly shouting now and keeps pulling at his mother's coat.

'Oh, alright, then, what is it? Sorry, Betty, but I'd better see what he wants. Now, Sam.' She turns to him at last. 'That was a bit rude, darling, wasn't it? But what do you want?'

She smiles down at him.

Sam is a typist who works in a large open-plan office. She is young and pretty and it is her first job. She is pleased to have it – jobs have not been easy to find – so she is keen to do her best and to impress her boss. In a quiet way, she is ambitious as well as being something of a perfectionist. She wants to do the job well and to be recognised for it.

Her boss is not a good manager. His skills with people are not advanced but he knows that he should show an interest, so a couple of times a day he walks through the office and stops at each person, looking to see what they are doing. He always follows a similar pattern. He stands and looks over the typist's shoulder at what she is doing for a few moments and then makes a comment. The comment is almost always critical. Then he will move onto the next person.

Sam dreads these visits. He does not always have something critical to say to her, perhaps one time in three, but the possibility is always there and it makes her nervous. For a few minutes after he has gone, she finds that her work is full of mistakes – she just doesn't seem to be able to think clearly or even to make her fingers flow as they should on the keyboard. Her boss has a very distinctive walk and she can hear it in the distance as he starts his rounds. She finds that her work begins to suffer when she can hear his footsteps and so it becomes increasingly likely that he will find a mistake and have something critical to say.

Sam is a man in his twenties, a school-teacher who likes his job and is quite good at it. He likes the children he teaches and gets on with them well. He is walking home from school when he is stopped by someone he has not seen since they were both at training college together. They weren't particularly friendly then, but knew each other and could not reasonably pass each other by without exchanging some words. They started to talk, or at least Sam did but found the conversation to be harder and harder going. His old acquaintance simply stood there and looked at Sam, not aggressively or oddly but simply unresponsively. He did not smile at what Sam had to say, nor did he nod or even grunt in reply to Sam. And he made no effort to chip in or make some contribution to the conversation himself. Sam found that he quite quickly began to run out of things to say, so he ended the conversation and continued on his way. 'Well, nice to see you – perhaps we'll meet again some time.' 'Yes, perhaps; good to see you.' Sam went on his way puzzled and feeling slightly let down.

Sam and Samantha are good friends. They are both at university, studying Law. They have an important examination in about a week's time which, in the way of Law exams, will take a great deal of work. They tend to work together or not exactly together, but in parallel. They have very different styles of work even though their abilities are similar.

Sam breaks his working day up into segments. He will work for an hour and then do something else for an hour – drink coffee, read a novel, go for a walk. Samantha tends to push on through those sorts of breaks. She might stop for a brief lunch, but in general prefers to stick at it. She certainly puts in more hours of work per day than Sam. In fact, by the end of seven days, they worked it out, obviously being aware of their different work habits, Sam had worked for just over 40 hours and Samantha had worked for 60. Assuming that they are of similar intelligence and ability, which of the two do you think would do better in the exam?

▶ Conditioning and learning

We all learn things, every day. Learning is a change that comes about through experience or practice. It is usually seen through a change in behaviour but also involves a change in what we think, in our attitudes or opinions or beliefs. On a given day, a person might learn a new route to drive to work or a new way of undoing a difficult window latch or learn something new about the political party that he or she is thinking of voting for.

Clearly, learning ranges from the very simple through to the highly complex. There is an enormous difference between learning to touch type and learning how to be a school-teacher, or between learning a new way to hold a cricket ball or learning how to drive a tank. A considerable amount of what we learn is through conditioning. Now, the word 'conditioning' has a bad press. It immediately hints at Pavlov and his dogs, the privations wrought on inmates in prison camps, the horrors of *Clockwork Orange* and the general idea of people exercising control over other people. And somehow the implication behind this is that conditioning is something that we can and should resist and that we have a choice in the extent to which we are conditioned.

To some extent, there is an element of truth in all of these possibilities, but, nevertheless, conditioning is an integral part of learning throughout life; we could not survive without it. In its various forms, it is merely the simplest and most straightforward learning that we do. If we were unable to profit from experience (probably the simplest definition of learning), then our survival would be problematic. To take a very basic example, if we did not learn how to obtain food in an edible form, we would inevitably die.

Classical conditioning

Here are Pavlov and his dogs (Pavlov, 1927). Classical conditioning is the most straightforward form of learning and simply involves the association of one thing with another, based on a response that is already built in or 'natural' to the person (or animal). Take the dogs. If food of some sort is put into a hungry dog's mouth, it will salivate. The food is a stimulus for the built-in response of salivation – the dog does not have to learn this. If, on each occasion just before you put the food into the dog's mouth, you turn on a light, then very soon the dog will come to salivate when it sees the light. The salivation to the light is a classically conditioned response.

Sometimes, in extreme circumstances, this type of response can be established very quickly. Most people have had the experience of eating something and immediately being violently sick. The next time and for many times thereafter that you see that type of food, you are likely to feel nauseous. Again, this is classical conditioning. What has been learned is an association between two stimuli, an association that had not existed previously. The dog learned to associate the light and the taste of the food, the person learned to associate the sight of the food and the taste of the food and being sick. To take another example, think back to the typist in one of the descriptions earlier. She learned to associate the sound of her boss's footsteps with his critical comments, comments that produced in her a negative emotional reaction. So the footsteps started to evoke that reaction as well and her work began to suffer.

Many aspects of classical conditioning have been studied, but two, in particular, are worth mentioning because of their obvious applications. There is the process of what is technically termed *extinction*. This simply refers to the fact that the new learning does not necessarily last for a lifetime. Think of a person who through painful experiences has become classically anxious when he walks into a dental surgery. If he then has to have a long course of treatment during which he experiences no discomfort, gradually the original learned responses will fade away – they extinguish.

The other pertinent aspect of this type of conditioning is *generalisation*. If the typist hears footsteps similar to those of her boss, she is likely to have a similar reaction. Similarly, if the 'dental' person walks into some other type of surgery with similar sights and smells, then he is likely to have a similar response. The responses have generalised. The more similar the new stimuli are to the original ones, then the more likely generalisation is.

Instrumental conditioning

Here we arrive at rats in boxes, *Clockwork Orange* and the brave new world in the form seen by Fred Skinner, the major proponent of behaviouristic psychology in the twentieth century (Skinner, 1938). Indeed, some psychologists have argued that instrumental conditioning covers most of the learning of all animals, certainly the human animal. Whereas classical conditioning rests on fairly primitive responses or reactions that are initially built in, instrumental conditioning involves the gradual shaping of behaviour from the simple to the more complex. It is thought to lie behind the way in which children learn to behave in ways approved of by society, or when adults go out and earn their living, or, more primitively, when a person trains a dog or tries to train a cat.

As it is intriguing to consider the similarity between rats in boxes and humans in houses or at work, and, for reasons of simplicity and expedience, rats in boxes have formed the basis for much of the study of instrumental conditioning, this is a good place to begin. Imagine a Perspex box of about 30 cm square. On one wall is a small tray into which food can be delivered and close to it is a small lever. A hungry rat placed inside the box will explore and, as part of this, virtually by accident will occasionally press the lever. If, when this happens, a pellet of food falls into the tray, the rat will eat it. After a few such occurrences, the rat makes the connection and presses the lever regularly, the food coming and being eaten equally regularly.

To introduce a technical term, the food is said to have *reinforced* the behaviour or the response of pressing the lever. The learning is shown through the increased rate at which the rat is pressing the bar, when, before the learning, it was occasional and haphazard. So, in that classical conditioning is a matter of establishing a connection or association between two stimuli, instrumental conditioning is a matter of making a response or a bit of behaviour stronger or more likely to occur. The core part of instrumental conditioning is reinforcement. For this type of learning to occur, there must always be a reinforcer, something that is rewarding to the organism and that will therefore have an effect on what it does.

Examples of instrumental conditioning in life are everywhere. Think of just these two. A child in class raises her hand and asks a question. If, before answering, the teacher smiles and says what a good question it was, she will be more likely to ask another question in the future. On the other hand, if the question is followed by sarcasm and criticism, she would be less likely to ask again – reinforcement or punishment. Or think of idly putting your hand down the side of the armchair and finding a coin there. My guess is that you will soon be trying the other side of the chair and the other chairs in the room and, surreptitiously, the chairs in most of the rooms that you go in. Your idle response of pushing your hand down the side of the chair has been reinforced.

Extinction happens in instrumental conditioning as well as in classical conditioning. Go back to the two examples. If, after the first couple of times of answering the question, the teacher simply ignores the child, raising the hand to ask will begin to stop. Similarly, if, after the first excitement, every time you push your hand down the side of a chair, there is nothing there (except crumbs), then you will soon stop. In both cases the behaviour has extinguished *because it has not been reinforced.*

Again, as with classical conditioning, instrumental conditioning also generalises. If a child is rewarded for asking questions in one classroom, she is likely to do it in other classrooms. If you find money down one chair, you will be likely to search in others. We also learn to discriminate. Questions asked in a classroom might not be asked in a church – the two settings are very dissimilar.

More important than matters of generalisation and discrimination, however, is the frequency with which the connections are made, that is, how often the reinforcement occurs. In real life, it is rare to be reinforced every time that we do something. A child is not always responded to so readily in the classroom. Parents do not always turn and happily engage with their children's requests or comments. We do not find money in every chair or settee. In other words, the reinforcements that we experience are called *partial.* That is, they happen only some of the time. This partial reinforcement has a very important effect. It makes the behaviour *stronger,* in other words, it makes it more likely to keep on occurring and less likely to extinguish. This all makes good sense. If just now and then you find money down the side of a chair, you are likely to keep on looking for a long time.

There is more to instrumental conditioning than reinforcement or a reward making behaviour stronger. Already, above, there was the example of punishment – the child being spoken to sarcastically on asking a question. Punishment has the opposite effect to reinforcement – it makes the behaviour weaker or less likely to occur. If a child is spoken to harshly or slapped for doing something, then he or she is less likely to do it again. If every time we greet a particular person at work, he simply scowls at us and passes by, we will stop trying to talk to him.

The trouble with punishment is that it only tells the person what not to do rather than providing an alternative. Reinforcement shapes behaviour in a positive direction. Also, what appears to be punishment does not always work as punishment. If someone is starved of attention, then even a snarly, unpleasant reaction from somebody might be better than nothing, so the person keeps on trying to make contact. This comment is hinting at the discussion of behaviour modification to follow.

▶ Behaviour modification

The brief descriptions of classical and instrumental conditioning suggest, correctly, that they are both types of learning that happen regularly throughout life. However, a large part of that learning happens between people. When parents teach their children, when teachers instruct their students, when people work together, conditioning, particularly instrumental conditioning, is happening all of the time. The question then becomes how consciously and carefully we turn conditioning into a series of techniques that we then use to help people to learn, or to train them or to change them. This happens throughout life, of course, but the moment behavioural control is described in this way, various ethical objections tend to be raised.

Take *punishment* as an example. Adults frequently punish children in one way or another. Employers punish employees. People in strictly run organisations such as the armed services are sometimes punished. People in institutions such as prisons are punished; indeed, they might have been placed there partly in punishment. Whether or not one raises ethical objections to one person trying to control another or modify another's behaviour through punishment, using punishment carries some disadvantages:

1 Punishment suggests nothing positive; it merely says 'don't do this' rather than suggesting what *to* do.

2 Punishment may well lead a person to withdraw from the situation entirely, if this is possible, and may also lead to other negative emotional reactions.

3 Sometimes, something that looks punishing might, in fact, be rewarding.

If punishment is considered for use in behavioural control, it is good to bear the following in mind:

1 Positive reinforcement is more effective if it can be used.

2 When using punishment, it best to combine it with positive reinforcement.

3 It is possible to use mild punishment almost informatively, to let someone know that they might be on the wrong track, rather than heavily – a frown rather than a slap to a child, for example.

4 If punishment is used, it should be associated quickly and obviously with what is thought to be the inappropriate behaviour, and with nothing else.

5 It is important to administer punishment instantly. Administered later, it simply becomes very ineffective. This point has some obvious implications if

punishment is used to control criminal behaviour – there are inevitably long gaps between the crime and the punishment.

Whether or not we approve of conscious attempts to influence other people's behaviour, society is based on them and to some extent we all engage in such attempts in daily life. When we respond to others, part of the reason for the response is to have an effect on their behaviour. If we want to get on well with someone, then we behave differently than if we were relatively unconcerned about our relationship with them. If we want someone at work or in our sports club or whatever it might be to do something (that is, to behave in a particular way), then we go about it with whatever techniques we believe might be effective. This is behaviour control or modification.

Punishment has already been considered because of its many implications. However, there are numerous other techniques of behaviour modification. The most important example is *positive reinforcement*. As has been suggested already, this is the essence of instrumental conditioning. It is the most effective and useful way of modifying a person's behaviour because it simply involves the reinforcing (that is, the rewarding) of whatever behaviour is in question. For it to be used, first the behaviour must already exist, even in a minor degree. Second, there must be a reinforcer that can be used. To take some obvious examples, if you want to reinforce a child for writing, then the child must first be able to make marks on paper with a writing implement. Similarly, if someone tries to positively reinforce another person for doing something simply by giving that person some attention (attention is a very important reinforcer), then there must be a positive relationship between them. Attention from some people is punishing rather than rewarding. Think of the typist and her boss again.

Extinction is also a common and effective way of exercising behavioural control. It has become such a significant part of attempting to shape the behaviour of children that it has come to be known as *time out*. As described earlier, it simply refers to the absence of reward or reinforcement where reward has previously been experienced. To take the commonplace example, to stop a child from doing something, taking his sister's toys, for instance, then he might be sent to stand in the corner, or sent off to his room. In other words, he is being given time out from a usually pleasant situation, a situation in which the behaviour in question cannot occur.

Behaviour control can be much more subtle than simply through reward, punishment and extinction. For example, it is possible to control anxiety by setting in place behaviours that are incompatible with it. If you teach someone (including yourself) to relax using a systematic programme of progressive relaxation and to apply what they have learned to situations in which they would normally feel anxious, then the anxiety is reduced. One cannot feel relaxed and anxious simultaneously. This might be achieved progressively, first by using imagined situations when in a relaxed state and then by gradually working through real-life situations.

A final example is *satiation*. This refers to the well-known maxim that it is possible to have too much of a good thing. You might really like chocolate and find yourself using it as a self-reward for all manner of things. However, if you were given a kilo of your favourite chocolate and asked to eat it until it was gone, the experience would be so unpleasant that chocolate would no longer be of any use to you as a reward. It would have lost its effectiveness.

It may well have occurred to you that so far much of this chapter on learning and conditioning has been written as though all learners (including the human variety) do not have cognitions or do not think. This is very much the tradition in this area of psychology, perhaps because much of the research work has been conducted using animal subjects, but also because, in the behavioural tradition, thinking is rarely considered. Conditioning can and does occur without thinking being involved. However, humans do think and, in fact, engage in a wide range of cognitive activity. Consequently, when they are in the midst of the circumstances that bring about classical or instrumental conditioning, they may well be aware of what is going on. This will clearly have an effect on the learning. For example, a person might well resist any attempts to change his or her behaviour. Or, alternatively, he or she might recognise what is happening, see its benefit and therefore learn more quickly.

It follows from this that it is perfectly possible for individuals to learn considerable aspects of behavioural *self-control*. Speaking well outside of the behavioural tradition, self-control hints at volition, inner direction, willpower and certainly a conscious awareness of what is happening. From a subjective viewpoint, such mechanisms are involved in bringing about changes in one's own behaviour. On the other hand, this can be characterised as using one behavioural response to control another behavioural response. An obvious and common example of this comes from slimming or dieting. Food is eaten less frequently or in smaller quantities in order to prevent over-eating. This is all dependent on attitudes and beliefs such as 'I don't want to look fat', 'All of my friends are slim and I want to look like them', 'I want to look like the people on television or in advertisements', 'To be overweight is to be unhealthy.'

There are many ways of bringing about behavioural self-control. For example, it is possible to teach oneself relaxation techniques and to arrange one's own hierarchies of situations that make one anxious and then to relax through them. Or one might imagine very unpleasant circumstances in order to stop or avoid a behaviour that one wants to be rid of. For instance, in attempting to give up smoking, one might imagine the details of horrible deaths that might result from lung cancer or emphysema. These are both techniques of self-control through classical conditioning.

Instrumental conditioning can also be used effectively on the self. For example, a married couple who keep on arguing but very much want to stop might set up a situation for themselves in which quarrelling is less likely or simply fades away. They might rearrange the furniture and so completely change the old cues that surrounded them when they argued. And if they still feel the impulse to argue, they might agree to go and stand in the corner of the bathroom, have their argument and then go back into the living-room or bedroom. Apart from the ridiculousness of this, it also helps them to realise that they have established control over their arguing and that if they can do this, they can control it sufficiently to stop altogether.

It is also possible to arrange some obvious reinforcers that help one to behave in ways that one feels are necessary but which one does not like. For example, someone who finds it difficult to study might break the work up into small chunks and follow these by reinforcers such as coffee breaks, reading a novel, going for a walk, or, in fact, whatever works for that person. Think back to one of the examples at the start of the chapter.

One of the positive aspects of establishing behavioural self-control is that if it is successful, it tends to increase self-esteem and self-confidence. This becomes a very positive cycle because it will lead to even more effective self-control. It certainly seems likely that if a person feels that he or she has been responsible for the change in his or her behaviour through his or her own efforts, then there is more chance that it will stick than if it has been brought about by someone else.

To summarise, the two types of conditioning are fundamental processes of learning and although they might seem very objective and not involving much in the way of thoughts and feelings, they nevertheless account for a great deal of what we learn. They also lead to what is one of the more useful applied aspects of psychology – behaviour modification. Behaviour *can* be changed either in oneself or in other people by judicious use of the principles of conditioning; it can be learned, maintained, strengthened, changed or made to disappear altogether. This is particularly useful when training children and when attempting to alter behaviours that are regarded by society as being inappropriate or harmful or regarded by the individual as being unworthy, unpleasant, injurious or generally unwanted.

▶ Complex learning – skills and tips

Although the details of both classical and instrumental conditioning can be very complex, the learning involved is quite simple. For the most part the behaviours or the responses are straightforward and easy to describe. However, much of what human beings learn involves either very complex behaviour or very complex material. For example, learning to ride a bicycle or drive a car or learning to acquire and develop social skills involves very intricate sequences of behaviour. Similarly, learning the material involved in completing a degree or learning to think in new ways, as one might when taking a degree, embrace very complex materials and processes. To try to account for these with conditioning is cumbersome. Other, much broader variables come into play.

To consider skills first of all, the pattern in which skills are learned tends to be similar from one skill and one person to the next. Certainly, one person might learn to type or to drive faster than another, but the sequence of learning tends to be very similar. There tends to be a rapid improvement at first, say, for the first 15 or 20 hours of learning, then the rate of improvement slows down to such an extent that there appears to be no learning at all. Such flat parts in the curve of learning are called *plateaux*. Then, suddenly, the rate of learning increases again for a while, until a second plateau is reached when, again, the rate slows down. The sudden increase usually means that some new level of the skill has been learned. For example, in driving, the first steep curve of learning might involve the acquisition of the various activities involved. Then, after a plateau, the second burst of learning might occur after the person has learned to put the various behaviours together in a co-ordinated way.

If you think about any practical skills that you have learned, you will recognise the plateaux that you experienced. You will also, perhaps, remember the frustration of them. At the time it seems as though you will never improve. Then, suddenly, you do and everything seems to be much easier.

An important aspect of learning a skill is the amount and distribution of time that you spend practising. The general choice (as in one of the examples at the start of this chapter) is between *massing* the practice and *distributing* it. In other words, you can plug away at it for hours without cease or you can work at it for a while, take a break, go back to it, take another break, and so on. In general, if the skills involve physical co-ordination such as in ball games or driving, then distributed practice is more effective. But if a great deal of thought is involved, then massed practice is often more effective. In general, as tasks become more complex, so the advantages of distributed practice lessen.

Another important aspect of learning complex skills concerns *parts versus wholes*. Is it more effective to learn a complex task altogether or to break it down into its parts and learn each of these in turn? There are a number of factors that influence the answer to this question.

The first point concerns intelligence. The more intelligent the person, then the 'whole' method will tend to be the more effective. Also, the advantages of the whole method increase with practice; similarly, the whole method is better if the practice is distributed than if it is massed. Then there is the material to be learned. If it is meaningful material, as when working for a higher level examination, for example, then again the whole method outweighs the part method. In general, although it might often be tempting (and sometimes useful) to break a task to be learned into its parts, the disadvantage of doing this comes from having to learn how to put the parts together once they have themselves been absorbed.

A further point that it is useful to bear in mind when learning complex material is that the beginning and end of any material are far more easily learned than the middle sections. In this case, if the whole method were being followed, then the beginning and end would be over-learned in order to learn the middle sections to a reasonable standard. Learning a poem (if anyone still learns poems) might be an example of this. So, if any material to be learned is of this sort, then the part method might be better.

A further important characteristic of material to be learned is its degree of *meaningfulness*. In general, the more meaningful the material to be learned, the more readily it is learned. If any material is patterned or organised, then it is far easier to learn than if it is not. Similarly, if one moves this idea up a notch and considers more complex meanings such as those involved in passages of prose, a similar effect obtains. Hence, if a person understands what has been written, then whatever is understood is remembered better than the words in the passage.

Feedback is also important. If a person is attempting to learn something, then the learning occurs more effectively if, from time to time, he or she is given feedback on how they are doing. This is particularly the case when learning some complex skill such as driving or learning a new sport. Some feedback is obvious – you know immediately if you drive over the kerb or if you reverse into another vehicle. But it is not so obvious how you might be doing in general or how well you are co-ordinating the various sub-skills involved. For this you need feedback from someone else. And if driving is replaced with a more complex skill such as learning how to behave in a meeting or learning to put people at ease when interviewing them, then detailed feedback from someone else is a necessity.

Finally, when considering complex learning, or the learning of complex material, is the matter of whether the learner is *active or passive*. To take a simple example, if one is learning material for an examination, is it better to just keep on reading it through or is it better to rehearse it for some of the time? The general answer is that active learning is more effective than passive learning. If you *do* something with any material that you are attempting to master, then the learning is likely to be more effective.

Work done some years ago on these types of issue suggests some obvious advice that can be followed by anyone who is engaged in so-called 'higher' education. Of course, sticking to the following advice is another matter, although the points listed all represent ways of being active rather than passive.

- When learning, don't relax too much. Don't sit in an easy chair or lie on the bed.

- Review material immediately after a class.

- Read actively rather than passively. In other words, think about the material rather than letting it flow past you.

- Read with the aim of answering questions.

- Don't simply memorise material but think about its implications.

- Ask yourself intelligent questions about the material.

- Take more notes than you need.

- Always record questions when they occur to you.

- Stay alert and attentive in classes.

- Study for examinations actively.

- If you have to learn some things by rote, recite them aloud.

Even though it is best to take an active stance towards this type of learning, most people would sooner be doing something else other than sitting there with their textbooks. It is therefore also worth remembering to build in plenty of rewards. An hour's work followed by a walk, a cup of coffee, a magazine, a crime novel, or whatever, for half an hour not only provides a break but is actually using a preferred activity to reinforce a less preferred activity. It is a fine example of behavioural self-control.

A final aspect of more complex learning is the importance of *prior beliefs*, something that takes us far from conditioning into a squarely cognitive area. In general, if one is learning new material, then one will almost certainly have some prior beliefs about some of that material, beliefs, for example, that some things are naturally associated. The learner tends to combine such prior knowledge with whatever new information is coming in to create a final appraisal. For example, if you believe that people who are dishonest in one situation are likely to be dishonest in all situations, then that is likely to influence how you evaluate the incoming evidence. The evidence may be distorted in that direction.

Such prior beliefs have important implications for the type of learning that goes on in schools and universities or any centres of higher learning. For example, if someone has a series of prior beliefs about the physical world, as most of us have, then the learning (and teaching) of physics will be influenced by this. If someone has prior beliefs about the nature of social relationships, then learning new social skills will inevitably be influenced by such beliefs.

▶ Summary

- Learning is change through experience or practice and ranges from very simple to very complex.

- Classical conditioning is based on learning associations between stimuli or events that were not previously associated and involves quite simple, rather primitive reactions.

- Reinforcement is crucial to both classical and instrumental conditioning. When reinforcement does not occur, the result is extinction – a gradual reduction or fading away of the learned response.

- Classical conditioning also generalises, in other words, it occurs in the presence or stimuli that are similar to the original stimulus.

- Instrumental conditioning is more complex than classical conditioning and includes much of everyday learning.

- Instrumental conditioning rests even more strongly on reinforcement than classical conditioning.

- Positive reinforcement leads to a strengthening of behaviour, an increased likelihood that it will occur.

- Punishment reduces the strength or likelihood of a response, and extinction and generalisation occur in instrumental conditioning, as in classical conditioning.

- Partial or occasional reinforcement leads to a much stronger learned response than continuous reinforcement.

- Behaviour modification is the application of the principles of conditioning to real-life problems in order to change people's behaviour.

- There are many good reasons to use positive reinforcement rather than punishment, not the least being that it is more effective.

- There are many forms of behaviour modification in many situations from dealing with abnormal or injurious behaviour to broad societal control.

- Behavioural self-control is the ultimate aim of behaviour modification.

- The complex learning of motor skills and higher-level material involves principles that go beyond those of conditioning and always includes plateaux in the learning curves.

- Matters of particular importance that influence complex learning are: massed versus distributed practice; parts versus whole learning; the meaningfulness of material; feedback; active versus passive learning; and the nature of prior beliefs.

▶ **Questions and possibilities**

- Make a list of examples of classical and instrumental conditioning that you have experienced. How have they worked?

- If you have children, think about ways in which you have consciously or unconsciously reinforced or punished or extinguished different behaviours in them. How might you have done things differently?

- What instances can you imagine of conditioning in everyday life, at work or at home?

- What are your views on attempting to modify other people's behaviour and on other people attempting to modify your behaviour? What are the possible moral issues involved with such attempts?

- Do you believe that it is possible to change any aspects of anybody's behaviour or are there some aspects of behaviour that are unchangeable? If you believe that some things are unchangeable, what distinguishes them from those that are changeable?

- What are your views on punishment? Do you agree or disagree that positive reinforcement should always be preferred to punishment or even to time-out?

- What have been your experiences with more complex learning? To what extent have you used some of the techniques described in this chapter? To what extent would you use them in teaching someone else?

- Active learning is clearly more effective than passive learning. Why do you think that this is?

- Think of some of the more complex learning that you have done and compare what has been best learned by whole rather than part methods. What is the difference between the two lists?

- Think of some instance in which your own prior beliefs have influenced your learning. To what extent do you think that the type or the strength of the beliefs matter?

- Do you think that all learning is encompassed by the two types of conditioning plus the more complex learning in which there is cognitive involvement? More extremely, do you think that all learning might be explicable in terms of one or other type of conditioning?

- Do you think that animals and humans learn in different ways? Do you think that adults and children learn in different ways? Do you think that people of differing intelligence learn in different ways? If you do think that there are such differences, what are they and how do they come about?

- Think of a situation either at home or at work in which you might have to teach somebody a new skill. Devise a programme to do so and think of why it would be successful or why it might fail.

CHAPTER THIRTEEN

Intellectual life

Memory and thinking

Scenes from life

Christine is in her early forties and is married with three children. She has a good job and has managed to balance her career and family to her satisfaction and theirs. She has a deepening relationship with her husband and, other than the usual teenage tribulations, a good relationship with her children. In short, she is a well-adjusted, happy woman who looks on the past with some contentment and on the future with some optimism.

Recently, she has begun to have sudden extremely vivid visual memories. It is as though a light suddenly goes on in her head and she can see a picture in great detail. The picture varies slightly in its detail but it is always of the same scene. A year previously she had been the first person to arrive at a road crash. It had been a particularly nasty smash with all but one of the members of a young family killed, their bodies flung all over the road. Everybody else involved was seriously injured, although some survived. At the time, Christine did what she could, calling the emergency services on her cellphone and, with other drivers who stopped to help, trying to comfort the survivors.

When she arrived home afterwards, she was very shaky and felt almost unable to drive for several days. Her family became even more important to her than they had been and she felt extremely protective of them. Gradually, the horrors of the incident faded, although it was something that she would never forget entirely. However, her memories seemed to have settled down until she started to suddenly be overwhelmed by the flashbacks to the accident; the scene would be there again without warning as though caught in a flashbulb. It would be there unpredictably and her work and sleep began to suffer. In the end, she seeks counsel.

Let's look at Jack's problem again. *Jack is in his early forties* and, like Christine, is happily married with a close-knit family. His career is going well and life in general is without much difficulty for him. He remains interested in his work, has a number of outside interests and enjoys time with his family in the evenings and at the weekend. The only fly in the ointment of his life is a rather traditional one. From the time that he first started going out with the woman who was to become his wife, he has never seen eye to eye with her mother.

Both he and his wife Jane saw her as interfering, judgemental, critical and generally the sort of person who would always be putting on some or other pressure by hints and innuendo. She lived in a different town, so, at a distance in space and time, he and his wife could laugh at it. They were careful, though, in doing this because they felt it to be important that they not influence their children too much. She was, after all, their grandmother. At times, though, this became very difficult because they deplored the way in which she constantly tried to impose her way of thinking on them.

In the way of these matters, it did not always remain at a distance. Inevitably, they had to see his wife's mother from time to time, the worst of these occasions being when she came to stay. Her husband had died a few years previously, so his steadying influence was no longer there. She had become worse than ever, almost developing into a caricature of her former self.

Jack and Jane are arguing, not strongly, but arguing, nevertheless, about the same old topic. Should they invite Jane's mother to stay, or not? The argument continues in a good-natured way until, as usual, they compromise, decide to ask her next month rather than this, and determine that Jane will write a letter asking her to stay and that Jack will post it tomorrow. Acting while the matter is still in her mind, Jane writes the letter and passes it to Jack for posting on the way to work tomorrow. Jack agrees and puts the letter in his pocket.

Three weeks pass and one evening Jack and Jane receive a phone call from Jane's mother, even more irritating than usual in its tone. She makes no mention of the proposed visit. Jack and Jane speak about it afterwards and Jane mentions how odd it is that her mother should 'be like that' when she will be coming to see them the following week. She has a sudden thought: 'You did post that letter, didn't you, Jack?' 'Yes, of course I did.' He is mildly resentful that Jane should even ask.

Later, Jack has second thoughts and checks the pocket of his jacket. The letter is still there. He has some explaining to do.

From these two aspects of memory (or forgetting), what follows will illustrate two different types of thinking.

Picture a workplace, a huge do-it-yourself store that contains a large number of employees. It is a congenial place to work and is divided into two main sections, each of which has its own manager. Although the majority of the staff work well in the two teams and seem to be reasonably happy with their jobs and their prospects, in each team there is one young woman who is clearly underperforming.

They have remarkably similar profiles. They are in their twenties, reasonably intelligent and basically quite good at what they do. However, both of them are upsetting customers – there have been a few complaints – by treating them in an off-hand way. The contrast with their work-mates makes things worse, because the establishment prides itself, rightly, on its good customer relations. They also very rarely smile or attempt to make conversation with the other employees and generally act as a drag on the atmosphere. They are simply not pulling their weight, either in the details of their work or in the development of their respective teams.

The two managers took a completely different approach to dealing with the problem, although each attempted to progress the matter through a series of meetings. One launched straight into a detailed analysis of the workplace and the demands of the job. He very carefully involved the young woman in his analysis, asking her what she thought the job entailed, including how best to deal with the customers, particularly given that the company had a clear policy and sets of guidelines about how to do this. His aim, as he made clear to her from the start, was to sort out where she was falling down on the job, having pointed out to her that she was clearly not pulling her weight.

The second manager also had a series of meetings with his young woman employee. However, his approach was quite different. He again began by saying that there was clearly something wrong, but emphasised that she did not look happy in her work and gently tried to find out from her what was wrong. He was equally open to it being something in her private life as in her working arrangements. His general style was to try to find out what was wrong, from her perspective, and then to attempt to generate with her ways in which things could be improved for her.

After a few weeks of pursuing their respective ways to solution, the two managers compared notes. The first had noticed no improvement at all and was still trying to wrack his brains to think of something. He was beginning to think that the fit between the person and the job was impossible and that she might have to go. The other manager reported that he had seen a definite change in his young woman, something that had been commented on by her co-workers. In fact, he had worked out from what she had said that she was simply not being stretched by her job and that this was making her unfulfilled in it. So he found a way to give her a little more responsibility.

The difference here is between convergent and divergent thinking, or, in everyday terms, between thinking inside the square and outside the square.

▶ Types of memory

The sub-title of this chapter is 'Memory and thinking', but at the outset it is important to say that learning, memory and thinking are intimately interrelated. It is hard to conceive of learning, even the simplicities of classical conditioning, without memory being involved. Similarly, we know that human beings (and, perhaps, some other species to some extent) think. It follows, then, that it is also hard to imagine learning and memory occurring without thought. Or when thought occurs, as it does most of the time, then memory must be involved and learning at least implicated. In other words, the division between this chapter and the last is somewhat arbitrary.

Although there are different types of memory, each of them involves three stages. These are: encoding, storage and retrieval. In other words, these are: putting the information in so that it is in a memorable form, storing it once it is there, and finally being able to gain access to it (as rapidly as possible). Say that you have just read a novel and then in a week's time someone asks you if you have read it and, if so, what you think of it. To begin with, you have somehow put the novel into your memory – you transformed the written word into some other form in your central nervous system. You then retained it there for a week. Then, finally, you were able to gain access to what you had stored in order to be able to transform it again but this time into the spoken word, a word that was a mixture of what you remembered of the novel and what you thought of it.

The major difference between types of memory (in which these three stages work slightly differently) is between *working memory* and *long-term memory*. Working memory holds items for just a few seconds. So, having just read a page of a novel and being questioned about it in detail immediately afterwards, you would probably do quite well. Asked the same questions about that one page a week later and you would probably remember very little. (Working memory is different from *iconic memory*, which is a detailed image of something that lasts for just a few milliseconds, whether this is visual, auditory, or involving the other senses.) Remembering some of the gist of the novel and its main characters a week later would be an example of long-term memory.

Interestingly, there is also a difference in the types of long-term memory that are used to store different kinds of information. For example, remembering the gist of a novel is a different style of memory from remembering how to swim. There are also differences between *explicit memory* and *implicit memory*. Explicit memory is what happens when we try to remember something consciously; implicit memory is memory for skills.

The encoding involved in the first stage of working memory can take various forms. For example, remembering someone's name might be from the sounds of it being spoken or a visualisation of it or the semantics that might underlie it, in other words, what associations it brings to mind for you. In the extreme (and very rarely), some people have eidetic imagery. If they are shown a picture or a page of writing, they can hold the entire visual representation in their heads and scan through it, reading off whatever they wish.

The storage part of working memory has a very limited range, exemplified by the phrase 'the magic number 7 plus or minus 2'. That is, the range of working memory covers somewhere between 5 and 9 items. Of course, if you can chunk the material into meaningful units, then the number of individual items might go considerably beyond 7 + or − 2. Compare: 124312331442 and 111222333444 or 123412341234 as memory tasks. Or: tmheimnokriyng and thinkingmemory.

Of course, after a brief time of holding onto a few items in working memory they disappear, or are forgotten. There are two reasons for this: they either decay with time or they are interfered with by other items that come in. For example, if you look up a telephone number, you will probably remember it long enough to dial but it will quickly fade away after that. On the other hand, if you look up the number and as you begin to dial it someone says another telephone number to you, then the one you looked up will be interfered with and disappear.

Assuming that information has made it into your working memory, it seems to be there in an immediate sense if you need it. You do not have to go searching for it, or at least only for a very brief moment or two. In fact, if you do have to search for some time, then the information has probably gone from working memory.

Working memory is extremely important for thought, particularly when the thinking involves attempting to solve a problem. The obvious example is the doing of mental arithmetic, but there are many other such problems throughout daily life both at work and at home. It is as though working memory provides a sort of blackboard in the mind from which we are able to read items for a brief time. A similar example comes whenever we use language, say, in a conversation or in reading. When conversing, we have to hold in working memory whatever the person has just said while we are formulating a reply. Similarly, when reading a novel or any sort of document, we have to hold in working memory some material while we are processing other material and putting the two together.

Whereas working memory covers just a minute or two, the span of long-term memory runs from a few minutes to the whole of one's life. One might be able to remember the details of a document throughout a day but would be unlikely to remember them a month or even a week later. On the other hand, aspects of one's own or one's family's biography one might remember throughout life.

With long-term memory the primary means of encoding relies on meaning. Specific aspects of what is remembered are often forgotten but we tend to remember the gist or the general meaning or impressions gained. Of course, if we make a conscious effort to learn things, then we might have encoded more than meaning. The rote learning of poetry is a clear example of this. Similarly, we also remember things like the sound of someone's voice or the smell of their hair or even their general demeanour. These are not actually meanings but seem somewhat related to meaning. There are various encoding techniques for improving long-term memory that will be discussed later.

Forgetting items from long-term memory is obviously a lack of retrieval. The question is whether this is due to a loss of the material itself or an inability to access it. It might still be there somewhere but we just do not seem to be able to get at it. It is a very common experience to attempt to recall something and fail. Often it is the name of a person, a film, a book, or whatever. Then, later, the name suddenly pops into mind. In fact, sometimes we might even use the technique of trying *not* to think about it in order the more readily to retrieve it. The 'tip-of-the-tongue' phenomenon is one of the most tantalising forms of this type of lack of retrieval. It is a situation in which we know that we know what it is that we are trying to remember, but it seems just out of reach, although we can produce all manner of associations to it.

The major reason for retrieval from long-term memory not working well is *interference*. Trying to remember a friend's new telephone number is difficult – there is interference from the old one. Occasionally, people change their first names. 'Would you mind calling me X now? I have always wanted to be called that so I am changing my name.' X becomes almost impossible to remember, there is such interference from the original name and when it is remembered it is almost impossible to use, it seems so 'wrong'. Not everything is made difficult to retrieve from long-term memory by interference. Some items seem to just disappear altogether.

An interesting aspect of long-term memory concerns the links between encoding and retrieval. In general, it is easier to remember something if the attempt is made in the same context as that in which it was learned. This context might be external – the place we were in at the time – or internal – the state that we were in at the time. For example, it is sometimes easier to remember something that was learned after we had had a few drinks if we were attempting the retrieval after a few drinks as well. The fact of this context-dependent memory is made very apparent when meeting someone with whom one is very familiar in a completely different context from the usual one. More often than not the person's name seems to have completely (and embarrassingly) disappeared.

▶ Forgetting

It is not possible to consider memory without also considering forgetting – they are opposite sides of a coin. So far, it has been clear that much forgetting occurs either through interference or from the gradual fading of the memory. But these are by no means the only influences on forgetting. Emotional factors also play a part, an example being the flashbulb memory and the forgotten letter described at the start of the chapter. If you consider your own memories and think of those that are the most vivid or compelling, then it is likely that they will have a strong emotional component, negative or positive. We think about or rehearse emotion-laden events more than those that are emotionally neutral and so we are likely to remember them more readily than neutral events.

Flashbulb memories are extraordinarily clear memories that surround the circumstances of a highly significant event. For example, many people remember exactly where they were and what they were doing in great detail at the time of a tragic event. Good examples are the assassination of President Kennedy, the death of Princess Diana or the destruction of the Twin Towers. It seems as though a special type of memory is set off by such events. If such a memory involves personal and horrific circumstances, then the person may also experiences vivid flashbacks of whatever it was that occurred.

Anxiety can also have significant effects on memory, as it can on many aspects of our psychological functioning. An everyday example comes from forgetting the name of someone you know well because of the pressures of the social situation in which you are having to introduce them to someone else. The name has suddenly disappeared and it is almost as if you are looking at a stranger. In the extreme, people might even forget their own name or get it slightly wrong when introducing themselves. Another all too frequently experienced example of the influence of anxiety on memory comes with examinations, particularly those for which one might be ill-prepared. The horror of seeing a question that one knows nothing about can drive out memory of the answers for those questions that one knows perfectly well. It is almost as though the memory freezes. This is probably some sort of interference, the extra thoughts and feelings that come from the anxiety seeming to drive out the information that is required.

One of the most interesting effects of emotion on memory comes with the idea of *repression*, first suggested by Freud (1933). This is exemplified by the man who forgot to post the letter to his mother-in-law. Freud's idea was that some experiences (particularly if they occurred in childhood) are so emotionally fraught that to bring them to mind is so painful that they are completely blocked. They can only be uncovered, or so the theory goes, when some of the emotion associated with them has been dealt with. The unfortunately commonplace examples of this type of memory failure have been seen in cases of childhood abuse.

▶ How to improve memory

We have various types of memory that have evolved in such a way that they enable us to engage with life more readily. Nevertheless, we forget a great deal, either through the decay of memory, interference from other information that we constantly have to process, or through various emotional influences. What, then, can be done about this? Is it possible to use strategies in order to improve memory? The general answer to this question is 'yes'.

Improving span

Although 7 + or − 2 items is the average memory span, we are not necessarily
stuck with this. It is possible to improve one's working memory span by practice
and the judicious use of chunking. This is best achieved by using material
that one knows well, in other words, material that is well embedded in long-
term memory and using 'chunks' of this to help expand day-to-day working
memory. For example, if you are a darts player, then you will probably automatically know a great many combinations of numbers that add up to or
subtract from 301 or 501, whichever of the two forms of the game that you play.
If, for some reason, you then need to remember sequences of numbers, the
type of chunking that the darts knowledge provides will allow you to remember
longer sequences than someone without such knowledge. Of course, most
people do not have this particular knowledge, but they do have some over-
learned knowledge that might well be of help in improving memory span for
some items.

Improving long-term memory

Improvement to long-term memory is, perhaps, more important than improving
memory span through practice. Over many years, a number of methods known
as *mnemonic systems* have been developed to aid long-term memory. For example,
the method of *loci* involves first committing to memory a series of places that
you know very well, a typical series being the places that you come to as you walk
from your front door through the various rooms in your house. Then, if you have
a series of items to remember, you form a strong visual image of each of those
items in a sequence of the places that you mentally walk through. If you memorise items in this way, it is easy to 'walk through' your house and bring to mind
the strong images that you have created and so remember the items that it would
have otherwise been difficult to recollect.

A second method involves *key words*. If, for example, you are trying to learn
a vocabulary from a foreign language, you might form a strong association to
each of the foreign words and then use that image to bring up the word. To take
an obvious example, the French word for bread is *pain*, a word for which it is
easy to create an image. Or take the French word for house – *maison*. For this,
you might form the image of a stonemason building a house. And so on.

A similar word system is that of *peg-words*. In this case you learn a list of words
so that you know it very well and number it from 1 to, say, 10. Then you might
form unusual associations between these 10 words and 10 items that you have
to learn. A common list that is used in this way comes from the nursery game
– 1 is a bun, 2 is a shoe, 3 is a tree, and so on.

Forming associations is also a significant way of improving memory. If you
read an article and wish to remember it, then ask yourself several questions
about it and its implications. The more you ask yourself and the more you think
about its ramifications, then the more likely you are able to remember it. *Context*

is also important. Simply, it is easier to remember something if you put yourself in the same context in which you learned it. And it is important to remember that this context might be external – the place where you first saw the material – or internal – the state that you were in at the time.

Also, it is possible to use various self-imposed *organisations* on material that you have to learn. For example, if you have to learn a list of words, then weave them into a story. Similarly, if you have to learn material that is already organised, such as in a textbook, then it helps to impose your own organisation on it, rather than simply reading it through and using the organisation already there. This reflects back on the importance of being active when learning. In fact, the notion of being active also applies to the practice of retrieval. It is possible to practise the retrieval of items that you might have to retrieve during an examination, for example. The practice of actually dredging up the information helps when it is done later. This is something akin to the *mental practice* of various physical activities that is engaged in by sportspersons. It is perfectly possible to practise your sport while never leaving the chair.

The best-known combination of these memory techniques, particularly when used for the sort of material that is to be examined, is the *PQRST* method. You'll notice that this letter sequence is very easy to remember, for an obvious reason. Again, this makes use of a very active approach to learning and memory. The letters stand for: preview, question, read, self-recitation and test, and need no explanation. If you follow through PQRST with material that you have to learn for an examination, then you will recall it better than if you do not.

Finally, there is what is known as *constructive* memory. This refers to what we do (perhaps automatically) when we attempt to remember complex information that might be in novels or stories that are told to us about events in life. We form active constructions around it, using our general knowledge, stereotypes that we might hold and various schemas about the world that already exist for us. Although this type of construction might distort the material somewhat, it also ensures that it is remembered.

▶ Types of thinking

As already mentioned, learning and memory are inevitably closely related to thinking, that is, the representation of information in the mind.

Problem-solving

Of the various types of thinking, probably the most commonly used is problem-solving or reasoning, something that we do when we use past experience to solve a current problem or to reach a particular goal. Of course, problems vary in their nature. Some are well structured, such as the best way to drive through the city to get to a particular destination. Others are less well structured, such as how to turn my teenage son from a surly brute into the pleasant 10-year-old that he used to be.

Well-structured problems are easy to solve, usually by looking up information in various sources of reference, or even looking into one's own memory. Less well-structured problems are more difficult and usually involve insight. This means that the various aspects of the problem need to be looked at in a new way in order to approach a solution. An insight-based solution might come suddenly to mind but this only follows a great deal of work and thought. Problems that at first sight appear to be about one thing might turn out to be about another, and it is only through this realisation that they can be solved. Take a simple (and perhaps foolish) example that appeared many years ago in a psychology textbook. If the letters P, O, L, K are pronounced poke and the letters F, O, L, K are pronounced foke, then how do you pronounce the white of an egg? Did you think 'yoke' or albumen? More complex versions of this type of intellectual sleight of hand are often found in the various urban myths that relay round the world. They usually involve having to think of a set of problems in an entirely new way, a way that the telling of the story does not suggest.

The example above is also an instance of the effect of *mental sets* on problem-solving. One is set up to think yoke rather than albumen. Such sets can get in the way of correct problem solutions because they constrain flexibility. A similar difficulty comes from what is called *functional fixedness*. This occurs when we are stuck with only one way of looking at something. A simple example would be to see a book as only something that is read rather than something that can be used to prop open a door, to prop up a chair, to put with other books in order to stand on, to press leaves in, and so on. There is a sense in which the opposite of functional fixedness is creativity, which will be dealt with later.

Clearly, some people are better problem-solvers or better at reasoning than others, particularly in certain domains or areas of life. These people are usually referred to as experts. What distinguishes the expert from the non-expert is the sheer amount of knowledge that they have and the relatively sophisticated way in which this knowledge is organised. It is a combination of these two characteristics that enables people to be expert problem-solvers. It follows, then, that the more knowledge you are able to amass about something, then the more readily you will solve any problems that arise in that area. In other words, as far as is possible, you make yourself into an expert. One does not have to be an expert to solve problems, but it helps.

Although problem-solving is the main aspect of everyday life in which reasoning is involved, it is also possible to break reasoning down into various types. The two major types of reasoning are *deductive* and *inductive*. Deductive reasoning goes from the general to the particular. Deductive reasoning is the type most often used by detectives when solving crimes; it is based on contingencies. If one thing happens, then it follows that something else is likely to happen and yet another something else is not. Such reasoning, when broken down into its elements, also takes the form of syllogisms. All birds have wings; all winged creatures can fly; therefore birds can fly. The third statement is a perfectly correct deduction from the first two, the problem being, in this case, that not all birds do have wings – the initial premise was incorrect.

In many instance of real life, we do not have clear initial premises (whether they are right or wrong), so then we have to apply inductive reasoning. This goes from the particular to the general. Going back to the previous example, if someone is learning that birds usually fly and then sees a flightless bird, he or she has to revise the general notion. We build up inductive reasoning through observation of examples, a process that, like science, is unending. Deductions are final, whereas inductions are never-ending because it is not possible to know all of the instances of something.

In the end, it should be said that mostly we manage to problem-solve and to reason reasonably well. We make mistakes, of course, but whether or not we know terms such as deductive and inductive reasoning, we can still engage in both activities. There is, however, another and highly significant type of thinking – creativity.

Creativity

Creativity involves apparently making something out of nothing. 'Apparently' is an important word here, because there has to be background to everything that is done or created – ideas, solutions, new ways of doing things, do not come from an entirely blank slate. But what actually happens when someone writes a novel, makes a work of art, finds a new way to bowl a cricket ball, makes a scientific discovery, or develops a new way to harness power?

One way to look at this is to take people who are known for their creativity and to ask them questions about the process that they typically go through when they are 'being creative'. This is an obvious thing to do but is, nevertheless, relatively clumsy. If you ask someone about their creative moments after the event, can they remember it as it really was? If you interrupt them during the creative process, will this ruin the process? In spite of these awkwardnesses, there are some surprisingly consistent patterns that have been observed.

The creative process appears to have four major steps that usually occur in the same order. They are:

1 *Preparation.* This involves the setting of the scene, the identification of the problem and the gathering of information that might be relevant to it.

2 *Incubation.* This is, perhaps, the most unusual part of creative activity because it involves apparently doing nothing. It is as if no conscious effort is being put into the problem. The problem is ignored and the person does other things or, perhaps, just does very little.

3 *Illumination.* This is the moment at which there comes a sudden creative idea. This is the 'aha' or the 'eureka' experience, something that is very like the moment of insight mentioned earlier. It usually involves a sudden recasting of the problem in a new way that leads to a solution. This moment at which illumination occurs is not predictable and little is known about how the breakthrough occurs or where the idea comes from. This is not to say that it is

mystical but merely that nothing is yet known about how and why an idea seems to just bubble up into consciousness.

4 *Verification.* This final phase of creativity involves the evaluation, checking, testing and possible revision of the ideas produced at the moment of illumination. This is the rounding off of the creative process and will involve logical thought and the type of reasoning described earlier. The result may, of course, be that the new ideas are rejected. Ideas might be new and creative but they might not always be practical, for example.

Another way to look at creativity is to consider the characteristics of creative persons. Do they have anything in common and, perhaps, more importantly, can people become more creative if they practise? Characteristics shared by creative people include:

1 A strong independence of thought and action.

2 A keen sense of humour – perhaps this is not surprising since much of humour is based on seeing familiar things in new ways.

3 A strong interest in the novel and the complex rather than the familiar and the simple.

4 An ability to tolerate ambiguity, that is, not minding shades of grey.

5 Self-confidence.

6 A disregard for the conventional.

7 Finally, and most importantly, perseverance. This last characteristic is the most significant of all, something without which creativity is very unlikely to occur. All creative people who have been studied show great perseverance. They hang onto problems and keep worrying away at them, not obsessionally, but simply with great application.

Creativity is not simply a matter of having certain personal characteristics, however. Also important is context and having a great deal of knowledge and intellectual prowess and motivation. If this all sounds impossible, then take heart. There are a number of steps that can be taken to increase your own creativity. The following list comes from Sternberg (1986) who has done more than anyone in recent years to study intelligence and creativity.

If you wish to improve your creativity, try the following:

1 Concentrate on an area that you really like and enjoy – don't choose to try to improve creativity in an area that bores you or makes you restless.

2 Follow your own path. Naturally, it might be useful to listen to advice and feedback, but evaluate these in your own terms and make your own decisions about the way to go.

3 Be self-critical but, nevertheless, hold to a strong belief in what you are doing. Do not be put off by what others say if they regard it as less than worthwhile.

4 A crucial part of creativity is choosing the appropriate problem and defining it carefully. Make sure that the choice is not only a sensible choice but also one that appeals to your own sense of values. It does not matter what others think, but only your own sense of what is important.

5 Use every type of thinking that you can to feed into your creativity. You might want to think laterally or divergently, to keep creating analogies and metaphors, but also find a place for more traditional ways of thinking. Anything might help.

6 Get help from those around you by choosing people who are likely to be encouraging and supportive of your attempts.

7 Make yourself an expert in the field, that is, gain as much knowledge as you can and then try to go outside it or beyond it or to stretch it.

8 Be committed. That is, persevere; keep at it.

As should be obvious, these ways of improving creativity all hinge on a huge independence of thought. Such independence is not sufficient in itself. You will not become more creative simply by going off in some direction that is different from everyone else. You also need to take into account the details mentioned. But, like everything else, it takes work.

▶ Summary

- There are strong links between learning, memory and thinking.

- All types of memory involve three stages: encoding, storage and retrieval.

- Working memory is like a blackboard for the mind that has items on it for just a few seconds before they are either erased or pass into long-term memory.

- Iconic memory is a detailed image (usual visual) that lasts for a few milliseconds.

- Explicit memory is involved in consciously trying to recall something and implicit memory is memory for skills.

- The storage part of working memory can normally carry only 7 + or − 2 items of information.

- Long-term memory lasts for either a few minutes or for the whole of life (with items such as biographical details).

- Forgetting from long-term memory occurs mainly through simple disuse or decay, or from interference from other items.

- Forgetting also depends on emotional factors such as trauma, anxiety and repression.

- There are various methods that can be used to improve long-term memory, such as mnemonics, key words, peg-words, loci and context. The best of these for use when dealing with the type of material that has to be remembered for examinations is the PQRST method.

- A basic everyday type of thinking is problem-solving or reasoning – the use of prior experience to solve current problems or to achieve goals. Insight is crucial to problem-solving.

- Deductive reasoning goes from the general to the particular and inductive reasoning from the particular to the general.

- Creativity usually involves four steps: preparation, incubation, illumination and verification.

- Creative people tend to share a number of characteristics such as being very independent in their thinking, able to tolerate ambiguity and capable of great perseverance.

- Although there are large individual differences in creativity, it is not fixed and can be improved by using a series of techniques.

▶ Questions and possibilities

- What things in life have you found it particularly difficult to remember? Why do you think that this was so?

- Have you developed any techniques for expanding your span of working memory? If so, write them down so that they are explicit. If not, then what techniques could you develop that would work well for you?

- Why do you think that there is a different type of memory for skills such as riding a bicycle or driving a car or playing a sport than there is for all other material?

- Do you think that you and the people in your family or that you work with have good memories? Are there differences? Why is it that some people seem to have better memories than others? Are there any aspects of your own memory that you find puzzling? Having read this chapter, can you make more sense of them?

- Do you find some things easier to remember than others? What is the difference between the two types of item?

- Test your own working memory and that of your friends and family. Do they all fit into the five to nine span or are some of them less or more than this?

If their working memories have a span of fewer than five items or more than nine, why do you think this is?

- Why do you forget things? Is it due more to disuse or to interference? Do emotional factors ever get in the way of your memory? What are they and are these factors worse at some times than at others?

- Think about any flashbulb memories that you have had. Why do you think they occurred?

- Are there some things that you imagine that you will never forget? Why do you think that this is and what distinguishes these items from those you are confident that you will forget?

- Have you ever experienced repression? What is it about the original situation that led you to repress it?

- Think of any situation that you have experienced in which you and other people have remembered things differently. Why do you think that this happened?

- What are your personal devices for improving your long-term memory? Are they similar to any of those mentioned in the chapter or have you developed your own unique technique? If you have never used such a technique, choose one of them and try it out.

- How good are you at problem-solving and reasoning? Do you see differences between yourself and those that you know well in these abilities? What problem-solving strategies do you use?

- Think of moments when you have been solving problems when you have had sudden insights. What do you think has brought about these insights? Do you think that it is possible to improve the likelihood of having insights and, if so, how would you do it?

- Have you ever experienced particular hindrances to your problem-solving or reasoning ability? What has brought these about? Are they different from those of other people that you know?

- Have you experienced the four steps of the creative process? In what areas? Are you equally creative in all areas? In fact, do you regard yourself as a creative person?

- In your view, what are the main differences between the creative and the less creative people that you know? Do these characteristics fit in with those described in the chapter?

- In Western history, there have been clearly more creative works (in the public eye) performed by men than by women. Why do you think that this is so? Do you think that there is a real difference here?

■ What do you think of the list of ways to improve creativity? Would you add to the list in any way? How, if at all, have you managed to improve your own creativity?

■ What do you think happens at the moment of insight in problem-solving or illumination in creativity? Similarly, what is going on in the period of incubation?

◀ CHAPTER FOURTEEN ▶

The lifespan

Bringing up children

Scenes from life

It is a pleasant summer day and 4-year-old Harry is playing in the garden with his cousin David, who is also 4. They were born within a few days of each other to sisters, themselves only a few years apart. They visit each other regularly and the children know each other well although in recent months they have not been getting on as well as they used to. The typical pattern of one of these visits is that the two youngsters play while their mothers talk. Occasionally something happens and there is an interruption and then things revert to play and talk as before.

After they had been playing in the garden for a while, playing quite separately but not getting in each other's way, Harry and David accidentally bumped into each other and both of them started to cry. They had had a bit of a shock and were not much hurt, simply upset. Harry's mother immediately heard this and went to see what was wrong. She gave Harry a bit of a cuddle, wiped his tears and sent him on his way back to play. David's mother sat where she was and watched her sister comforting Harry. She ignored David, saying when her sister came back, 'You're too soft on Harry. Look, David's stopped crying already.' Harry's mother did, indeed, look and saw David snivelling a little and casting glances in his mother's direction, glances that his mother did not notice.

A short while later, after the children had been playing quietly together, they both came up to their mothers and in the way of young children were insistently trying to capture their attention. It was not a good time because the conversation had reached a particularly interesting 'Well, she said to him and he said to her' sort of point. After a moment or two Harry's mother stopped her conversation and turned to her son, but David's mother quickly superseded her, almost as though competing. 'What is it, darling?' she asked David, but her tone was irritable. He started to talk to her and she only half-listened and then told him not to be so silly and to stop bothering them. Meanwhile, Harry's mother had listened and quietly given her son an answer to his question.

The day finally went wrong for everyone with some shrieks from the garden. Both mothers went flying out to see what had happened. There was a small garden pond and Harry and David were both half in it, fighting as ineffectually as 4-year-old boys do. David's mother darted to the edge of the pond and dragged her son out. 'What on earth do you think you are doing? You don't fight and you don't get into the pond. What is wrong with you? You are a thoroughly bad child. I've no idea what I'm going to do with you.' Meanwhile, her sister quietly extricated Harry from the pond, checked that he was unhurt and said 'You know that you shouldn't be in the pond. What went wrong? Come on, let's go into the house and dry you off and you can tell me what happened.'

There, then, are two very different styles of dealing with 4-year-old boys. Do you think such differences would have any lasting effect? Do you think that they might affect the boys' future relationships?

Now imagine another Harry and David. Again, they are cousins and they are out playing together in the park. They are entirely engrossed in a fantasy involving imaginary Colt 45s, bows and arrows, and covered wagons drawn up in a circle as a group of settlers and cowboys are being attacked by a band of Apaches. The two boys are whooping and hollering as they run through the bushes trying to make good their escape from the Indians. They fetch up behind a tree, deep in a lonely part of the park, and pause for a moment, panting and slightly wild-eyed. David looks down.

'Hey, look what's here. Look what I've found.' He bends down and picks up a wallet; it is brown leather and quite new.

'Wow, I wonder what's in here.' He begins to open it.

Harry says, 'No, you shouldn't do that – we ought to take it to someone.'

'Why not? Why shouldn't we see what's in it? I'm going to, anyway.'

David opens the wallet while Harry looks on, uneasy but interested. David spreads the wallet wide open and both boys see that it is packed with money.

'Wow, look at that. We're rich. We'll share it, but I bags most of it. I saw the wallet first.'

'I'm not sure that you did see it first. You just picked it up. I might have *seen* it first,' said Harry. 'But we mustn't keep the money, anyway. It belongs to someone and they have lost it. We ought to take it to the police station, or at least take it home. The money isn't ours.'

'What does that matter? Finders keepers.'

David looked around. Everywhere was quiet. 'Nobody's seen us. Come on, let's just keep it and we'll leave the wallet here. No one will know and think what we could buy with the money. Come on, I'll let you have half. We won't get caught.'

> 'No, it's wrong. It's stealing. We shouldn't do it.'
>
> Harry was quite clear.
>
> 'Well, I'm going to keep it all, then.' And David went running off clutching the wallet.
>
> This time, there are two very different styles of morality. It is not simply that David wants to keep the money and Harry doesn't. They seem to be working to two quite different moral codes. What do you think the differences are and why might they have come about?

Human development is a huge topic and is concerned with how people change with changes in their age and experience. It is not simply a question of children; development goes on in varying degrees throughout the lifespan. As we all know, life throws various things at us that have to be dealt with – this never stops – and our ability to deal with anything that comes varies from time to time and usually improves with age and experience. This is all part of the developmental process.

There are many ways to look at human development and there is a vast amount of material on the topic. It is sometimes driven by pure research and sometimes driven by very practical questions. For example: what are the effects of the diet of a pregnant woman on the development of her child? Are children desensitised by television violence? In what ways is a child's relationship with his or her mother important for later life? In this chapter and the next, some of the highlights of lifespan development will be touched on, but, as usual, from a perspective of practicality.

The more interesting issues and problems of development will be touched on rather than the somewhat pedestrian description of what happens when. Whatever happens during the course of development is the result of an interaction between what we inherit genetically (even though it might not appear until later in development through the process of maturation) and what we learn. The question of whether nature or nurture is more important will not be considered. It might make for good discussion, but the answer varies enormously from area to area and ability to ability and really does not much matter.

▶ Birth and infancy

The human womb is obviously a quite well-protected place, but there are, nevertheless, many things that can go wrong during pregnancy that can have lasting effects on the child. So, although there is natural protection, there is a great deal that can be achieved to boost that protection from the outside.

To return to an earlier question, diet can make a difference. So a basic aim during pregnancy should be to maintain a balanced diet. It may be that the cravings for very specific foods that some women experience during pregnancy represent the body's way of prompting that balance. If you are suddenly desperate for spinach, a vegetable that you normally cannot stand, it probably means that you are deficient in iron.

There is also the linked matter of alcohol and other drugs. That too much alcohol can lead to foetal alcohol syndrome is well known by now and it is self-evident that any excess of any drug might well have an effect on the embryo. A salutary reminder of this comes from the effects of thalidomide, and another from children being born addicted to heroin because of their mother's addiction.

Efforts should also be made to avoid viruses, smoking (another drug), radiation and too much in the way of vitamin supplements. Finally, in another type of category, any type of stressful event, which will, of course, vary from person to person, should also be avoided. Prolonged stress during pregnancy can have deleterious effects on the developing embryo.

There is a sense in which when a child is first born it is even more vulnerable than in the womb. The protection of the womb is no longer there but the infant is still just as dependent on the mother (or some other caregiver) as he or she was a few hours ago. Infants do have some basic abilities, of course, otherwise they would be unable to develop at all. They have basic perceptions and are able to make basic discriminations. Perhaps the most complex of these is that from very early on they can distinguish the elements of faces from the rest of the world – clearly a very useful ability since they are so dependent on creatures with faces for their survival. At a more primitive level, they also have various necessary reflexes such as sucking and eye-blinking. And at a more sophisticated level, they can think and gather information, although both processes have a long way to go before reaching the sophistication of even a 5-year-old.

It is the first 18 months of life that are usually regarded as embracing the infancy period. During this time various important developmental milestones are passed. These begin very simply with the child being able to recognise the smell of the mother's milk and end with the complexity of being able to walk up steps, something that most children can do by about the age of 18 months.

Whatever milestones are being reached and passed, most infants (unless there is something wrong with them) can be counted on to be keen to learn. Of course, there are huge variations in this, but the general keenness is there. However, for environmental or for social reasons, there might be constant failure in any sort of support for learning that might otherwise have occurred. The result of this is that the child learns to be helpless, perhaps because he or she *is* helpless. This is the result particularly if a child spends the first year or two of life in a bleak, unstimulating environment. Imagine, for example, the pictures that came from Romania a few years ago of children that had been raised in some orphanages. The result of the experience of learned helplessness is the eventual social anxiety. If this goes on long enough, then the result of that can be the development of childhood depression. It is very important during the first 18 months of life to provide as stimulating an environment as possible, including the social environment. As will be seen later, it is also crucially important that this environment be secure.

In the first years of life, in parallel with the physical maturation, the core part of development centres on personality. This occurs through a mixture of temperament and attachment, the form of nature and nurture during these stages. Temperament ensures that there are huge differences in children, emotionally and socially, right from the start. Some children are active, some are naturally cheerful, some are sluggish and unresponsive, and some seem to be angry from the word 'go'. Sometimes these early characteristics set in for life and sometimes they change vastly during childhood.

Whether or not in-built differences in personality change depends to some extent on cultural factors. Of particular importance here is the manner in which caregivers gratify their children's needs and the extent to which they use punishment as a mechanism of control. However, by far the most important influence on personality development is attachment.

Because human infants are completely dependent on adults for their survival, it is inevitable that some form of attachment occurs through the dependent relationship. Or, to put it an alternative way, it may be that the nature of the attachment influences the kind of dependent relationship that develops. The basic dimension of attachment is security. Is the infant securely attached or not? How important is the nature of the attachment that develops during the early months of life, in what could, perhaps, be seen as a critical period? In other words, does the type of attachment that occurs early on have influences later?

The kind and degree of attachment can be measured in a number of ways. Parents know about attachment through the amount of crying, smiling, vocalisations, following (either with the eyes or the whole body when this is possible), greeting, lifting the arms, clapping, burying the face in the adult's shoulder, hugging, and so on.

The main psychological measure of attachment, though, was developed by Ainsworth (1979) in the 1980s. It is generally known as the 'strange situation'. Basically, it consists of a standardised series of strange (strange to the child, that is) situations that the child is put through in such a way that observations can be made of how he or she interacts with the caregiver (usually the mother) when having these experiences. All of the situations involve separation from the mother and then, later, a reunion. How does the child handle the separation when in a strange situation, and then, how does he or she handle the reunion?

The strange situation studies all lead to one of three possible types of reaction by the child, each of which is easily recognisable in daily life. It goes without saying that the way in which the caregiver deals with the child, from the start, leads to the development of one of the three attachment styles:

1 *Secure.* The child protests when the mother goes and then searches for her for a while. On reunion, the child is delighted.

2 *Insecure-avoidant.* The child is not upset by the strange situation, does not cling to the mother and is generally indifferent.

3 *Anxious-ambivalent.* In this type of reaction the child clings to the mother and shows great distress when she leaves. But there is very little joy expressed on her return. The child's general demeanour in the strange situation shows anxiety and disorganisation.

In day-to-day life one of the aspects of early child care that is of most concern to concerned parents is the effect of *day care*. Does it have an effect or not? It is, after all, a strange situation, at least to begin with and it does involve the caregiver leaving the child. The most significant point is that in general children are not much affected by being put into day care, as long as it is of good quality. There might be some minor emotional effects to begin with but these, it might be said, are offset by some positive social experiences. Of course, if the day care is of poor quality, this might have some obvious negative effects, but these would not necessarily have anything to do with separation from the caregiver.

What is actually meant by 'no effects' in this context? If day care is of good quality, then the quality of attachment to the caregiver is unaffected, and neither is emotional security. Of supreme importance in all of this is the caregiver's sensitivity to the child. Generally, insensitivity of various sorts will lead to one of two types of insecure attachment and this will override any effects of short-term separation that come about through day care.

Secure attachment lays the groundwork for life. For example, it both represents and then leads further towards a harmonious relationship between parent and child. This, in turn, means that the child is more receptive to socialisation in general, that is, to learning the ways of being, the general cultural norms and rules, of his or her society. So, it is through a secure attachment that a child most readily learns to develop self-control, emotion regulation and a conscience.

Secure attachment also goes beyond this to being important in the creation and maintenance of close relationships. In short, a secure initial attachment to the caregiver will be very influential in the capacity to develop secure romantic attachments later on. Insecure early attachments are likely to lead to later insecure romantic attachments. However, fortunately, the effects of this are not impossible to overcome. This will be returned to in the next chapter.

▶ Later childhood and adolescence

There are, of course, enormous developmental strides made throughout childhood and adolescence. Think of the huge difference (at least for most people) between the still very dependent 5-year-old boy or girl and the gauche 15-year-old boy and the relatively sophisticated 15-year-old girl. And then the differences between 15-year-olds and young adults a few years later. Huge numbers of developmental milestones are passed in those years, only a few of which will be touched on here. They are, however, the more obvious and the more important to be aware of.

Piaget and cognition

It is impossible to read or think about children's development without considering the influence of Piaget on our understanding. His main contributions were in the area of how the child develops the capacity to think (Piaget, 1952). Of course, the ability must be there from the start, otherwise nothing would develop. However, it is clear that different modes or styles of thought characterise different ages. By the way, the ages and stages are not strict; there is considerable individual variability.

Between infancy and adulthood, Piaget describes four stages of cognitive development that are based on modes of thinking that are qualitatively distinct from one another. The development from one stage to the next is based on two processes that are germane to all developing thought processes – *assimilation* and *accommodation*.

Assimilation means incorporating new information into something that already exists. For example, if a young child in the early stages of speech has learned the word cat when referring to the family pet and then points to a dog in the street and says 'cat', assimilation has occurred. The child has seen similarities between the family pet and the dog in the street (small, furry, four legs, etc.) and used the same word. In this case, further refinement is obviously necessary.

Accommodation is almost the other side of the coin to assimilation. It means changing or modifying an existing way of thinking to take into account new information or input. In the example of the cat and the dog, the child will soon accommodate to other refinements; not only the difference between cats and dogs but also the differences between cats and kittens, domestic cats and wild cats, and so on. All of the balances that develop in thought, including the processes of assimilation and accommodation, are upset when a new stage is reached.

The stages of cognitive development are characterised by these four distinctive patterns of thought:

1 *Sensorimotor thought*. In this first stage, the infant is dealing practically and overtly with the physical and social world. During this period (roughly from birth until 2 years) the child will learn, for example, that objects do not disappear when a screen is put in front of them. So, if a marble rolls under the fridge, it remains under the fridge. If the child's father seems suddenly to have disappeared behind a newspaper, then he has not disappeared altogether. In other words, they learn the principle of *object permanence* which is one of the many practical ways in which they learn that the world is orderly. The stage ends with the development of symbolic thought.

2 *Pre-operational thought*. This is the stage (from about year 2 to year 6 or 7) when representative thought begins. This is best exemplified by the idea of *conservation* which is missing from this type of thinking. Take a piece of clay

and roll it into a ball. Then take it and roll it into a sausage shape. In the pre-operational stage of thought, the child will not know that the amount of clay has not changed, but might think that there is more when it is rolled out into a longer length. Similarly, pour water from a short, fat glass into a tall, thin glass and the pre-operational child will not know that it is the same amount of water. Or imagine two sticks 30 cm in length that you show to a child and then cut one of them up into 10 3-cm lengths. You give those to the child. Depending on what stage of pre-operational thought the child has reached, the child will think that he or she has more than you (10 pieces rather than the one stick) or might begin to think that they are the same amount if he or she is about to pass into the concrete operational stage.

3 *Concrete operational thought.* As they pass through this stage of the development of thought, children master various concepts or processes, although, as the name suggests, they do this at a concrete level. In other words, they are not able to abstract and fully conceptualise their understanding, but they *are* able to work with all aspects of conservation. So, to take the examples above, the concretely operational child will have mastered a sense of identity about objects or amounts. So, the amount of clay is the amount of clay, whatever shape it is moulded into, and the water is the same water whatever shaped receptacle it is poured into. During this stage, the child also learns about closure, reversibility and associativity. An example of closure is the idea that choosing all of the apples and choosing all of the oranges is the same as choosing all of the fruit (as long as there are only apples and oranges). Reversibility means that any operation can be reversed. So, if the clay is rolled into a ball from a sausage, then it can be rolled back into a sausage. Associativity means that to speak of all the apples and oranges is the same as to speak of all the oranges and apples.

4 *Formal operational thought.* It is not until the age of about 12 or 13 that this stage develops, *in those people in whom it develops at all.* In other words, not everyone reaches this stage in their ability to think and some people do not reach this stage until their late teens or early twenties. The problem is that concrete operations are not quite enough. They do not allow the capacity to think abstractly, to deal with the future, or with possible futures in the form of hypotheses or probabilities. This requires far more sophistication than comes from the idea of conservation in its various forms. That some people never reach this stage could be due to a number of reasons. There may be a genetic limitation that makes it impossible for an individual to think in this way. Or it may be that the environment is so limited as to restrict this possibility. Of course, if this is so, it could be reversible. Finally, it could be that the stage of formal operations is reached in some areas of endeavour, for the individual, but not in others. In any event, Piaget suggests that in its various forms, the stage of formal operations reflects the highest level of cognitive ability that can be reached.

Although Piaget's views of cognitive development have been very influential and have clear practical implications for how parents deal with their children's thought processes, there are some limitations. These tend to be to do with the type of questions that are asked of children when they are involved in studies of the various types of thinking. As soon as they are described, they appear to be obvious, but in the midst of undertaking an experiment, matters can become less clear. It is useful to describe some of these difficulties because they have broader implications for any questioning of children by adults. The precise words that are used and the nature of the relationship between the adult and the child can make a large difference in the answers.

Think of this example. If you do a conservation test with a child and ask a question of the form, Which one is longer, shorter, bigger, smaller, etc.?, and then ask the question again a little later, the fact of the second question might imply to the child that the first answer given was wrong. He or she might therefore swing to the other answer. Another possibility comes from the fact that, in general, children like to please adults, so they might answer questions in a way that they believe the adult wants them to answer. Or to extend this a little, a child might give the adult an answer that the child thinks that the adult thinks that a child would give. In other words, they might answer questions in such a way as to appear more naïve than they are. As already mentioned, these matters apply not only to how any adult might test a child's stage of thought development, but also to how adults question children in general.

Moral development

Closely linked to cognitive development throughout later childhood and adolescence is moral development. An important part of growing up is to assimilate the rules and conventions of society, in other words, to absorb its moral code or whatever part of it applies to your part of society. Again, it was Piaget that had much to say about this, but it is Lawrence Kohlberg's stage theory of moral development that has been most influential. The link with cognitive development is clear if it is remembered that Kohlberg (and Piaget) regarded moral development as dependent on types of moral *reasoning*:

1 *Pre-conventional morality*. At this earliest stage of moral reasoning, right and wrong are viewed in terms of sheer expediency. The aim is to avoid punishment and to maximise gain or reward. So, it is important not to break rules because if one does and is caught, then one is punished. In other words, one gains by following rules and one also gains by making bargains about rules with other people. You keep to your side of the bargain because whoever else is involved keeps to their side, and everyone gains. There is nothing abstract about this level of morality, there are no principles involved. Everything is about relative power and the possibility of punishment and that is how everybody sees the world, or so the pre-conventional thinker believes. As a brief

exercise, try to think of any adults that you know who might never have gone beyond this level of moral reasoning.

2 *Conventional morality*. This is the typical type of moral reasoning that develops during adolescence. This is basic conformity to the law, to a moral code and to various moral rules. This is the level at which most adults remain. Here, then, the aim is to do 'right' because this is the only way in which the system can survive; one's individual needs or wants become subsumed under what is best for society. At this level, then, the simple idea of expediency has been left behind, but the person is still stuck following a system, albeit for more altruistic reasons, rather than being able to think more abstractly to change a system or to create a new one.

3 *Post-conventional morality*. This type of moral reasoning is not unlike Piaget's stage of formal operations in thinking. It involves abstract thought, with moral values being personally chosen, depending on principles such as what is good for humanity or how social justice can best be served. Here, then, the interests of the majority supersede those of the individual, but not by blindly following a set of existing conventions but rather because the rule has been worked out and set up by the individual. At this level of moral reasoning, from time to time the individual might be in conflict with the rules/laws/moral code of society if this happens to interfere with the basic needs for humanity. An extreme example of this that arises occasionally is cannibalism. This is clearly against the moral code of much of the modern world, but there are circumstances (air crashes in remote places, for example) in which this principle might have to be compromised if the people concerned are to survive. At this point, the fundamental human need to survive overwhelms a long-standing moral rule and the rule is changed, albeit temporarily.

If someone has reached the post-conventional level of moral reasoning, then they are able to see a moral code for what it is and to put this together with the human condition. This means that a conventional moral code can be broken if circumstances demand and a 'higher' moral code is brought into play. So, even the extreme of 'thou shalt not kill' becomes compromised either by the exigencies of a situation (this man is about to rape my daughter) or by a 'higher' set of principles, e.g. a jihad in Islamic faith. Try to think of instances of post-conventional morality outweighing conventional morality. Interestingly, it may be the case that some people act as though reasoning at the post-conventional level, even though they are merely replacing one set of behaviours with another with no thought of the morality involved. This might well happen in warfare, for example.

Social development

Although almost every aspect of development continues throughout the lifespan even though the pace of that development might vary from time to time, many capabilities reach their peak in late adolescence, after which their development might better be described as a decline of sorts. One very important exception to this is social behaviour, which tends to show improvement over the lifespan, even though, again, the rate of improvement might slow at times.

Early on in childhood and then through adolescence, the importance of the peer group to social development is central. Much of the time with the peer group is spent in what might be called play, of one sort or another. The importance of play is that it allows things to be tried out in a context that, by definition, is not serious – obviously, the moment that play becomes serious it is no longer play. Frequently, the sort of play that occurs in childhood strongly involves fantasy. This in itself is interesting in that children who are securely attached tend to have richer and more frequent fantasy play which also tends to be linked to a greater cognitive maturity.

One of the main ways of looking at a child's social development is to consider their popularity. This can easily be done using a *sociometric* analysis. If you work with children, this is straightforward to try. Simply ask each of the children which three children they would most like to play with or walk home with or have to a party, and which three they would least like to play with, walk home with or have to a party.

The results of this type of exercise place children into one of four categories. *Popular* children are chosen positively by many others and negatively by very few. *Controversial* children receive many positive *and* negative choices. *Socially isolated* children receive very few positive or negative choices. And *rejected* children receive very few positive choices and a large number of negative choices.

In general, the degree of popularity enjoyed by children is related to their social skill; the more socially adept they are, then the more popular they are likely to be. So, the one thing builds on the other, with the chance to relate to peers and siblings being very helpful. Interestingly, however, even though 'only' children do not have a chance to relate to siblings, there appear to be no long-term deficits or disadvantages that come from being an only child. In fact, in some instances only children seem to gain intellectual, artistic and academic advantages over those with siblings, even being more mature and socially sensitive.

Social development continues through adolescence again largely via the influence of the peer group. In some instances the peer group may consist of cliques or even gangs. Typically, the adolescent changes socially through a sequence of changing peer groups, although not all adolescents will necessarily experience all of these. But the usual sequence is: same sex groups, heterosexual cliques and crowds and finally couples.

There is strong social pressure on the adolescent to conform, particularly since when going through this difficult phase of life many adolescents would prefer not to stand out from the crowd. The pressures to conform to the changing groups lead to the development of standard heterosexual interactions and dating, although there are obviously some homosexual exceptions to this.

During this time of life, part of social development concerns *gender identity*, or the extent to which a person sees himself or herself as male or female. This is a very complex matter because culture tends to have an entire system of beliefs, opinions, behaviours, attitudes, values and so on, that are regarded as going with being male or female. And there are large variations in these systems from one culture to the next and from one time to the next within a culture.

Sex typing refers to gaining the general characteristics that a particular culture regards as appropriate to being male or female. This is not the same as gender identity. So, for example, I might have a strong sense of myself as male but, nevertheless, not mind expressing attitudes and behaviours that are considered to be more typical of females in my culture. Think of people that you know where there might be an apparent discrepancy between gender identity and sex typing. Perhaps the most interesting aspect of gender identity is that it is not fixed but can be changed or modified. Such changes have been seen developing in Western culture during the past few decades in which some women have taken on more male characteristics and some men have taken on more female characteristics. For example, some women are more assertive in the workplace than they once were and some men are more socially and emotionally sensitive than once they were.

Love and attachment

One of the most significant social developments for many people towards the end of adolescence (although for some it may not happen until a little later) is the formation of an attachment to or a close relationship with another person. People fall in love.

Love itself is a huge and fascinating topic about which writers of fiction and poetry have probably done rather better than psychologists. Before talking a little about the attachments that make up romantic love, it is important to say that this is only one type of love. There are others. A psychologist called Richard Sternberg (1986) provides a very full breakdown of the various types of love relationship.

He suggests that love (and liking) are based on the three dimensions of intimacy, passion and decision-commitment, which in each case might be present or absent. This gives eight possibilities and these were discussed in Chapter 6:

1 Non-love – this is a casual relationship in which all three aspects are absent.

2 Liking – intimacy only.

3 Infatuation – passion only.

4 Empty love – decision-commitment only, but just from one person, in one direction.

5 Romantic love – intimacy and passion.

6 Fatuous love – passion and decision-commitment.

7 Companionate love – intimacy and decision-commitment.

8 Consummate love – intimacy, passion and decision-commitment.

From this list, it is easy to see that many people experience a number of these, if not all of them, as they move through late adolescence into adulthood, including the pain of infatuation and fatuous love. The most significant types for most people are, perhaps, romantic love that then grows into consummate love. The way in which this develops for someone takes us back to the initial attachment styles described earlier. They tend to become played out again in the romantic attachments that develop later.

The avoidant-attachment style rejects intimacy, preferring instead to be private and independent. So the person with this style is unlikely to form a satisfactory enduring relationship. The anxious-ambivalent style is made up primarily of anxiety over possible rejection or abandonment and a concern about being unworthy of love or of not being loved enough. The securely attached person by contrast is comfortable with intimacy, mutual sharing and general closeness.

It is easy to see how these types of attachment in adult relationships would arise out of the initial attachments in infancy and also that the secure attachment is far superior to the other types. The most important point to make, however, is that these attachment styles, although influential from childhood to adulthood, are not set in concrete. They can be changed. It is possible to move from an avoidant or an anxious-ambivalent attachment to a secure attachment as a relationship develops. This possibility is, of course, made considerably more likely if an insecurely attached person falls in love with a supportive, understanding partner. Gradually, insecurity can give way to security in the relationship and the influence of the early years is overcome. Presumably, however, it is also possible that someone who begins a relationship securely attached can come unstuck through the ambivalence of a partner.

▶ Summary

- Development is concerned with how people change with age throughout the whole of the lifespan.

- All development is a result of nature and nurture, heredity and environment, in varying proportions, the relative amounts not being of great significance.

- Various circumstances in pregnancy can have a lasting effect on the child after birth, for example, diet, alcohol, drugs and even stressful events.

- There are a number of milestones throughout the first 18 months of life from becoming used to sucking a nipple through to walking up stairs.

- Personality develops through a mixture of temperament and attachment, temperament referring to there being large psychological differences between children from birth, for example, in the degree to which they are active or passive.

- The child's first attachment is crucial in many ways. Styles of attachment have been studied using the strange situation test.

- There are three types of attachment – insecure-avoidant, anxious-ambivalent (also insecure) and secure.

- Early attachment has a huge influence on later life, through all social relationships to romantic relationships in adolescence and adulthood.

- The main figure in our understanding of cognitive development is Piaget who described four stages: sensorimotor, pre-operational, concretely operational and formally operational, although not everyone reaches the final stage.

- Moral development or the development of moral reasoning also occurs in stages: pre-conventional, conventional and post-conventional.

- Social development is highly dependent on peers and siblings throughout childhood and adolescence, even through cliques and gangs.

- Popularity is very much dependent on social skills, although there appear to be no permanent disadvantages of being an only child.

- Part of social development is the development of sex typing and gender identity.

▶ Questions and possibilities

- Think about the children in your family or those of your friends. Do you think that there are temperamental differences between them? Can you see any genetic influences to account for this in their parents?

- What was your own first attachment like? Which of the three types of attachment does it fit into? What sort of effect do you think that it has had on you? Do you think that a mother (or father) can influence the type of attachment conditions or environment that they provide for their children?

- Can you see links between your own first attachment and any romantic attachments that you have had? If you were to want to change your typical pattern of attachment, how would you go about it?

- Think about any children that you know, including your own if you have them, and consider what stage of cognitive development they are at. Do you know any adults who have not reached the stage of formal operations? Why do you think that they have not reached that stage?

- Do you think that people stay at their particular level of moral reasoning in all situations? What might make them drop down a level? What are the types of situation that would make you change down to the pre-conventional level of moral reasoning? Do you have moral principles that place you squarely at the post-conventional level? What are they and are they unshakeable in any circumstances?

- Think of people that you know who are only children. Do you think it has influenced them in any way? Are these influences positive or negative?

- What are your views on adolescent cliques and gangs?

- What are the advantages and disadvantages of encouraging people to behave according to their sex?

- What do you think brings about differences in the strength of gender identity? Do you think that differences matter? What would be your reaction if your son seemed to like constantly dressing in his mother's clothes or your daughter always refused to wear skirts?

- Would/do you encourage your son to behave more assertively and even aggressively than your daughter and your daughter to be more socially sensitive than your son? Why?

- Have you experienced the eight types of love relationship described by Sternberg? What category do you think that your love for your children or your parents fits into? How about your 'love' for a close friend?

CHAPTER FIFTEEN

The lifespan

Growing older

Scenes from life

Nick was 16 and worried about everything, from a spasmodically spotty face to stumbling over his words when he talked to girls, from desperately wanting to be a few centimetres taller to wondering why his father didn't seem to like him much and why his mother was such a fusser, from concern about being tired most of the time to a feeling of apprehension about the future. None of this showed on the outside, if the spots were discounted.

The day had started much like any other day, with a silent family breakfast, although when Nick thought about it he was not sure why breakfast was always silent. Then it was off on the bike to school for a routine day, plodding from lesson to lesson, playing a bit of a scratch cricket game at lunch-time and listening to the usual exaggerated tales of sexual conquest, fuelled more by fantasy than reality. Then home with a bag laden with books for a definite hour or two of homework before going out to meet Maureen, or so he hoped.

In the early evening, his mother was strangely quiet; she was usually quite garrulous later in the day. And his father was bordering on the morose, or so it seemed to Nick, and kept glancing at his wife. Nick started one or two attempts at conversation at dinner-time, but they went nowhere, so he stopped making the attempt. After a moment or two of wondering what was up with them, his thoughts, with unerring inevitability, turned to Maureen.

As it worked out, Nick did see Maureen that evening and she seemed to be quite responsive to his attempts to make her laugh. She was a few months older than Nick and seemed to him to be very sophisticated. His feelings for her were a mixture of unadulterated lust, of which he was vaguely ashamed, and a sort of worship, with her standing untouchably goddess-like on a pedestal. Even when Nick could manage to get his tongue round the words that tumbled around in his mind, the very mixed feelings that he had for Maureen seemed to make the spots on his face break out by the moment. He spent a couple of hours with Maureen and even managed to put his arm round her for a while, without any resistance. He felt as though he was growing up at last, a wave of genuine maturity, and walked home with a great sense of optimism about the future, not just tomorrow evening when he was to see Maureen again, but the future in general.

Nick's parents were waiting for him when he arrived home. He looked at them and could see something was wrong. His feelings of optimism disappeared. 'We have to talk to you, Nick.' His father's voice was grave.

'What's up? What have I done?'

'Oh, Nick, you haven't done anything. It's nothing like that.' His mother's voice was quieter than usual.

His father said, 'Nick, your mother's very ill. She's got, well, she's got . . . cancer.'

A great wave of emotion came over Nick, feelings that he could not describe. He just sat there and looked from his mother to his father, a sense of desperation coming over him. His world was changing; stability was going. 'We don't know what's going to happen, Nick. I've got to have more tests and then we'll see.' His mother was calm but beneath it Nick could sense her fear.

'Well, Mum, I'm here and I'll do whatever I can to help.'

After some more conversation in which the three of them were closer than they had been for a long time, perhaps closer than they had ever been, Nick went off to bed. He felt bereft. He was sure that his mother would die and felt enormously sorry for her and profoundly sad. Above all, he wondered if he would be able to cope. He felt young and in need of his mother, of being looked after, of the world to stay still and to be like it had always been. He felt as if he were 5 years old again. Then, as he was drifting off into sleep, he thought again of Maureen and he felt older, more mature and the sense of optimism returned. But in his dreams that night, he was surrounded by blackness, of monstrous beings pressing in on him, as he became smaller and increasingly helpless.

Alan and Terry had been good friends for years. They worked in the same job as school-teachers in a secondary school. One taught mainly Geography with a few other social studies thrown in, and the other taught mainly History with a few extras. Neither had been particularly ambitious or had sought posts of extra responsibility. In fact, they had rather avoided doing anything extra in their jobs, being quite content to have a relatively easy life, watching their children grow up (they each had two) and having the few extras in life provided by working wives. Their wives were also similar women, very pleasant and family-oriented with quite traditional home-based values with no great ambitions to drive them on.

That the two men had remained friends throughout their adult lives was, perhaps, due to their lack of general competitiveness. Neither envied the other's minor successes (there had been no major successes for either of them) and they had always found it very easy and companionable to talk things through with each other. They were now in their late fifties and had begun to mention retirement which, for both of them, would happen at 60. Neither could see any point in working further.

For the first time that they could remember, Alan and Terry found that they were disagreeing, not violently, but consistently. Terry was quite clear that he was making some very definite plans for his retirement. He wanted to spend a year travelling with his wife, if they could afford it, and according to his calculations, they would be able to. Then he wanted to settle down to do some of the things that he had never had the time to do. For some reason that he had long forgotten he had always been interested in eighteenth- and nineteenth-century crime, but had managed to read very little about it over the years. So, he aimed to collect early editions of writing about it and even perhaps to write something himself, if he found that he had something to say. The thought excited him and he was quite animated when he spoke about it to Alan. He also tried to persuade Alan and his wife to come with him and his wife on their trip.

Alan was not interested in the trip and had quite different views about retirement. He argued to Terry that retirement was a time of doing very little, after having worked all his life. He just wanted to 'sit back and enjoy myself'. 'But what will you do?' Terry couldn't understand Alan's viewpoint. 'Oh, I'll have plenty to do by the time I've read the paper and been out to do a bit of shopping, have a cup of coffee somewhere. The time will pass easily and I'll enjoy every moment of it.'

In the months leading up to retirement, Terry could not shift Alan's way of thinking. Nor could Alan's wife, who agreed with Terry that Alan should be putting more thought into it than he was. The day came and Alan and Terry managed to combine their retirement celebrations. There was a good farewell party for them both, nice things were said and they both received the genuine good wishes of their colleagues at school. In a quiet way, they had both been respected.

Terry and his wife went off within a couple of weeks on their grand tour. They had bought a motor-home, fully kitted out, and set out with more excitement than they had felt for years. They felt very close and their children, now adults with families of their own, felt very pleased for their parents and from time to time had the odd thought about there being more to them than they had imagined. Meanwhile, Alan and his wife settled into a sort of domestic routine that, within a couple of months, found them being increasingly short-tempered with each other. Alan's wife eventually found herself another part-time job, not that she needed the money, but she did feel that she needed to be out of the house and, if she were honest, away from Alan.

At the end of a year, when Terry and his wife returned, quite fit-looking and keen to get on with their various plans, Alan had been taking anti-depressants for some months and was oddly sombre. For the first time that Terry could remember, he and Alan seemed to have nothing to say to each other, even though they tried. After an evening that the two couples spent together, Terry's wife commented, 'Don't you think that Alan's looking old? He seems to have aged a lot since we were away.'

▶ Maturity

For many years, it was only children that were studied by developmental psychologists. Then, interest also began to centre on ageing and the elderly. Eventually, the entire lifespan began to feature, including the relatively quiescent middle years.

Considering adult life as a whole, it is dotted with various milestones, transition points in life that occur for many, if not most, people. Such transitions points will vary, of course, from time to time, historically, and from culture to culture. The obvious milestones are: becoming married or in an equivalent (semi)permanent relationship; gaining a measure of financial independence; having children; having the children leave home; having grandchildren; retiring; losing a spouse.

Interestingly, within any culture there are social beliefs about how each of these major events or transitions should be dealt with. The message to people is that essentially they should 'act their age'. This means moving through the various stages at appropriate speeds, neither too fast nor too slow and being able to deal with the transition much as anybody else in the culture would. Whatever stage one is going through during the middle years of adulthood, so there is also a general progression taking place. One's social power and competence gradually increase but this is unfortunately counterbalanced by a gradual decline in psychological and physical capacities.

The best model of the transitions of development throughout the lifespan was put forward by Erik Erikson in 1971. He saw the entirety of human development as characterised by eight stages. As these are described, it would be useful to think of people that you know who are going through one or other of them, and also to think of yourself and how far you have progressed through the stages. The other way to describe these stages is as psychosocial crises or developmental tasks. In effect, the psychosocial conditions that develop for most people need to be solved before the person can move through into the next facet of maturity:

1 *Trust and mistrust* are the two opposed elements in the first stage; this stage occurs during infancy. The mistrust comes from the child's sudden appearance into a difficult world and this is resolved by the attachment to the mother, or main caregiver. Of course, there may well be further conflict if the trust is sometimes misplaced. In any event, the sense of trust that develops in this first stage provides hope that then lasts throughout life.

2 *Autonomy and shame/doubt* are the conflicts of toddler-hood. This is where the child begins to develop a sense of will. How the parents handle this is crucial. The ideal is that will is allowed expression but not to the extent that it is wilful. It has to be within socially acceptable limits. Like all other aspects of parenting, this is a delicate balance to achieve.

3 *Initiative and guilt* characterise the pre-school phase. Again, it is a balance between these two that is needed for a satisfactory transition and a reasonable degree of maturity to develop. The child is learning to take initiative within what is socially acceptable, the result of which is a genuine sense of purpose.

4 *Industry and inferiority* is the conflict of middle childhood during the school years. On the one hand is the sense of pleasure from working and on the other are the feelings of inferiority that come from unfavourable comparisons with others. The stage is all to do with competition and co-operation at school and if traversed reasonably well should lead to a sense of competence.

5 The struggle to find *identity* and to deal with *identity confusion* is what characterises adolescence. This is the *identity crisis* that so much has been written about. The struggle that any adolescent experiences, according to this way of looking at things, is to find a coherent self. This is, perhaps, not so difficult in some simpler societies in which the transition from childhood to adulthood occurs relatively quickly and where the roles of adulthood are clear and circumscribed. In Western society, the choices (of what sort of adult to be, what sort of self to develop) are immense and frequently do not mesh. Thus the crisis. Do I want to be a person who seizes the main chance for self-advancement or a person who puts others first? Should I enjoy every short-term advantage I can find or seek out long-term goals? Is it better to keep everybody happy or to always express my own basic feelings? The choices are legion. The resolution of this crisis is through the formation of a firm sense of 'who I am', a faithful sense of self.

6 The struggles of early adulthood, according to Erikson (1971), are to do with attaining *intimacy* versus remaining in *isolation*. Having attained a reasonable sense of self, the developing person becomes ready to subsume or merge that

self into or with another person. The extent to which this happens successfully leads to intimacy and the extent to which it does not leads to relative isolation. In our society, this might also be seen as the search for a mature love. This sixth crisis, then, concerns the search for a partner.

7 The period of middle adulthood is taken up with *generativity*, the lack of which leads to *self-absorption* or *stagnation*. In the middle years of adulthood, then, an individual is concerned with accomplishing things, things that might or might not be socially significant. These might be personal or social or familial goals. Everything is fine if goals are accomplished and are found to be satisfying. The crisis is prompted if they are not satisfactory. For example, if a person who has worked in a job with some sense of commitment for 25 years is suddenly made redundant, there is an obvious questioning of accomplishment. Similarly, if a couple, in middle age, become alienated from their children, there is again a sense of failure. An important way to resolve the crisis of generativity is to realise one's personal limitations. Not everything that one attempts will necessarily make a successful contribution to others or to the future in general.

8 The final crisis that anyone who lives to be relatively old has to deal with involves the search for *integrity*. If this is not successful, then the person has to struggle with *despair*. This is not unlike adolescence in that it involves another identity crisis, in which we reflect on ourselves and our position in the larger scheme of things. If this crisis is weathered successfully, then the result is a degree of wisdom. Towards the end of life it is important to feel some sense of satisfaction and fulfilment. In our very rapidly changing society, again, as in adolescence, this is a difficult time. It is easy for skills, abilities and accomplishments acquired and attained earlier in life to be superseded by new ways of doing things. In this context it is harder to find a satisfactory resolution to life than it would be in a society that changes more slowly. All societies change, but Western society changes at a faster pace than any others have done throughout history.

Whether or not Erikson is correct in his listing of these developmental rites of passage, these eight crises that apply to all of us, is uncertain. They make good sense and it is easy to see them reflected in the people around us, any one of whom, at whatever age, is likely to be struggling with one or other of the crises. Unfortunately, not everyone negotiates all the stages successfully. To do so requires a great deal of work and self-analysis, particularly during adolescence and old age, when the crises are squarely about identity.

Erikson's psychosocial crises point clearly to human development occurring across the lifespan. It is not something that is complete by the age of 20. It also points to the importance, in our society, of certain key aspects during the adult years, in particular, marriage, career and old age.

▶ Marriage and identity

Marriage or its equivalent long-term relationship brings about a huge change in ways of life. Whatever form a marriage takes, it must involve a sorting out of roles, that is, who does what and when. Where do the responsibilities lie? This may seem a minor matter, but to anyone who has experienced it, it is not. To settle into living with another person, in an intimate relationship, requires considerable adjustment.

The aim, of course, is that both partners are happy with whatever is the resulting pattern of roles. When this does not happen, there remains dissatisfaction and the potential for disruption. There seem to be three major styles of cohabitation: traditional, egalitarian and a collegial partnership.

The *traditional* style has husband and wife (they are usually traditionally married) adopting quite distinct roles. The husband makes the big decisions and brings in the money and deals with whatever they do in their spare time. The wife looks after everything domestic, including bringing up the children.

In the *egalitarian* system each partner assumes no specialised role. They both do everything, but at different times. It is almost inevitable that some specialisation develops in the end. Finally, as ever in these types of classifications, the third type, the *collegial* partnership, is a mixture of the other two. Here there is specialisation but not along traditional lines. Each does what he or she finds comfortable. In the extreme, the traditional roles might be completely reversed with the wife being the major bread-winner and decision-maker and her partner being the 'house-husband'.

Of major importance in an enduring 'couple' relationship is, of course, its likelihood of success. It would be easy to argue that this is related to the type of role differentiation that occurs. This may well be so, but it is, perhaps, fairer to say that the type of role differentiation and the couple's degree of satisfaction with it and the probable success or failure of the relationship are all dependent on some underlying factors. These may well be to do with the degree to which they are matched ideologically, for example.

To take the USA as an example (although it may be the extreme example), one half to two-thirds of American marriages end in divorce and some other enduring marriages are unhappy. What is it, then, that makes marriages or long-term relationships happy? Why do some succeed and others fail?

The general and most important characteristic of happy couples is that they 'like' each other; they are 'best friends' and confidants. When they talk to other people of what they do, they tend to say 'we' rather than 'I'. Nevertheless, they value *interdependence*. It is important to understand the meaning of this word. It does not mean that they are simply dependent on each other, nor does it mean that they are independent of each other. Rather, it means that they respect and enjoy each other's independence but are, nevertheless, somewhat dependent on each other for intimacy. In other words, as the term suggests, they are interdependent.

In practice, this takes several forms:

1 From time to time, they mention their commitment to each other and to the relationship.

2 They argue constructively rather than destructively. That is, they look for solutions to problems and for ways forward.

3 They listen to each other respectfully, that is, they genuinely listen rather than appearing to listen while thinking what they are themselves about to say.

4 They try to solve any problems rather than reiterating the difficulties.

5 When they argue, they do not dwell on past hurts but look to the future.

6 They tend to use positive comments about each other and the future and to use humour a great deal.

This is a description of some of the behaviours of happy couples in successful long-term relationships. Turning the coin over, these ways of behaving in a relationship could be seen as prescriptions for happiness, actions to aim at if one wishes to develop a satisfactory and enduring relationship. Although they might come easily to some couples, for others they take work.

In Western culture, because of the typical differences in upbringing between girls and boys, female partners tend to feel more responsible for bringing these things about than do males. Of course, there are exceptions to this general rule but it does hold in many cases. This is not to say whether it is right or wrong. It is simply the result of upbringing. For this to change, then, the general style of upbringing would have to change and any such change would follow from a change in basic values in society. There is some evidence that this change is slowly coming about as women gain equality with men in the workforce and as more couples move to an egalitarian or collegial relationship.

In general, the satisfaction that married women experience in their marriages declines during the years of child-rearing. Interestingly, this depends to some extent on the degree to which the men engage sensitively with their children and their upbringing. The greater this involvement, then the greater is the satisfaction experienced by both husband and wife.

Many of the aspects of marriage mentioned above interact. So, the children of a couple whose relationship is harmonious tend to be more content. This, in turn, prompts even greater concordance between the couple, and so on. Discord between parents is a major source of discontent in children, which again leads to a less satisfying relationship between the couple. No doubt, any marital discordance is reflected to some extent in the style of child upbringing that they practise which, in turn, impacts on the type of attachment bonds that are formed. It is easy to see from this type of progression the way in which problems in attachment work their way through from one generation to the next.

▶ Career

The last but one of Erikson's life crises takes place over a long period of time, roughly between the ages of about 20 to 60 or more. This is the time during which, as well as developing a relationship and possibly having a family, people are concerned with their working lives, the progression of their careers. Employment, then, is a dominating force in adult development during the middle years. Depending on one's job, anywhere from 35 to 60 or more hours per week are spent working or thinking about or worrying about work.

There are a number of ways of looking at career development, one of the better being that of D.E. Super, put forward in 1990. This model is interesting because it links psychological changes with various stages in a career, beginning with entry into a career until retirement. Of course, the pattern discernible in a person's career is to some extent dependent on the nature of their work. For example, a factory hand's career is likely to be far more circumscribed with less chance of development than that of a school-teacher.

Super suggests that there is (potentially) a four-stage process to career development, at least in those people who are career-minded:

1 *Exploration.* In this first stage after a person has entered a job, there is a great deal of sampling of what is possible and indecision about the most appropriate way to develop. This is a time of settling, in which a person is trying to find a match between personal aspirations and whatever might be possible in their chosen field. At this early stage, resolution might even have to involve changing the field of work.

2 *Establishment.* Having found a good match between personal abilities and workplace possibilities, the person might now seek advancement and promotion. In other words, this is the time during which a person who wishes to have a career starts to advance it firmly. It is during this stage that it is possible to see some people become very ambitious and single-minded in pursuit of high achievement.

3 *Maintenance.* This is a time of consolidation. Whatever gains were made during stage two are now being realised and enjoyed. Ambitions decrease to some extent and the person slows down. Of course, some people may not go through this stage but continue with the drive of stage two throughout most of their working lives.

4 *Disengagement.* As might be expected, the final stage in a career is one of gradual decline or disengagement. The first part of this stage is a gradual withdrawal from the job in a psychological sense. The person is no longer as actively engaged, no longer so committed, no longer looking to the future for potential changes. There is sort of distancing as though the person is anticipating no longer being in the position. The second part of this stage is retirement which brings us to the beginning of Erikson's final life crisis in which personal identity again becomes at issue.

Retirement can be a time of considerable stress. For many people, their identity has been correlated with their job for many years. Asked to describe themselves, many people will quickly start to talk about what they do. 'Well, I am a . . .' or 'I work at . . .' and so on. Suddenly, this is no longer possible. The retired person has to learn to introduce themselves in a new way. Interestingly, this often takes the form of 'Well, I'm a retired . . .', so once again they are trying to define themselves by their work, even though that work has ceased.

Any of life's transitions is difficult, but the transition to retirement can be made easier if it is approached with clear personal goals. If retirement is seen as a new beginning at something different in life, then it seems easier to bear, indeed, might even be looked forward to. If a person ducks from thinking about it until the day when he or she suddenly finds himself or herself suddenly not going to work, then it can be very difficult and can also put a strain on marriages. A couple might well have found good ways of living together given 40 or so hours a week when they are apart. Now, unless they make some special provision, they could be together 100 per cent of the time. This takes some adjustment.

Interestingly, there is some suggestion that the course of retirement is similar to that of working life in that it can consist of four phases, although if careful preparation is made it does not have to follow this course. The first phase is a sort of euphoric enjoyment ('free at last'), followed by a more depressing period of realisation or disenchantment with the whole thing. After this, the options are explored more realistically and a more stable time ensues, not unlike the third phase of working life. Finally, there is an ending phase which might be in some form of care or might, alternatively, involve going back to work, although, perhaps, in a different sphere than previously.

Perhaps the most important aspect of retirement to consider is the question of the type of goals that are set. If one's goals are mainly material, retirement is usually not very fulfilling. Staying in the workforce for longer is, then, a better option. On the other hand, if one's goals are personal, then these might well be better fulfilled in retirement than during a working life – there is simply more time. Those who work out a series of realisable personal goals are more likely to have an enjoyable retirement than those who do not. It is worth bearing in mind that some of these goals might well be social (see below and Chapter 6).

▶ Old age and death

Old age is not easily defined. It begins at different times for different people, although what exactly 'it' is, is hard to say. Clearly it is a time of decline, although arguably every year from the early twenties onwards might be described similarly. It is also to some extent a matter of attitude. Some people reach a particular age, say 60, and regard themselves as officially old at that point and so start behaving in an 'old' way. There are stories of people of that age who are perfectly fit and healthy booking themselves into rest homes simply because they think that is the right thing to do at that point. They become old overnight.

There are obvious changes that occur with advancing years, both physically and psychologically. One way of looking at such changes is that they either represent or reflect a growing disengagement with life in general or, perhaps, a disengagement with one's own capacities to deal with life. This might well be so for some people as they age. However, an alternative way of looking at the ageing process is that disengagement is forced on the person through lowered physical capacities, retirement and/or illness. In spite of this, with increasing age, some people strive to become even more involved with life in spite of whatever decline they might be subjected to.

A common reaction to increasing years is what has come to be called socio-emotional selectivity. That is, people become more to enjoy the present rather than planning for the future, for obvious reason – the future appears to be shorter than it has previously. So, greater emphasis is placed on having strong relationships with family and friends, rather than casual social encounters. Some people become more socially focused and less likely to engage in perfunctory social encounters. Couples who develop this approach to ageing also tend to become closer in their relationships. In this social sense, ageing can be a beneficial process.

A dominant aspect of ageing is death. With increasing years, people's thoughts inevitably turn to their own ending more than they did in earlier years. The fear of death, if it occurs at all, tends to peak in the fifties and then to decline. The reason for the peak is that people see the deaths of those around them as the incidence of heart attacks, strokes, cancer and other life-threatening events increases. Thereafter, there are a number of approaches to the possibility of death. Some people withdraw from the world a little and enter the world of memory and reflection. Others do not, but remain actively engaged to the end. One's style of approaching death probably reflects one's style throughout life.

Elizabeth Kubler-Ross (1969) describes five stages of impending death, not dissimilar to her stages of grief. However, not everybody experiences these stages and those that do, do not necessarily go through them in the same order. They are: denial, anger, bargaining, depression and acceptance.

It is possible to take an entirely positive approach to old age, rather than accept what it brings and play any of the roles that society might expect of the elderly. For example, a great deal can be done with diet and exercise to offset both physical and psychological decline. Obviously, it cannot be halted or reversed, but it can be slowed down. Decline due to diet or to lack of exercise is relatively straightforward to remedy and can make a huge difference to quality of life.

The possible changes to social life in later years have already been mentioned. In some ways, after retirement there is more time per day (even though there might be less time overall) in which to consider things social. Improved social lives can be built on the many experiences that people have had as they have gone through the previous stages and crises of life. In general, during these later times, people also know themselves better than they have previously. This can even help in one of the most difficult times of all, when a long-time partner or spouse dies.

One of the most interesting aspects of later life is the cognitive. The general belief is that capacities such as memory and problem-solving decline with age. While this might be so in some cases, there is also strong evidence that this type of decline can be offset by keeping motivation and interest high. So, for example, keeping on reading and doing crossword puzzles or playing word games keeps a person's word-finding and word usage ability high into old age. It is thought this type of activity can even repel the onset of such conditions as Alzheimer's disease to some extent.

One way of dealing with the cognitive (and other) ravages of increasing years has become known as 'selective optimisation with compensation'. What this rather clumsy phrase refers to is the recognition of losses and the selection of psychological capacities that might compensate for them. For example, a greater experience of strategies in board games or card games might be used to compensate for slightly slower decision-making. Or, if an older person is still engaged in sport, then a good knowledge of strategy and tactics can help to compensate for reduced speed and reaction time. More generally, a decreased capacity to react quickly can be considerably compensated for by a longer time of preparation. And the decreased demands on one's time that come with retirement and advancing years mean that there is more time to prepare, at least in the short term. This is simply a matter of sorting out what has declined and what has not and optimising one's strengths.

Finally, it is important to say that it is never too late to develop *new* interests and activities. Whenever a capacity or ability declines or in some way drops off, it is possible to see this as an opportunity to develop something new that falls within one's capacities. This is not a matter of foolishly fighting the inevitable, but more of optimising one's life at all stages and through all crisis points, not merely those to do with ageing and eventual death.

In general, then, passing through the adult part of the lifespan is no easy matter. From a child's or an adolescent's perspective, adulthood might seem to be a time of relative stability; perhaps it is in comparison with the identity turmoil of adolescence. However, issues that surround establishing (or not) a long-term relationship, having children (or not), establishing and progressing through a career (or not), coping with bolts from the blue, such as redundancy or any other form of major loss, facing retirement, dealing with the death of partner or spouse, dealing with the inevitable declines of old age, and facing one's own eventual death, are none of them easy.

One way of looking at these difficult times and events of transition is that our ways of coping with them depend largely on the approaches that we might take. As the Buddhists would suggest, there is suffering involved in everything; it is an inevitable part of life. How we deal with suffering is up to us. If each of the major life events of adulthood is seen as providing opportunities for learning and as interesting challenges for personal development, then passing each milestone can be viewed as an achievement. There is also the constant comfort that, whatever else might decline with age, our social skills are likely to go on steadily improving, if we allow them to.

Summary

- There are milestones throughout life that indicate various transition points.

- Erikson (1971) describes eight stages from birth to death that involve life crises that have to be dealt with. The most difficult of these involve identity and occur in adolescence and retirement.

- Marriages (or long-term relationships) are fundamentally about the division of labour and roles and take a great deal of work.

- There are three types of role divisions that tend to develop in marriages: the traditional, the egalitarian and the collegial, this being a mixture of the other two.

- Happy couples like each other and tend to be best friends. They know how to argue constructively and to sort out problems without rancour.

- In our society women feel more responsible than men for the success of marriage, but, nevertheless, about half of all marriages fail.

- A series of psychological changes occur throughout the various stages of career development, from getting a first job through to retirement.

- Retirement is a particularly difficult time of life. People vary considerably in their approach to it but it is dealt with better when there are clear, personal goals that guide it.

- There is an inevitable physical and psychological decline with old age, although to some extent being old is socially defined.

- With advancing years, some people disengage from life, and some have to disengage from some aspects of life (due to illness, for example).

- There is greater social selectivity and subtlety in old age than earlier in life.

- The fear of death peaks in the fifties and then declines; there are huge individual differences in how it is faced.

- Diet, exercise and cognitive work can offset the effects of ageing to some extent.

- It is possible to see old age as providing an opportunity to develop new skills and interests.

Questions and possibilities

- Which of Erikson's life crises are you dealing with at the moment? How are you doing? What stages are your family and friends at? How are they dealing with them?

- How would you go about helping someone go through a life crisis, particularly one involving identity?

- In your life so far, what have been the most difficult milestones to pass? What made them particularly difficult?

- Compare your own long-term relationship(s) with those of your friends and family. What types of division of roles characterise them? Why do you think that different patterns develop of the sharing of labour in enduring relationships?

- In your observations, are there differences between the adult development of couples who have children and those who do not? What brings any such differences about?

- To some extent, long-term relationships and small family circles are a product of the present time within Western society. What are your views on alternative social structures? Do small nuclear families necessarily represent the best background for development across the lifespan?

- Do you recognise the career stages that have been described in this chapter? Which stage are you at and what are your plans for progressing to the next? What difference do you think having a career or not having a career would make to adult development? In poorer societies or in poorer parts of relatively rich societies many people have no opportunity for establishing a career, they simply have to work to survive. What difference might this make to their development through life?

- Think of people that you know who have retired from full-time work. How have they dealt with it? What different strategies have you seen used? Do some of these strategies lead to greater possibilities than others for growth and development in later years?

- Many people have plans and dreams for their own development throughout adult life. Frequently, these plans might even be formed in childhood or adolescence. What do you believe to be the main factors that prevent these plans from being fulfilled?

- When people that you know reasonably well have died, naturally rather than in an accident, what different approaches have they taken to their own deaths? What approaches have been taken by those close to them? What do you think about your own death? If this is something that you shy away from dwelling on, why might this be so?

- Do you think that decline is an inevitable part of growing old or do you think that old age is a matter of attitude?

- Many people do not look forward to being old. Why is this so, given that a moment's reflection shows that any stage of adult life brings its particular problems? Difficulties of old age are simply a new set of problems.

- If you reflect on your own development in life so far, what do you consider to have been the major sources of influence on it? Do you believe that these influences have 'set you in your ways' so that no change is possible as you go through the remainder of life?

- How is it possible to influence your own development?

CHAPTER SIXTEEN

When things go wrong in life

Scenes from life

Geoff was at work as usual. He worked in an open-plan office with several others around, each with a desk and a computer. He was good at his job, although mildly stretched by it. His life outside work was not wonderful. He had recently experienced the break-up of a relationship and his flat was not all that he could wish. He was in his late twenties and vaguely wondered if life should actually be offering more than he seemed to be getting from it, but the thought did not stay with him all of the time.

During the day, he left his desk for a while and when he came back found a couple of handwritten notes attached to his computer screen. The messages were strangely cryptic and he did not recognise the handwriting. He puzzled over them for a few minutes and then put them to one side. After this, every few minutes he would return to the notes and gradually began to wonder if someone was getting at him in some way. The more he pondered on this, the more likely it became. He thought about his colleagues and how, in fact, he did not get on with them very well. He often felt excluded from general discussions and sometimes had the feeling that people had been talking about him as conversations faltered when he joined a group at coffee time.

These feelings built up during the day although he mentioned them to no one. His mood became blacker towards 5 o'clock and he packed up for the day feeling as though the weight of the world had settled on his shoulders. As he left the building, one of his work-mates, Andrew, fell into step with him, someone whom he usually liked rather more than the others. 'How's it going, Geoff? I thought that you looked a bit low today.'

Geoff immediately thought, 'I'll bet it was him who left those notes. What's he up to?' He could feel the anger bubbling in him.

'What d'you mean?' His voice came out loudly and aggressively. 'There's nothing wrong with me. What're you on about?'

Andrew felt rebuffed, but continued, 'Come on, Geoff, I can see something's up. D'you want to talk about it?'

'No, I bloody well do not. Mind your own business. Leave me alone. You're always getting at me.'

Geoff strode off abruptly in another direction and made his way home, feeling that everyone was looking at him. The world seemed to be pressing in on him, a dark force out there that he could not pin down, somehow trying to overtake him. Things were no better in his flat. The more he thought about things, the more certain he became that his work-mates were out to do him down in some way. His anger at this bubbled and smouldered throughout the evening and when he eventually went to bed, his sleep was broken and tortured.

The next day, his mood continued in this great blackness until about midday when he suddenly felt it lift. Within half an hour or so, he felt very different and was simply left with the feeling that he had recovered from a migraine. This had been an attack of paranoia.

Emily is in her forties and was being assessed at a hospital, under her own admission, for gut-wrenching pains in her stomach, as she described them. She had not been to the hospital previously, so they had no background medical records for her. When asked about previous conditions, she was very vague and unhelpful in her replies. She was a very unco-operative patient, nothing seeming to be to her liking until she met one particular doctor. She took to him and suddenly became co-operative as he examined her and tried to determine exactly what was wrong.

Eventually, though, after a series of questions about her diet and about whether she had had any history of stomach ulcers, she again became aggressive, even shouting at the doctor about there never having been anything like that in her family. And so it went on after they had admitted her. Each day, she would spend some time being almost obsequiously pleasant to some people, getting them clearly on her side, but then would round on them, throwing back any act of kindness shown to her in an almost vicious way.

Eventually, even though the nurses who had to deal with Emily became sick of her, they managed to track down some medical records for her. They found that she had had a long history of appearing at various hospitals, seeking admission and treatment for a very wide range of problems. Although all of the patient notes were written in a relatively guarded way, it was obvious that Emily always treated people in this unpredictable way. Her history also showed a similar pattern with her family members and friends. Emily was suffering with a borderline personality disorder and so leading all of those who tried to help her to despair. In the end, she was very difficult to help or even to feel any sympathy for.

To describe someone as abnormal depends on the circumstances. What is abnormal in one culture or at one time might not be abnormal in the next culture or a few years later. One way of looking at abnormality is statistically. This equates the abnormal with the rare. At first sight this might seem reasonable. In Western culture, the two types of reaction described at the start of this chapter are relatively rare. Fortunately, either for themselves or for those around them, not many people suffer from paranoia or from borderline personality disorder. But, there again, even fewer people win a Nobel Prize or run a 4-minute mile. This is even more abnormal, but such achievements do not have anything negative about them.

Another way of defining abnormality is very pragmatic – it is whatever is labelled abnormal by the majority of people within a culture – a social definition. This means, for example, that killing someone is abnormal; but not in times of war. To take another example, to decide not to seek medical treatment for a serious condition is abnormal. However, it is not abnormal among, say, Christian Scientists or members of similar religious groups. Even paranoia might be seen as normal among a group of spies.

A further problem with terming something as abnormal and then classifying it in some way, for example, as schizophrenia, can lead to self-fulfilling prophecies. If someone is classified with a label that is within the abnormal range, then this creates expectations among those around them about how they will behave and leads not only to the greater likelihood of such behaviour but also puts them at enormous disadvantages in life. Such classification and labelling typify current Western views of abnormality.

Abnormality is also defined as whatever is maladaptive for the individual *or for those around the individual*. If you are so anxious that you are unable to leave the house, this is clearly maladaptive for you. If you are consistently inconsistent in the way that you deal with others, then this is clearly maladaptive for them. Again, however, what is maladaptive for the individual or for society changes from time to time and place to place. Linked to this way of looking at abnormality is seeing it as whatever causes personal distress to the individual. Many people who are classified with one of the 'mental' disorders are certainly distressed emotionally. However, if someone close to you dies or if you lose your job or if someone writes off your uninsured car, you are likely to be personally distressed, but this is unlikely to be seen as abnormal.

In our society, all of these ways of looking at what is abnormal tend to be used together in order to decide whether or not someone's behaviour is abnormal or if they are suffering from a mental disorder. Much of the remainder of this chapter will be spent describing some of the main disorders *as they are classified in our society*. It is important to bear in mind several points, however, when reading these or any similar descriptions of such disorders.

1 They are very much restricted to Western culture at this time in its history.

2 They are rarely seen in as clear-cut a fashion as they inevitably seem to be when they are described.

3 To label someone with a particular mental disorder might be convenient but such a label explains nothing and might in itself put the person at a serious disadvantage in life.

4 The major classification system of abnormality used in the Western world comes from the American Psychiatric Association (1994) – it is the *Diagnostic and Statistical Manual* (in its fourth iteration) (DSM-IV). Whether there are sufficient similarities between American society and European society, let alone antipodean society or Eastern society, as to make the DSM-IV equally applicable to all is arguable.

There are various axes to the DSM-IV, but the most significant of these are Axis I and Axis II, referring to *clinical disorders* and *personality disorders*. A list of such disorders follows, but only some of the more common (and more interesting) will be described in this chapter.

Axis I disorders: disorders of infancy, childhood or adolescence; cognitive disorders such as dementia and amnesia; substance-related disorders; psychotic disorders such as schizophrenia; mood disorders; anxiety disorders; somatoform disorders (that is, disorders about the body); factitious disorders (in which symptoms are feigned or consciously produced); dissociative disorders (temporary alterations to consciousness); sexual disorders; eating disorders; sleep disorders; impulse control disorders (such as compulsive stealing or lying); adjustment disorders.

Axis II disorders, describing various types of personality dysfunction: anti-social; avoidant; borderline; dependent; histrionic; narcissistic; obsessive-compulsive; paranoid; schizoid; schizotypal.

A final point to be made by way of introduction concerns the links between physical and mental disorders. In the everyday world this is a common enough distinction. But there are problems with it. For example, although something like chicken pox is clearly centred in the body (the spots are obvious), where is a disordered personality centred? Again, the only possible answer to this is 'in the body'. What else is there? This might, then, mean restricting 'mental' disorders to anything that goes wrong that involves the brain. There again, however, there is a problem. It can be argued, and, indeed, is argued, that *any* disorder, disease or even accident has a mental (or, perhaps, it is better to say, psychological) aspect. This might be before, during or after the illness or the accident. For example, not all broken legs occur merely by accident; some personality types might be more prone to such 'accidents'. Also, it is obvious that there are psychological effects of having a bodily illness or being laid up following an accident, and equally obvious that it takes some time to 'come right' afterwards.

Perhaps, then, it is a matter of the balance between the physical and the psychological (even though the psychological must be physically based, as well). This balance can vary from time to time and person to person within one disorder. For example, a stomach ulcer might have its main cause in the food eaten or it might have its main cause in living a stressful life. Whatever the balance of causes, it remains a stomach ulcer. So, to say to someone 'It's just psychological' or 'It's all in your mind' is nonsense.

These points apart, the brief descriptions of 'mental disorders' or behavioural 'abnormalities' that follow are more psychological than physical, although they must have a physical substrate – they are, after all, occurring in the human body. However, to say that they must have a physical underpinning does mean that they have a physical cause – the cause might well lie in the environment, in thought processes, in emotional or motivational processes, and so on. Of course, all such processes are also grounded in the physical. Other than the spiritual, there is no choice.

▶ Anxiety disorder 1: phobias

Anxiety and panic disorders were discussed in passing in Chapters 2 and 3 and stress will be considered in the next chapter. This leaves phobias and obsessive-compulsive disorders to mention here. Phobias are persistent irrational fears of something – it can be anything, an object, an event, a setting; anything that upsets the individual. All that the word irrational means in this context is that the fear does not make sense to others who do not share it, and that there appears to be no clear basis for it.

The main types of phobia are:

1 *Simple*, involving a single thing such as dogs, spiders, or darkness, even in some cases being bizarre in the extreme, for example, the fear that one's knees will suddenly bend backwards (kneebophobia).

2 *Social*, fear of criticism, ridicule, embarrassment, and so on, leading to avoidance of all groups.

3 *Agoraphobia*, intense fear of open or public places.

▶ Anxiety disorder 2: obsessive-compulsive disorders (OCDs)

These anxiety-driven disorders take the form of persistent (unwanted) thoughts or impulses to perform certain actions that cannot be resisted, usually in order to be rid of the thoughts. 'If I walk through this doorway 17 times, then I'll stop thinking over and over again that she doesn't love me.' The thoughts and actions involved in OCD are unwanted and not enjoyed at all. The person knows that the behaviour is foolish, nonsensical or pointless, but cannot desist from doing it. He or she might know that they have just checked every window latch in the house and know that they have turned off all electrical appliances, but they just have to go and check again, and again, and again . . .

If you think of these types of anxiety disorder or panic attacks and think of those people you know (perhaps yourself) who have suffered from them, what makes them into a disorder? We all become a bit obsessional at times, or a bit panicked or certainly a bit stressed. We all have specific fears, of heights or spiders or beetles or moths, or confined spaces, for example. But they are not debilitating and the level of anxiety is not so high that it dominates. Similarly, if those around us think our anxiety is justified by the cause (say, an exam or a job interview) and in its level (not too extreme) and in its consequences (doesn't make much difference to a person's life), then it is not abnormal.

▶ Disorders of mood

Somewhat like anxiety, mood disorders are concerned with debilitating disturbances in emotional state. The person might be extremely depressed or jumpingly manic. These are extreme reactions; they don't just involve being 'fed up' or 'a bit scatterbrained'. The various disorders of anxiety are quite common, but so is depression, occurring at some time in the lives of between 10 and 20 per cent of people in Western society.

Depression includes some or all of the following symptoms, which are a mixture of emotional, motivational, cognitive and physical – anhedonia (loss of pleasure), sadness, feelings of hopelessness and negative notions of the self, poor concentration and memory, passivity, lack of initiative, loss of appetite, poor sleeping, fatigue, aches and pains. Most of us are somewhat depressed on some occasions when things go wrong; we fail exams, do not get jobs, lose someone close to us, and so on. But if you experience all or most of the above symptoms in one hit, then you are depressed, and you know it.

There are various types of depression, or, perhaps, it is better to say, various causes of depression, that can be distinguished. For example, depression might come primarily from an external event, such as career reversal, or from an internal event such as a neurochemical imbalance. Depression might be the main problem or might be secondary to something else, such as extreme anxiety. It might occur with advancing years or after giving birth, and some depressions seem to occur seasonally for some people (seasonal affective disorder – SAD). This is as 'real' a disorder as any other and appears to be the result of very short winter days in some of the more northerly northern hemisphere countries.

Most people who become depressed do not also become manic, but a few do, although obviously at different times. Those who experience such mood swings are suffering from what has come to be known as *bipolar disorder*. Such mood swings might be quite rapid or might occur only occasionally. When in a manic phase a person becomes highly excited, hyperactive, constantly talking and seeing no need for sleep. This is far more than the exuberance that one might experience with normal elation or joy. In a manic phase the person is dancing about on a high wire, full of grandiose ideas and plans and might well go and spend huge sums of money or take completely impractical trips. He or she might become hypersexual, bankrupt, fired, divorced, all of which is a great deal to put up with in exchange for needing less sleep than usual.

There is a clear link between mood disorders and suicide, the majority of those who commit suicide having been suffering from depression. Far more suicide attempts are made by women than men, but men, when they attempt it, tend to be more successful than women, largely because of the more extreme methods that they adopt. The largest increase in suicide rates is among adolescents and young people, even more so if they happen to be in college. The primary characteristic of adolescents or young people who attempt suicide is social isolation, both from family and friends.

Drug abuse is also highly related to suicide, but the direction of any causal links is unclear. Drug abuse might make suicide more likely or it might be that people turn to drugs in an initial attempt to cope with the depression. Some of those who commit suicide simply want to end their lives because they can see no other solution to their problems. Others want to draw attention to the horrors of their personal circumstances – this more manipulative motivation is sometimes known as para-suicide.

▶ Schizophrenia

Schizophrenia is *not* split personality. The 'split' suggested by 'schizo' is between the person and what is normally considered reality, rather than something within the person. It can take many forms, with each instance being unique, but always involves some or other disorganisation of personality, distortion of reality (through hallucinations, delusions and blunted emotion), and usually means an inability to function in daily life. It seems to occur in most cultures that have been studied and affects about 1 per cent of people, equally divided between the sexes.

Both thought process and content may be disturbed in schizophrenia. Words may be said in a very loosely associated way that makes very little sense to anyone else and the thought sequence might be influenced by the sound of the words rather than by their meaning, gleaning, leaning, weaning, dreaming, beaming, scheming, and so on. This seems to be largely due to an inability to focus attention and in so doing cut out whatever might be irrelevant. As well as thought processes going awry in this way, thought content can also become disorganised or lacking in insight. There might well be delusions (beliefs that are based on misinterpreted reality). For example, the person might believe that some outside force is taking over their thinking (from outer space or through the radio or the television) or that particular people or groups of people are out to get them.

Such delusions of persecution are usually termed paranoid. So, a paranoid person is someone who is suffering from delusions of persecution, not someone who is simply afraid of something, as is moving into common (mis)use currently. Such paranoid delusions can lead to extremely aggressive acts, when the person comes to protect himself or herself against the object of their para-noia. Such instances are very rare and most schizophrenics are a danger only to themselves rather than to others.

People suffering from schizophrenia also experience large-scale perceptual distortions. The perceptual world can seem different from usual (brighter, more intense, louder, smellier, and so on). Their bodies might seem to be distorted and in the extreme they might have hallucinations, in which they might actually be sensing things that are not there. The most common of such hallucinations are auditory, usually in the form of voices that tell the person what to do. Hallu-cinations can be very frightening, particularly when they occur, as they some-times do, as part of a delusional belief system.

To some extent, as with most forms of mental disorder or abnormal behav-iour, we can recognise it in ourselves. Most people have a minor paranoid episode occasionally and we all have hallucinations every night when we dream. Imagine what it would be like to be dreaming in that way when one was going about one's ordinary life. Similarly, most of us have voices that go on in our heads when we are working, writing, talking or whatever we might be doing. But we know that the voice comes from within, that essentially it is our own silent voice. Imagine that the voice was being critical of you and also telling you what to do in the strongest terms and that you *thought that it came from the outside* rather than the inside.

Emotionally, a person suffering from schizophrenia seems to be dead or at least unresponsive. There may be reactions going on within but nothing is being shown. Or sometimes, the expressions displayed appear to have nothing to do with the circumstances that surround the person. Going along with this is some-times very unusual motor activity in the form of odd facial expressions, strange sequences of hand or arm movements, manic-like frenzies of activity and com-plete immobility even in an unusual posture.

The DSM-IV lists five major types of schizophrenia, although no single case is likely to fall with complete clarity into any one category:

1 *Disorganised schizophrenia* is replete with delusions and hallucinations, flat or inappropriate emotional display and sometimes large mood swings.

2 *Catatonic schizophrenia* has long times of complete immobility and detach-ment.

3 *Paranoid schizophrenia* is characterised by threatening or critical voices of persecution or aggrandising voices of grandeur. Many events are interpreted as though they are of special significance for the person.

4 *Undifferentiated schizophrenia* is simply a category for anyone who does not quite fit into the other categories.

5 *Residual schizophrenia* describes someone who has had a schizophrenic episode and still shows a few signs, but nothing more.

In its more extreme forms, schizophrenia is the most 'abnormal' of abnormal mental functions. Although this is not a book that is aimed at canvassing all of the theoretical accounts that have been given of various conditions, it is worth saying a little of some of these ideas with respect to schizophrenia.

A psychodynamic theory suggests that it all comes back to a mother who is cold and dominant, while also being rejecting but overprotective, rigid and moralistic and afraid of intimacy. A similar type of view (the double bind) suggests that schizophrenia develops in those who in their early years are put into double binds. That is, they are simultaneously given contradictory messages. For example, they might be told by their mother 'I love you' but this is said in a cold voice while the mother flinches away from physical contact.

Labelling theory suggests that once people are labelled as schizophrenic, then they start to behave as schizophrenics, so something that starts off simply as being a little unusual gradually becomes more extreme simply because of the label and the expectations that go with the label. Cognitive theory has it that schizophrenics are simply trying to make sense of the unusual sensory experience that they *actually* have. Humanistic explanations suggest that schizophrenia does not actually exist, it is simply a particular way of viewing the world and is not (akin to) a disease or that schizophrenia is merely a label given to people whose attempts to live in the world are not much liked. Perhaps the most telling of recent accounts of schizophrenia is that it results from too much dopamine (a neural transmitter) in the system.

▶ Dissociative Identity Disorder (DID)

DID is the disorder that is mixed up with schizophrenia in everyday language. It involves multiple (that is, split) personalities. Each personality that develops has its own identity (age, name, characteristics, memories, etc.) and takes control of the person while it is present. Then another takes over. Frequently, the alternative identities have characteristics quite different from the original personality. For example, they might be hostile and aggressive rather than gentle and unassuming.

Particular types of dissociative disorder are amnesia and fugue. In dissociative amnesia a person suddenly loses all recall of events that occurred during and after a particularly traumatic event. Although being able to live fairly normally in the world, the person might also have forgotten his or her name and address and the relevant details of other family members. After anything from a few hours to a few years, the person suddenly snaps back into full memory. With dissociative fugue, the person responds to a traumatic event by suddenly beginning an entirely new life, new identity, new job, new relationships, everything, with absolutely no memory of what went before.

DID usually results from extreme childhood trauma, most often involving child sexual abuse and tends to begin at about 4 to 6 years of age. It seems as though such children self-hypnotise themselves into the creation of another identity and this helps to rid them of some of the emotional turmoil that their life circumstances are forcing on them. If, later, there is another emotional trauma that their identities cannot cope with, then they might create yet another identity that allows them to cope. Sometimes one of the personalities might know about the other, but frequently they are all hidden from one another.

The most famous instance of DID, or multiple personality disorder, as it was then known, appeared in the book and movie *The Three Faces of Eve*, based on the true case of Chris Sizemore. DID always demonstrates a lack of integration of identity, memory and consciousness in general. It is simply as though a difficulty is dealt with by creating another personality that can manage this, whereas the usual one cannot. The child learns to cope by dissociating the memory of the painful events from memory altogether and one way of achieving this is by creating another personality that does not have those same memories.

Instances of DID are always fascinating, but they are relatively rare. The chances are that you have not known of such a case personally. It is also possible that some of the reported cases may be false. Given the usual association of DID with childhood sexual abuse and the now well-known difficulties involved in recovering memories for traumatic childhood events, there are clearly problems in finding exactly what has or has not happened. Similarly, given that people who experience DID are highly suggestible, the disorder may have been over-diagnosed in them merely because of their suggestibility.

▶ Personality disorders

Personality disorders have a large classification to themselves. This is, perhaps, surprising since one might well ask: what can possibly be wrong about a personality? A personality simply is a personality. Sometimes, however, personality traits become highly maladaptive and inflexible, so much so that they seriously impair the person's ability to function in the normal world. Although they can be extraordinarily disruptive to the individual and to other people, personality disorders are, nevertheless, seen as not as extreme as disorders of mood or as those in the schizophrenic range. It is as if mood disorders, schizophrenia and DID are regarded as being outside of the person's control, whereas there seems to be some doubt about personality disorders.

One problem with personality disorders is those who experience them may well not be motivated to change because they do not feel particularly upset or anxious. There is no loss of contact with reality and no special disorganisation of behaviour. These again might be reasons why the general feeling is that people could control their personality 'disorders' 'if they wanted to'.

There are several personality disorders listed in the DSM-IV and, as always with any classification system, in reality they are not as clear-cut as the descriptions suggest. Often there is overlap. Each will be briefly described in turn. As the descriptions unfold, think about whether or not you have come across such personality types and, indeed, whether or not you recognise some of the characteristics incipiently in yourself. It would be surprising if you did not. All aspects of personality are on a continuum, so most people will personally recognise some of the characteristics that, *in the extreme,* can lead to a diagnosis of personality disorder.

Anti-social personality

This personality disorder has been listed first because it is, perhaps, the best known. Hundreds of books, mainly in the crime fiction genre, have been written that feature what used to be called psychopaths or sociopaths. These are the extremes of the anti-social personality. The short description of this type of person is that they appear to have no conscience. Although superficially charming, what they do is determined exclusively by their own desires or wants. Such persons act on impulse, driven by immediate goals and gratifications and show no shame, guilt, embarrassment or remorse for any actions that might harm others. Inevitably, such people are insincere, unreliable and untruthful even though reasonably poised and apparently at ease socially.

In general, the anti-social personality is someone who has no empathy, who never puts himself (it is most often a man) in someone else's place. The reasons that someone has (it would be inappropriate to say 'suffers from' – it is others who suffer) an anti-social personality are a mixture of genetic and environmental. There is evidence of a genetic component, but this will probably only manifest itself given an environment that also promotes anti-social behaviour. Even as children, those with this type of personality tend to see all social behaviour as aggressive, including viewing accidents as intentional if they themselves become harmed. Vicious cycles of aggression develop.

In practice, an anti-social personality may not be physically aggressive. However, with the series of characteristics described, such a person might well end up very successful in the business world, leaving a trail of damaged relationships and hurt people in his wake.

Borderline personality

The second of the more extreme personality disorders and one that has received considerable attention recently is the borderline personality. It is not very aptly named because it suggests that someone has a personality that is only acceptable in a borderline way. However, the borderline is between neurotic traits (extreme anxiety, emotional instability) and psychotic tendencies (as in schizophrenia).

The keynote of this disorder is instability; instability is all aspects of personality. Moods and emotions might swing from anxiety to depression to anger, all in the extreme. The person's view of themselves swings from huge self-aggrandisement to equally large self-abasement. Relationships with others are appalling, swinging from believing the other person to be wonderful to loathing and rejecting them to the full. Relationships (say, with a new therapist or a new acquaintance) tend to start off in a completely committed way, as though offering new hope for the future. But then, with a hyper-vigilant attitude, the person seems to be looking for the smallest sign (a glance, a cancelled meeting) that can be taken as rejection. The reaction is extreme anger and depression.

At even more extreme moments, persons with the borderline personality disorder may engage in self-mutilation (usually cutting themselves). They also occasionally suffer psychotic withdrawals from reality in which they lose all sense of time and place. Because of the extremes to which 'borderline' cases swing, they also tend to be diagnosed with other disorders such as depression, generalised anxiety, agoraphobia, and so on. Whereas the anti-social personality disorder is more common in men, the borderline disorder is more common in women.

Borderline personality disorder is not well understood. The usual accounts of it stress it as involving a build-up of huge defences and as deriving from very unsatisfactory early relationships, particularly those in which the child is not encouraged to develop a sense of self. It is for this reason, perhaps, that they are so sensitive to the reactions of others – it is as though they are reacting to themselves, even rejecting themselves (hence the self-mutilation).

Finally, again it is instability that is at the core of this disorder. 'Borderlines' tend to see themselves and others as either all good or all bad and never put the two together; they simply veer from one to the other. Everything is at the extremes and those extremes vary from moment to moment. It is easy to see why those with a borderline personality are very difficult to deal with, either by their families and friends or by health professionals.

The other personality disorders will be dealt with in less detail than the two so far considered. They are, perhaps, less interesting than the anti-social and the borderline, although, when extreme, they can be just as difficult to deal with. It is worth noting that there is some overlap between some of these disorders and some that were discussed previously, for example, there is an obsessive-compulsive personality. The difference is that those that are described below are all concerned primarily with personality.

Other kinds of personality disorder

- *Paranoid personality.* As the name suggests, this person tends to be suspicious of everyone else. He or she expects to be treated badly and blamed for everything bad that happens while blaming others for everything bad that happens to him or her. Of course, we all probably have moments like this, but the paranoid personality has such reactions all of the time and in the extreme.

- *Schizoid personality.* This is a personality disorder that rests on poor relationships. The person seems to be incapable of forming relationships, largely because of an extreme indifference towards other people's reactions.

- *Schizotypal personality.* This disorder is hard to distinguish from a mild form of schizophrenia. The person suffers from illusions and behaves in very unusual, bizarre ways. He or she may believe that he or she is in contact with things supernatural and moves on from this to other forms of magical thinking.

- *Narcissistic personality.* With this disorder, individuals have a highly aggrandised view of themselves. They are completely self-absorbed and self-centred, never considering others in their personal relationships. Similarly to those with anti-social personality disorder, they appear to have no empathy for others. The narcissistic personality tends to use other people and to be only concerned with his or her successes and how best they can be achieved.

- *Histrionic personality.* As the name implies, this is an attention-seeker, someone who behaves as though acting out a play on the stage of life in the constant presence of an audience. Like the narcissist, the histrionic personality tends to be shallow, demanding and manipulative, apparently displaying a great deal of emotion, but with little to it in the way of depth.

- *Avoidant personality.* Here is a person who is consumed with the possibility of rejection, so much so that he or she is very reluctant to enter into any close relationships. This is the type of person who keeps asking others what is wrong with him or her and why they are so useless. In other words, they have very low self-esteem and are simply too anxious about the outcome to be genuinely close to anyone else.

- *Dependent personality.* Like the avoidant personality, a person with a dependent personality disorder is lacking in self-confidence, but this takes the particular form of being unable to assume responsibility for him- or herself. Loved ones come to predominate in this person's life, as he or she puts their needs first, largely for fear of losing them if this were not done. This means that such a person (usually a woman) is extremely sensitive to criticism.

- *Obsessive-compulsive personality.* This is the extreme perfectionist, a person who is obsessed with order, rules, styles of behaviour, habits, and so on. Such a person tends to be heavily invested in their work and to want everything about that work to be exactly, precisely just right. One outcome of this is that interpersonal relationships suffer; it is as if there is no time for them in such a highly ordered life. The major difference between this *personality* disorder and OCD is that there is no feeling of extreme anxiety if the rituals are not followed as there is in OCD.

Finally, it should be borne in mind that the personality disorders are genuine disorders. They are not simply the small impulses that we all experience in a day-to-day sense. There are times when we are all a little narcissistic or overly sensitive to criticism or anti-social or changeable in our moods or even histrionic. However, such moments are aberrations and soon pass. For the person suffering from a personality disorder, they do not pass; they are part of their make-up and without help they will not change. It is not possible simply to 'get a grip' of a personality disorder. It needs outside intervention and in the case of some of the more extreme forms of the anti-social and the borderline personality disorders, even this intervention might not prove to be effective.

▶ **Summary**

- There are many ways of defining abnormality, including something that is statistically unusual, or something that is simply labelled as abnormal by the majority of the population or something that is causing distress to a person or to those around.

- Abnormality or mental illness is always bound to a particular time and a particular culture.

- The major way in which abnormalities are classified in the Western world is through the DSM-IV, based in the USA. It is a medically based classificatory system and may well lead to self-fulfilling prophecies.

- There is a sense in which any disorder, even one of clearly physical origin, has its psychological components. This would be the case even with an accident that might have psychological aspects before, during and after the event.

- A major area of mental disorder comes through anxiety when it is extreme. The anxiety disorders include generalised anxiety disorder, phobias, panic disorders and obsessive-compulsive disorders.

- Mood disorders consist mainly of depression and bipolar disorder in which depression alternates with mania. The major symptoms of depression (which is very common) fall into the emotional, motivational, cognitive and physical areas.

- There are strong links between depression and suicide.

- Schizophrenia is characterised by a split from reality. This can take many forms including hallucinations and delusions. There are distortions in perceptions, cognitions and emotions, and even in the extreme of motor behaviour.

- The major types of schizophrenia are: disorganised, paranoid, catatonic, undifferentiated and residual, but any one case is unique and may not be easily categorised.

- Dissociative Identity Disorder is split or multiple personality in which the person is protecting the self from traumatic situations by developing an alternative personality. This is a rare disorder and usually results from childhood abuse.

- There are 10 categories of personality disorder, the most extreme and most interesting being the anti-social and the borderline, both of which are very hard to deal with either for friends and family or for health professionals.

- All types of abnormality or mental disorder (particularly the personality disorders) overlap with everyday experience. They are simply more extreme and frequently more debilitating so that to recover from them the individual needs professional help.

▶ Questions and possibilities

- Reflecting on your experiences of life to date, what instances of abnormal behaviour or mental disorder have you observed? What do they have in common? In other words, what, for you, defines abnormality?

- If you see someone behaving in an abnormal way, does this seem threatening to you? If you do make links between behaviour that is out of the ordinary and a potential threat, why do you believe that this is?

- What would you say to someone who maintained that mental disorder was due to demonic possession?

- What are the major differences that you can think of between everyday anxiety and anxiety that might be labelled as abnormal? What signs would demonstrate to you that someone else was suffering from an anxiety disorder?

- Think of any instances of phobic behaviour that you have seen. Are these genuine and debilitating phobias or simply someone expressing a dislike? If a family member or a friend was suffering from a phobia, what help would you attempt to give them?

- Have you ever experienced generalised anxiety, that is, anxiety that does not seem to be attached to any particular event or circumstance? How do you think that such anxiety comes about?

- What do you think are the main differences between being depressed and simply feeling down or between being manic and simply feeling elated? Do you believe that it is possible for someone to simply 'snap out' of a depression? If not, why not?

- Think of people that you have known who have suffered from depression. What do you believe to have been the causes? Do these causes have anything in common? Why do you think that depression is so common in our society? Is it likely to be as common in other (say, Eastern) societies?

- Which of the various explanations suggested to account for schizophrenia do you consider to be the most likely?

- Have you ever experienced any of the splits with reality that characterise schizophrenia, even in minor form? If you have, what do you think might have brought them about?

- Can you imagine a culture in which schizophrenic ways of behaving were the norm? Is it possible that schizophrenics in our culture are simply out of joint with the place and the time?

- Have you or anyone that you know ever experienced something so psychologically traumatic that it might have prompted some sort of dissociation? In this sense, are reactions such as day-dreaming a mild form of dissociation? Relatedly, do you ever feel that there might be a Jekyll and Hyde aspect to some people, that at times their personality changes?

- Work through each of the 10 personality disorders and make two lists – one of people that you have known that fit into the category and one of any impulses you might have felt in that direction. What do you think might have prompted any such impulses on your part?

- Do you think that any of the personality disorders would preclude someone living a relatively normal life, even though people around might be suffering?

- To what extent have your previous views of abnormal behaviour or mental illness been shaped by society in the form of news items, fiction, and so on?

- To what extent do you believe that people should be obliged to receive treatment for mental illness? What criteria would you use in making such decisions?

CHAPTER SEVENTEEN

A healthy life

Self-help

Scenes from life

Jack was 45. Married for 20 years, he and his wife and three teenage children had settled into a familiar sort of routine, with nothing more than the usual stresses involved in mid-life and adolescent children. In other words, home life and marriage were reasonably settled for Jack; neither overly exciting nor especially dull. He had not thought about it much, but if he had, he would not want to make many changes.

Work was stressful for Jack. He had been in the same job for some time but the company had been restructured around him several times and on each occasion he had worried about keeping his job and then found that he was having to work even harder afterwards. He was just about managing but finding that he had little time for anything else. For the last year or two he had also been steadily putting on weight and was becoming quite portly. As a young man, he had been reasonably sporty, but now his activity seemed to be restricted to mowing the lawn at weekends and getting up and down from the couch during the week. He had recently noticed that he was short of breath simply from walking upstairs to the bedroom.

Having, by chance, seen a magazine article whilst waiting for an optician's appointment, Jack decided that he had to take matters into his own hands. The facts and figures quoted in the magazine worried him and he realised that if he continued along his present route, he might not live much longer. He was still smoking, not often, but a few every day. No one at home liked him doing this, but he felt a great release from it. Now, suddenly, he saw himself as heart attack material. He discussed this with his wife and they worked out a good programme of healthy eating for him. The children were amused by this but rallied round and helped. He started to exercise, getting up an hour earlier and going for a walk. After a few weeks, the walk turned into a slow jog and he even bought himself a tracksuit. The children were even more amused but, again, continued to be supportive. And he had stopped smoking immediately after leaving the optician's room. He simply threw his packet of cigarettes into the first bin that he saw.

Two months later, Jack weighed 7 kilos less than he had, his belt was two notches in, his children were looking at him in a new light and his relationship with his wife seemed to have improved. He had also become slightly less attached to the various stressors at work; somehow, he seemed to be treating it all more lightly than before. In general, Jack felt very good about himself, almost that he had taken on a new lease of life.

Rosie was 23. She had left school, never quite coming to terms with academic work, although doing reasonably well at it when she could stay relaxed. She had worked for a few years in minor office jobs and then decided that there was more to life for her. So she had begun training as a teacher, a career she had often thought about. She liked young children and enjoyed dealing with them and helping them to learn to see the world from varying perspectives. She very much enjoyed their freshness and enthusiasm.

She was in her second year at teacher's training college and had been doing very well at all of the practical work, especially the placements in schools. Everybody said that she was clearly 'cut out' to be a teacher. However, the academic side of things was not going so well. She found the material easy enough and could learn it readily enough, but as soon as a series of assignments were due and examinations were looming, then she started to become so anxious that she found it difficult to concentrate.

It was coming up to the busiest time of year for assessments and they were all beginning to crowd in. To make matters worse, she seemed to have developed a cold, or perhaps it was even a variety of influenza, that she could not shake off. It had been waxing and waning for some weeks, never quite disappearing. It made it very difficult to concentrate on her work and even to sleep at night. She was becoming more and more lethargic, her energy seeming just to be disappearing by the day.

Rosie could not stop thinking about her physical state and how it was interfering with her work. She was desperate to do well; she so much wanted to be out there, teaching. But she was also beginning to feel physically unable to do things, bumping into doorways, knocking things over and forgetting her keys or her bag. All the while, the assignments and the exams were looming ever closer. Each time she thought about them, so she became panicky and her cold seemed to worsen. The really frustrating thing for Rosie was remembering being in a similar state in the previous year and then all of her physical ailments clearing up after the last exam was over. If only she could keep going and keep doing the work until it was finished again. It all seemed impossible.

As mentioned in a previous chapter, any illness, disease or accident involves psychological factors at some or all of its stages. Health psychologists are interested in these relationships and in how people become ill, how they stop themselves from becoming ill, how they become well again once they have been ill, or how they deal with chronic illness, and finally what the relationships are between life circumstances (particularly stressful life circumstances) and illness.

Leading a healthy life depends on a deceptively straightforward set of conditions. They are:

- sleeping sufficient hours each day – the amount varies from person to person;

- eating breakfast;

- not eating between meals;

- staying at a reasonable weight;

- not smoking;

- drinking alcohol barely or not at all;

- having regular physical exercise.

Of course, one might ask the question – why would one want to stick to these prescriptions? Many of them preclude quite enjoyable things. Some people fully engage in sitting around eating, drinking, smoking, staying up late and not exercising. The major answer to the question is that life is prolonged (as well as being more comfortable while it lasts).

To take some of these matters in turn, smoking is extremely costly to any society because of its serious effects on health. These effects can also be indirect as well as direct (lung cancer, emphysema, etc.) through, for example, leading to reduced lung capacity which in turn makes it less likely that a person will exercise.

Although there is some evidence that very moderate drinking of alcohol might reduce mortality slightly, heavy alcohol consumption clearly increases the risk. Again some of the risks are indirect. For example, after drinking too much, there is an increased risk of having a motor accident, of being burned in a fire or of drowning.

Dieting has been mentioned in an earlier chapter, and these days in Western society many people know a great deal about diet; enormous amounts are written about it. The problems associated with poor nutrition are huge and widespread. Obvious examples come from narrowing of the arteries through cholesterol deposits, the likelihood of these being increased by eating certain foods. In general, though, the evidence about the significance (positively or negatively) of high-fat diets is mixed. Similarly, there are links between hypertension (high blood pressure) and diet and hypertension increase the risk of strokes and coronary heart disease. Probably, in the midst of many fads and fancies, the important point to make about nutrition is that a good diet is a balanced diet and contains a variety of foods with not too much in the way of saturated fats.

Exercise has an effect on most of the aspects of a healthy life so far mentioned. Weight, cholesterol and blood pressure are reduced and there are positive effects of physical exercise on self-esteem and the consequent reduction of stress. Of course, strong physical exercise also carries a risk of injury, but this risk might be preferable to the risks that are run by the absence of exercise. The question becomes: just how much exercise is 'good'? The answer must vary from person to person and there are also numerous views on this. For it to be useful, though, it must be regular, last for a reasonable time and be aerobic – that is, it should get the heart rate and respiration up. (Anaerobic exercise – short bursts of energy – does not increase oxygen consumption and therefore does not much increase heart or lung fitness.)

The final aspect of staying healthy does not usually appear in any list of prescriptions, perhaps because it seems to be something that is less under the control of the individual than matters like diet and exercise. It is the *risk of accident*. Accidents (particularly road traffic accidents) are among the highest causes of death and injury in industrialised countries, and relatively high in developing countries. In people aged 15 to 24, about 50 per cent of deaths are from accidents.

Think it through a little and it becomes obvious that accidents are to some extent under personal control. For example, the risk of accident increases a great deal when a person is under the influence of alcohol or drugs, the taking of which is voluntary. Other background factors are less under personal control. For example, one cannot do very much about one's age. Similarly, males are three times more likely to have accidents than females, and, mostly, we can do little about our gender. Of course, this is probably because, in Western society, men are more likely than women to work in relatively high-risk jobs.

There might also be personality differences in proneness to accident. For example, people who are high in aggressiveness and competitiveness are more likely to have accidents than those who are low on these dimensions. Similarly, high sensation-seekers are inevitably more likely to have accidents than low sensation-seekers. Controlling the likelihood of accidents is not easy, but there are two possible ways of going about it. Efforts can be made to change the environment to make accidents less likely – speed restrictions on the road are an obvious example of this. The other possibility is through changing our own attitudes towards any situation, such as driving, in which an accident is likely to occur.

▶ Dealing with stress

The topic of stress was touched on briefly in the chapter concerned with emotion regulation. The point was made that stress is difficult to define and, indeed, has been through many definitions over the years. This is, perhaps, because it is something that is both within and without the person. Certainly, some circumstances (such as losing one's job, a marriage break-up, moving house, having a child with a chronic illness, retiring, etc.) are stressful to many people. But all of these events are not necessarily stressful to everyone and nor are they stressful to the same degree in everyone. So, there are large individual differences in stress reactions. Stress is the result of an interaction between the individual and the environment, and for a highly readable analysis of stress, see Overton (2005).

An obvious cause of stress reactions is *disasters*, single, cataclysmic events either for the group (an earthquake, tsunami, tornado, etc.) or for the individual (major traffic accident, shooting, rape, etc.). Such events can have a major impact on both the immune system and emotional reactions and general psychological functioning (lack of sleep, inability to concentrate, etc.). Major *life events* can also have similar effects, although, again, it should be emphasised that there are large individual differences in reactivity.

Disasters and major life events are obvious. Less obvious as background conditions or causes of stress reactions are *daily hassles*, events such as losing keys or wallet or handbag, being stuck in rush-hour traffic, having a succession of minor problems with the car or with the plumbing or with electronic equipment. Again, such events can, in some cases, lead to a greater propensity to illness, presumably through lowered immune function. They also might have indirect effects on health by leading to increased likelihood of smoking and over-eating and decreased likelihood of exercising.

Whether stress is *acute* or *chronic* makes a difference. For example, to have to work extra hours during the course of one week in order to get a particular job done is very different from having to work extra hours over a period of months or years. Even with chronic stressors, though, there are large individual differences in reaction. Some people become quite used to living with chronic stressors, such as poverty, over-crowding, noise, and even vast and enduring overwork. In this context, it is also important to realise that stress is not always negative. To have some stress in life is, for many people, positively motivating.

The particular type of chronic stress mentioned above, that which comes from enduring overwork, can lead to *burnout*. This is similar to depression. The individual feels emotionally exhausted and, as part of this, emotionally distant from other people, particularly at work. There is difficulty in sleeping and appetite may be disturbed. There is a clear sense of being unable to achieve anything that should be achieved or that the person used to achieve, in the job.

Stress, then, even though it is difficult to define, has both bodily and psychological aspects. The physiological reactions in stress were best demonstrated in broad terms by Hans Selye (1956) with what he termed the *general adaptation syndrome*. He described this as the typical reaction to stressful circumstances. It has three phases:

1 *Alarm.* This is the emergency phase in which the fight or flight system kicks in. The body is reacting to deal with the threat.

2 *Resistance*. Chemical changes have occurred and the body is coping, although at this point its vulnerability to other stressors is increased.

3 *Exhaustion*. Bodily resources are now run down and there is increased proneness to illness or even death, depending on the severity of the circumstances.

While all of this is going on at the bodily level, psychologically the individual is also finding methods of coping with the stress. These methods are based on initial appraisals of: what does the event mean for me, will it be harmful? And, then, will I be able to deal with it? Dealing with it means either (or, more usually, both) emotion-focused or problem-focused coping. That is, faced with, say, a particularly stressful problem at work, the person might evaluate it and decide whether or not he or she can solve it as a problem. Can I change the work circumstances so that the problem goes away? If not, if there is nothing that can be done (for example, being stuck with a recently appointed boss who seems to have a personal bias against you, or having to continue to work long hours in order to hang onto your job), then the question is: what can I do to change the way I am reacting emotionally to this? As already mentioned, most stressful situations are dealt with by a mixture of these two types of coping.

Take another situation that some people find stressful – facing a difficult examination. A problem-focused approach would be to be systematic about the work done towards the exam, talk the work over with other people, go to all possible support groups and tutorials, and so on. An emotion-focused approach would be to try to reduce your anxiety about the exam by using relaxation techniques or by playing sport or by seeking social support by having friends to commiserate with you about it. Again, in this type of situation, many people would cope by using a mixture of the two methods.

Also, of course, some of the coping methods might have other consequences. For example, some people eat, drink and smoke more as a type of emotion-focused coping. This might have short-term gains but there are obvious longer-term negative consequences. Alternatively, a person might cope with the stress of an impending exam by thinking of something else or by talking to the people about anything else, or by going to the movies, or even by praying. Although, perhaps, emotionally comforting and acting to reduce the anxiety that the individual would otherwise feel, none of these strategies is likely to make performance better in the exam.

▶ **Personality and health**

A common belief is that stress increases the risk of various outcomes for health, or rather for ill-health, particularly in the area of heart disease and strokes. There is also some belief of a link between stress and proneness to cancer. Apart from being very much dependent on the definition of stress, there are large individual differences in any such relationships. The idea of individual differences brings personality into consideration. The interesting question then becomes: what is the relationship between personality and health (or ill-health)?

Throughout the past 30 years, in the area of health, the major distinction to be made has been between *Type A* and *Type B* personalities. Type A people tend to be always pressured by time and to be irritable and aggressive. They are competitive and desperate to achieve. Type B people are the opposite; more relaxed and easy-going, less competitive and aggressive. According to the original researchers in this area, Type A behaviour is linked to a greater risk of heart disease.

There is a great deal of general evidence to support the relationship between Type-A personality and proneness to heart disorder. However, a problem is that this type of personality has many characteristics. Is the risk of heart disorder due to one, some or all of them? Again, the general evidence here suggests that the major factor is hostility. The hostile type of person seems to be at greater risk of heart disorder than those who are less hostile. This is particularly the case when the hostility is confrontational rather than the type characterised by constant worry or complaint.

Although there are proven links between Type A personality and risk of heart disorder, there remains much that is unknown about the link. For example, very little is known about any such relationship in women; the majority of the research has been with men. Furthermore, Type A men in white-collar jobs are more at risk of heart disease than men in blue-collar jobs. Also, there are clear links between Type A personality or behaviour and high rates of smoking and drinking, relatively unhealthy eating and even increased risk of accidents. The question then becomes, is there a direct link between Type A and risk of heart disease or is there a complex interrelationship between all of the factors involved?

A further factor that enters this complex equation is stress. Type A and Type B personalities react differently to stressful situations. Type A people react more rapidly and more forcefully to stressful stimuli than Type B people. They also tend to perceive any threat as more personal than Type Bs. It is also reasonable to surmise that Type A people tend to increase their likelihood of being in stressful situations. It is almost as if their personality style prompts them to seek out more stressful situations.

Although, as was seen in previous chapters, personality is reasonably settled, it is not set in stone. To some extent personality is modifiable and so it is with Type A behaviours. Generally, we can alter our perceptions and emotional reactions by working on our cognitions. So, someone who recognises Type A tendencies in himself or herself might set various life-style changes in place, ranging from taking more exercise and learning relaxation techniques to broadly changing typical reactions to stressful situations. An example might be learning to be relaxed when standing in a supermarket checkout queue behind someone who cannot find the correct money or who seems to have forgotten the pin number on their card. In this situation, the Type A person would be tense with frustration and impatience and even potentially hostile. The control of any such way of reacting can only be good for the immune system.

Another type of question that has been asked in recent years concerns the possibility of a personality type that is prone to *cancer*. At present, the general answer is that no link has been found. One suggestion has been that a so-called Type C personality might be linked with cancer. This is the sort of person who is prone to depression, feelings of helplessness and with a very flat sort of emotional reactivity. However, to date, the evidence does not support this suggestion.

Another way of looking at the links that have been proposed between personality and various diseases is that such specific links do not exist: rather there might be *general disease-prone personality*. These would be people who score highly on a number of characteristics such as anxiety, depression and anger. Related to this, there is some indication that attitudinal factors also have a part to play in proneness to disease. For example, people who have a pessimistic approach to accounting for the events of life tend throughout their middle years to be in a worse state of health than those who take an optimistic approach.

Linked to attitude or approach to life and the proneness to disease is what is sometimes referred to as general *resilience*. Part of this is based on a person's view of *locus of control*. This refers to whether or not a person perceives himself or herself to have control over possible negative outcomes in life. Perceived control has positive outcomes and perceived lack of control has negative outcomes, even including an effect on the immune system. People can also be divided into those who believe that they are in control of events generally in their lives and those who believe that most things happen due to circumstances outside them – referred to respectively as internal and external locus of control. Needless to say, those who have an internal locus of control would be expected to be less disease prone than those with an external locus.

Again, generally, resilient or hardy people have a strong internal locus of control. However, they also have a firm sense of what they are doing in life – a sense of purpose. They are the sort of people who rise to challenges, seeing anything that changes around them as an opportunity rather than a threat. If people are highly resilient, then the impact of stressful events on them is less and tends to be less likely to lead to illness.

▶ Social influences on health

Social networks are very important in dealing with the type of stressful circumstances that might eventually have an impact on health or in dealing directly with ill-health and disease. There are a number of aspects to this, the first and most obvious of which is how many people that you might have in your network of social support. To some extent, the more the better. However, sheer numbers would not make up for a lack of any practical support from among them. In other words, the nature of the support is also important, as, also, is the individual's perception of that support. For example, if, from an individual's perspective, his or her family and friends only paid lip service to providing support, the lack of quality involved would be likely to have its impact.

The obvious way in which social support might have an influence on health is by helping the individual deal with stressful situations. This could be through both problem- and emotion-focused coping strategies. Straightforward practical problem-solving coping advice could come from family and friends as also could a friendly ear in which to speak and a friendly shoulder on which to lean – both providing emotion-focused coping.

However, it is also possible to imagine circumstances in which social support, depending on the kind of social support, might not be positive. If a family member contracts an illness and the family gather round and tell stories that they know of others who have had to put up with such an illness, then this might be less than helpful. In such circumstances, people are sometimes prone to catastrophise, to spread rumours as though telling true stories, and so on. In other words, the apparent social support might be more about the person who is offering the 'support' than it is about the person apparently being supported.

For most people at many stages in their lives, their social group is a strong source of influence and such influence might well impact on health. The most obvious time of life in which this happens is adolescence. At this stage, influences might be powerful to smoke, drink, take drugs, eschew exercise, and so on. However, such peer pressure or influence continues later in life. Think of the pressure of executive lunches or the idea that the only proper way to take a break from a manual job is to have a smoke.

In general, broad cultural factors also have a strong influence on health. An obvious example in Western society comes from the huge emphasis on slimness equating with beauty and fashionability throughout the previous two or three decades. No doubt this has not been the only influence on the development of eating disorders in women, with all the attendant health risks, but it has surely been an important factor. Similarly, although, in another sense, by contrast, the large-scale advertising of fast foods has surely added to the potential to be overweight and thus at a greater health risk. There are numerous examples of such influences, such as the influence on tooth decay in children or the advertising of sugar-based products.

▶ Pain

All but a very few people experience pain at many times in their lives. And pain has a very obvious adaptive value – it is a clear warning that actual or potential damage is occurring to basic bodily tissues. Again, though, as most people have experienced, pain is not as straightforward as this description makes it seem. Have you ever injured yourself playing sport and not noticed until later? Have you ever been in some extreme situation in which you have had to do something that would normally cause you great pain, but which, again, you have not noticed until later? Have you ever had a chronic pain, such as a toothache or broken bone or extreme indigestion, which seems to have disappeared from your awareness for a few minutes? It has not 'really' disappeared, but simply seems to have gone from your attention.

There are (at least) two parts to pain. There is a sensory side – a bee-sting hurts *at the point of the sting*, a tooth aches *in and around the tooth*. But there is also an emotional side to pain. Pain is always accompanied by an emotional reaction (anger, fear, unhappiness, and so on) and this reaction somehow interacts with the sensory side of pain. For example, if we feel a sudden pain in the chest and start to be afraid that we are having a heart attack, then the chances are that the pain will worsen.

Cognitions are almost always involved in emotions and each individual, depending on personal experience, develops thoughts, beliefs and opinions about pain. These, in turn, might well influence the pain. For example, if I am typically afraid of pain and what it might mean, then the experience of the pain is likely to be more intense than if I believe that I am the sort of person who can easily cope with pain.

This combination of sensation-based and emotion/cognition-based factors have been put together in the well-accepted *gate-control theory* of pain, suggested in 1965 by Melzack and Wall (1983). A potentially painful stimulus occurs (the bee stings, the shin cracks on the edge of the bath, the toe catches on the leg of the bed) but there is a sort of gate in the central nervous system that, by its degree of opening, determines the extent to which the pain is perceived. In other words, the mixture of emotions and cognitions going on in the brain sends messages to the spinal cord that makes the experience of the pain either more or less intense.

If the gate opens a little, then the threshold for pain is lowered, that is, less of a stimulus leads to a perception of pain. Other reactions might close the gate, raising the pain threshold and thus making it necessary for much more of a stimulus to occur before pain is experienced. To take an obvious example, if I am afraid of painful stimuli and catastrophise them, then the gate opens and I am more likely to experience pain quickly and readily. If, on the other hand, when I notice a potentially painful stimulus, I am able to relax and concentrate on other sensations, then I am less likely to experience intense pain – the gate has been closed somewhat.

The interaction between sensation and emotion/cognition in pain means that two very broad types of pain can be distinguished, even though both factors might be present in both types. Organic pain can be extreme and is what occurs when there is obvious damage to bodily tissue. Psychogenic pain is the type of pain (that can also be intense, severe and long-lasting) that occurs without any obvious physical basis. Of course, this might mean that, as yet, a physical cause for the pain has not been found. There are three major types of such pain. Neuralgia is an intense, shooting pain along a nerve, often in the face, for which no physical cause has been discovered. Causalgia is similar to neuralgia but consists of a severe burning pain in some part of the body. And phantom-limb pain is a pain that is sometimes experienced in a limb that no longer exists (through amputation) or for which there no longer exist any nerves.

As with most aspects of health or disease, there are possible links between pain and personality and various attempts have been made to establish such links. The problem, however, is the usual one of correlations saying little about causes. If, for example, a link is found between anxiety and proneness to experience pain, does this mean that the anxiety causes the intensification of the pain experience, or that the pain leads to increased anxiety, or both, or even that there is some underlying factor that is causing both?

Perhaps the most important aspect of pain to consider is how it can be controlled. This is particularly so where chronic pain is involved, that is, pain that goes on for months or years. The major methods are through: drugs, surgery, acupuncture, biofeedback, hypnosis, relaxation and guided imagery, counter-irritation (of another part of the body) and distraction. As should be clear, some of these techniques work on the sensory side of pain and others on the cognitive/emotional. Most of the techniques are to some extent effective, but each of them, with the exception of relaxation and guided imagery, has its drawbacks.

Teaching relaxation enables the person to lower their state of arousal and relax the muscles. This is usefully induced through meditation techniques. It can be used in conjunction with guided imagery in which people are trained to imagine scenes that help to deal with the pain. For example, one type of guided imagery involves the person being encouraged to imagine fighting the pain, wrestling it into submission, or another might be to imagine taking the pain and wrapping it up so that it becomes smaller and smaller and then disposing of it. Although the relaxation and meditation techniques work well in many cases of pain, the guided imagery tends to work less well where the pain is especially severe.

In the end, a person has to *adapt* to chronic pain and how well this adaptation occurs will determine how well the person copes with the pain. Such adaptation will depend on the type of factor or sources of influence discussed so far in this chapter. For example, there are background factors such as personality, personal beliefs and culture. There are also aspects of the pain itself, particularly its severity, and finally there are factors such as the nature and kind of social supports available to the person and even the degree of financial support that there might be.

▶ A specific health problem – smoking

In order to illustrate some of what has been discussed in this chapter, various health problems could be considered in more detail, but one that is frequently mentioned in the contemporary world is smoking. The illness-related effects of smoking have now been incontrovertibly established. Smoking has direct effects on all respiratory and heart and circulatory diseases, as well as lung cancer.

In Western society, people of different ages typically smoke different amounts, becoming more consistent with adulthood. It used to be that men smoked far more than women but now the pattern is changing with fewer men smoking than previously, but the number of women smoking remaining constant.

One of the interesting considerations about smoking is *why* people start to smoke at all, given that the very first cigarette or two are exceedingly unpleasant. It actually takes some perseverance to go on and become a smoker. Similarly, it is possible to see smokers going through the difficulties of continuing to smoke through a heavy cold and cough. This takes some doing, but many seem to manage it.

The reasons for starting to smoke are to do with things social and with personality. Socially, the availability of cigarettes is a factor that influences the starting and the continuing of smoking in young people. Perhaps stronger factors, though, are to do with self-image. So, for example, rebellious teenagers are more likely to begin smoking than less rebellious teenagers.

Although image might prompt young people to start smoking, it is other factors that probably maintain the smoking once it has begun. One important factor is thought to be withdrawal from nicotine, a clear biological factor. The symptoms that go along with nicotine withdrawal are not necessarily very strong but they are not pleasant. However, as anyone knows who has given up smoking, the idea of having a cigarette still has considerable appeal long after all the nicotine has disappeared from the system.

One suggestion is that people continue to smoke for a mixture of four possible reasons:

1 to gain positive feelings such as relaxation;

2 to avoid negative feelings such as anxiety or stress;

3 simply due to a habit;

4 in the service of a psychological dependence such as regulating anger or depression.

A further point is that smokers are extremely adept at reducing the cognitive dissonance involved in the knowledge – I smoke and smoking leads to lung cancer. They start *not* to believe the evidence, for example, or to justify their habit in other ways. Well, it is important for me to relax socially and this is the only way I know how to do it. Or they might decrease the subjective importance of the dilemma – well, you've got to go some time; it might as well be from smoking as anything else.

The important practical consideration about smoking is clearly how to stop smoking oneself or how to help somebody else stop smoking. In passing, it is worth saying that it is more difficult to stop doing something than it is to start it. Starting a new behaviour is usually done by degrees; there is a gradual build-up. It is difficult, although not necessarily impossible, to stop something by degrees. Smoking is particularly difficult in this respect because it tends to be linked to so many other things, for example, eating, not eating, drinking, different times of day, socially, in certain places, and so on. Thus, each of those occasions or places becomes a stimulus that suggests 'smoking', so each of them, in turn, has to be eliminated in its suggestive or discriminatory function.

The major techniques that can be used to help the cessation of smoking are: hypnosis, relaxation, self-talk, nicotine patches and rapid smoking. The latter is an interesting technique based on making smoking become aversive by having the person smoke a large number of cigarettes in a very short time, in order to make them feel sick. This is straightforward classical conditioning, putting together the behaviour of smoking with an unconditioned, aversive response – being sick. Self-talk is like the converse of rapid smoking, helping the person stick to the decision to stop smoking by reinforcing for themselves the positive benefits of so doing.

Apart from all of these individually based techniques to help in the cessation of smoking, there are also community-based programmes. These range from some types of advertising through to various types of ban on smoking in and around the workplace, the home, any public place, and so on.

Perhaps the most important final point to make in this chapter is that health is not simply a physical or biological matter. Psychological factors are heavily involved in it in all of its aspects. Stress, anxiety and emotion, in general, all have their effects on the immune system, health in general and in reactions to disease. Although this makes health a more complex matter than it was once thought to be, it also means that various psychosocial factors can be used in order to bring about positive changes to the health of individuals, from dealing with stress and the control of chronic pain through to increased chances of longevity.

▶ Summary

- Health is not merely a physical or biological matter but involves psychological aspects that can come into play before, during or after an illness, disease or accident.

- Particularly important in maintaining a healthy life are diet, exercise, the control of smoking and alcohol consumption, and weight control. All aspects of healthy or unhealthy living interact with the chance of having accidents.

- Stress is difficult to define because it is a mixture of factors internal and external to the person.

- Some situations lead to stress reactions more often and in more people than others, for example, any major environmental catastrophes and various types of loss – of a person, a job, a relationship, and so on.

- Daily hassles are also an important aspect of stress and if stress goes on for long enough, it can lead to burnout.

- Bodily, the three stages of stress are alarm, resistance and exhaustion.

- Psychologically, dealing with stress occurs through a mixture of emotion-focused and problem-focused coping.

- There are links between personality and health, the Type A personality being particularly prone to heart disease. However, Type A behaviour is also modifiable.

- There is no definite link between personality and cancer although there may be a general disease-prone personality.

- Social networks and broader cultural factors have an influence on health, particularly through social support and peer group pressure, respectively.

- Pain is a mixture of sensory and emotional/cognitive factors, the most accepted theory being that emotional/cognitive factors make a gateway for the extent of the pain reaction.

- There are various techniques for controlling pain that concentrate either on the sensory side or the emotional/cognitive.

- A specific and very common health problem is smoking, for which there are a variety of causative and maintaining stimuli and a number of techniques that can be used for cessation.

Questions and possibilities

- How do you fit into the prescription for healthy living? What changes would you have to make in order to fit into it more readily? What is stopping you making those changes?

- Have your patterns of exercise, diet, smoking and drinking, etc., changed over the course of your life? If so, what has led to those changes?

- To what extent do you believe that your own health, proneness to disease, immune functioning, proneness to accident, etc., are within your own hands?

- What are the main causes of stress in your life? What are the main causes of stress in the lives of your family and friends? Have these stressors changed over time?

- What is your preferred method of controlling stress? Make a list of instances in which you have controlled your own stress by using emotion-focused coping and problem-focused coping? Which do you prefer? Have different stressors led you to adopt these different approaches?

- What are the main daily hassles in your life? What can you do about them? Do you think that anything that you do might be causing a daily hassle for anybody else?

- Have you ever experienced burnout or seen anyone else that is experiencing burnout? What are its major characteristics? If a friend were experiencing burnout, what would you advise him or her to do?

- Design a stress-free environment for (1) your family, (2) your place of work. What are the main differences between your design and the reality?

- What characteristics of your own personality make you more or less susceptible to health problems? If there are some aspects of your personality that put you at risk, what do you think can be done about them?

- Do you know any people with Type A personalities? Do you perceive them as being at risk?

- If you found out that you had an incurable disease, how would you deal with that psychologically? How would you help others to deal with that knowledge about themselves?

- List the main instances in which your social support network has influenced your health. Have you ever been persuaded to do anything, either positively or negatively, with respect to your health on the basis of advertising? Have you ever done anything that is bad for your health but good for your image?

- List some of the main experiences of pain that you have had. What are the differences between them? Did you deal with them in different ways? If so, why did you do this?

- Do you think that it would be possible to control *any* sort of pain using psychological techniques?

- Design a programme that would enable someone to stop smoking or to stop over-eating or to take more exercise or to sleep for longer. Do you think that your programme would work? What might stop it from working?

A healthy life

Therapeutic help

Scenes from life

Imagine a psychotherapist working in the public health system who is conducting an initial interview with a patient. The patient has been referred to the therapist because of an eating disorder. She is clearly anorexic and has become so dangerously underweight that she is somewhat at risk both of extreme physical collapse and possibly of harming herself in other ways.

During the course of the interview, which is very much aimed at gathering information that might be helpful in understanding the person and finding a useful way forward for her, the therapist uncovers a very complex home situation. The woman, who is in her thirties, has two young children and is obviously very unhappy with the relationship she has with her husband. It emerges that much of this unhappiness stems from the way in which he keeps a large part of his life a secret from her. However, during the previous year or so she has learned that when he goes out at night, as he does frequently, it is to engage in various criminal activities. She had no idea of this earlier in the marriage.

As the interview progresses further, so the patient reveals a great deal of information to the therapist. This includes the fact that although she has repeatedly told her husband how she deplores what he is doing, even though it is swelling their income, he shows no sign of stopping. In fact, she points out to the therapist, her husband has planned a robbery for later in the week. She even knows and mentions the name of the person who is to be robbed.

At the end of this first session, the therapist has collected a great deal of information that might be useful in subsequent therapeutic sessions with the patient. She has even begun to make a formulation of the case; this being one of the initial tasks that she would normally do as early as practicable when seeing a new patient. However, the therapist is also faced with a very difficult moral issue. She knows that a crime is to be committed, or, at least, she believes that her patient is sure that a crime is to be committed. The therapist/patient relationship is usually regarded as sacrosanct, but in this instance, should it remain sacrosanct?

Malcolm is 42 years old. He is single and has had a sequence of unsatisfactory relationships. He seems to be able to start a new relationship easily enough, but it soon begins to go wrong and it is always the other person that ends the relationship, rather than him. The latest break-up has been particularly unpleasant from his perspective and he has become both anxious and depressed, so much so that he has sought therapeutic help. He is in a good job and so can afford the relatively expensive hourly rate of therapists in private practice. Asking around, he finds two names that come strongly recommended. He has no way to decide between them and so decides to go to see each of them for one session and then make his mind up which of them he will continue with.

The first is a very gentle man in his late fifties who seems to be extremely friendly and accepting of Malcolm and his problems. The session seems almost like sitting and having a chat with a sympathetic friend. The therapist quietly explores all manner of things with Malcolm, from the details of his most recent relationship right back to the type of relationship he had with his parents, particularly his mother. He also asks him a little about his dreams, how often he has them, what they tend to be about, whether or not they wake him up and so on. He also asks Malcolm a number of questions about how he is feeling in the therapeutic situation – how he is feeling here and now. And he probes Malcolm's answers quite deeply, not letting him get away with statements such as 'Oh, I feel alright'. He pushes for more and keeps returning to how Malcolm is feeling when he talks about particular events and circumstances.

The second therapist, whom Malcolm sees a few days later, is a woman in her forties. She is quite sharply dressed and has an air of rather brisk efficiency and competence. There is nothing vague about her; she seems confidently to know what she is doing. Her questions to Malcolm are much more business-like than those of the first therapist. She explores in some detail what went wrong in Malcolm's recent break-up and keeps bringing him back to what he did and what his partner did and how what they each did impinged on the other.

She asks Malcolm nothing about his dreams or his previous relationships or his early life, but is more interested in finding out from him exactly what he would like to achieve for himself in coming to see her. When he tells her that he has been feeling anxious and depressed, she wants him to spell out exactly how that has affected what he does and what precisely he has been thinking about it all.

Towards the end of the first session, the therapist begins to suggest to Malcolm other ways in which he might begin to think about what has happened to him. She even describes to him one or two techniques for making his anxiety reduce and ways in which he might try to behave differently from usual when he begins to think depressing thoughts.

After the two sessions, Malcolm is no nearer to making up his mind who to continue with than he was before. Each seemed to have something to offer. He liked the style of the first man and felt in sense 'better' after seeing him but he liked the practicality of the woman that he saw secondly. He felt that he had come away from that second session armed with something helpful to do in his day-to-day life.

▶ Dealing with the extremes

Therapists in all of their guises and with a very wide variety of techniques naturally deal with an equally wide range of mental health issues. However, the issues to which society pays most attention are at the extremes. In the Western world there is a long history of not dealing with the bizarre, unusual and, in fact, the least happy members of society with very much compassion. For many centuries, in one way or another, they were simply cast aside, as being under the control of demons or in some way possessed. To deal with such tortured people, the idea seemed to be to torture them some more and then hanging, burning or drowning them.

Then came mental asylums. Although such places of incarceration might seem more humane than what had preceded them, they were frequently dreadful places, in which the likelihood of improvement was minimal. Throughout the twentieth century they did improve and, again in the Western world, the attempt was then made to replace them with various forms of community mental health. The aim was to help members of local communities care for the mentally disabled. This was not very successful either and was replaced with a variety of programmes that are being more rigorously assessed than had been the previous practice.

There are various types of provider of mental health treatment. *Clinical psychologists* have a specialised psychological training and are able to undertake a wide variety of therapies, either with individuals or with groups, including families. *Psychiatrists* have a medical training and have specialised in psychiatric medicine. Although they might develop therapeutic skills, their major approach is based on drug intervention. *Counsellors* are, as the name suggests, trained (to a greater or lesser degree) in counselling skills. They undertake therapeutic interventions but not with the same degree of individual psychological knowledge as the clinical psychologist. *Psychiatric social workers* and *psychiatric nurses* also care for those with some of the more extreme mental health problems but their skills in psychologically based therapy are necessarily limited.

The type of matter that was highlighted in the first example at the start of this chapter frequently arises when dealing with the more extreme forms of mental disorder. There are always ethical problems concerning treatment. For example, many therapeutic interventions involve a very intimate discussion between therapist and patient and yet any personal involvement (particularly sexual involvement) between therapist and patient is clearly inappropriate. The difficulty is that many of the more intimate discussions that people are used to having in their lives are surrounded by a generally intimate personal involvement, but not in the case of therapist and patient.

There is also the question of privacy. Any interchanges between the therapist and patient have to be guaranteed with respect to privacy, much as it is with a doctor and patient or a lawyer and client. The exception comes, for example, when the law has been broken, or, in the case of the example at the start of the chapter, might be expected to be broken. Also, of course, the other main occasion when privacy might be put to one side is when the therapist sees that the patient is at risk of doing self-harm or harm to others.

Finally, there is the question of informed consent. If the effectiveness of various types of therapy is to be properly assessed, then it is important that methodologically appropriate investigations are carried out. Inevitably, these must involve patients. However, patients cannot simply be used as guinea pigs without their informed consent to be used in such studies. This may seem straightforward enough; they can simply be asked and if they refuse, they refuse. But there are very many different ways in which questions can be asked in order to bring about desired answers. Most therapists are likely to be very skilled interpersonally and so it would be relatively easy for them to shade their questions in numerous ways. This is a particularly subtle way in which privacy might be breached.

The other broad area of consideration that lies behind any treatment that is offered in institutions for those with mental health problems is that of culture and gender. Different ethnic and social groups within a culture appear in such institutions at different rates. Men and women appear at similar rates but for different disorders. For example, men find themselves seeking help more than women for substance abuse and women more than men for mood disorders. There is also a fundamental difference between men and women in Western cultures in that women are far more likely than men to talk to others (particularly their general practitioners) about any mental health problems they might be experiencing. In general, then, the therapist has to be aware of any and all of these ethnic and social differences if he or she is to remain appropriately sensitive to the patient.

▶ Biological or physical therapies

The many varieties of therapy divide into two main types: the physical/biological and the psychological. The assumption that underlies the biological therapies is that the causes of mental disorders are in the brain; they are reflected in brain physiology or biochemistry. Consequently, if appropriate changes are made to the physiology or the biochemistry, then the condition should improve.

The notion of cause is difficult, even without probing into its philosophical origins. It is quite clear that many psychological difficulties have their genesis in a person's early life, initial attachments, current life circumstances, and so on. Of course, whatever changes such experiences bring about must be reflected in the person's physiology and biochemistry. However, in these cases, to say that the physiology or biochemistry is *causing* the reaction or condition is perhaps stretching belief too far. In other cases, there might well be direct physiological or biochemical abnormalities that directly cause a behavioural difficulty or mental disorder. In any event, whatever the origins of the causes of various conditions, it is possible to treat them either biologically or psychologically.

Drugs

The most frequently used biological therapies are based on drugs that are aimed at changing either mood or behaviour. From the 1950s on, for example, people suffering from the more extreme schizophrenic conditions no longer had to be restrained in straitjackets. Their behaviour became more humanely controlled by the use of drugs, drugs that are also used to reduce the frequency of hallucinations. Similarly, at much the same time, drugs began to be developed for the relief of depression:

- *Anxiety-reducing drugs*. Mostly, drugs that reduce anxiety are tranquillisers (also known as benzodiazepines). Like alcohol, they depress the action of the central nervous system. They also reduce tension but raise sleepiness. Although the tranquillisers have proved to be very useful over many years in the control of anxiety, they have also been over-prescribed and frequently misused. Perhaps more importantly than this, they also only provide short-term solutions to the problem of anxiety; essentially, to follow the medical analogy, they are treating the symptom rather than the cause. Stop taking the pills and the problem has not gone away.

- *Anti-psychotic drugs*. Anti-psychotic drugs work on the dopamine system in the brain, by blocking the dopamine receptors. Their use is based on the view that schizophrenia is due to increased activity in the dopamine system. Such drugs do *not* cure schizophrenia but they do help to reduce many of the symptoms that are particularly problematic for the person, for example, having hallucinations and strange thoughts. Anti-psychotic drugs do not work for all schizophrenics and they sometimes have side-effects such as the flattening of emotional reactions. The choice might, then, be between hallucinations and strange thoughts and some degree of happiness, or fewer hallucinations and strange thoughts but with reduced happiness as well.

■ *Anti-depressants.* Anti-depressants work to elevate mood. They have their effect through working on two neurotransmitters in the brain – norepinephrine and serotonin. Two quite distinct mechanisms are involved. One type of anti-depressant blocks an enzyme that destroys norepinephrine and serotonin and the other prevents the re-uptake of these neurotransmitters and so prolongs their effectiveness. (Re-uptake is an automatic process of the drawing back of neurotransmitters into the nerve endings that released them initially.) As with most drugs, there can be unpleasant side-effects from anti-depressants. Common ones are, for example, a very dry mouth, constipation and blurred vision.

■ The search is constantly underway for new anti-depressant drugs, perhaps because depression is so common in the Western world. Some drugs in this class have, however, been used for many years. The most long-standing example is lithium. This works on approximately 50 per cent of those who have bipolar disorder, but even after 50 years of study its action remains unclear and it can have severe side-effects.

■ *Ritalin.* Ritalin is a stimulant drug used to treat hyperactivity in children in disorders such as Attention Deficit Disorder (ADD) and Attention Deficit Hyperactivity Disorder (ADHD). It decreases disruption and increases attention, but, again, there are side-effects. Also, like almost any drug, it has come to be misused by adults.

It is worth repeating the point that even though the therapeutic use of drugs is widespread and extremely useful, no drug therapy deals with the disorder. It simply cuts down some of the symptoms. Apart from this obvious drawback, drugs used in therapy may also have unpleasant side-effects and, for the most part, such drugs cannot be used by pregnant women or by those who have various other medical problems.

Electroconvulsive therapy (ECT)

ECT involves the passing of a mild electric current across the brain and has an effect not unlike a mild epileptic seizure. Nowadays it is used only in very severe cases of depression and is administered in a far more precise and well-conceived manner than was once the case. Before 1960, it was very widely and very crudely used with widespread and sometimes disastrous side-effects involving memory loss, for example. Its present usage sometimes still leads to some memory loss, but this has been minimised with the very low dosages of electricity that are now administered. Interestingly, although it can have a very palliative effect on severe depression and has been used for well over half a century, the mechanism through which it has its effects remains unknown.

▶ The placebo effect

As well as giving those who are in psychological pain drugs to help alleviate the pain, the effectiveness of any such drugs has to be assessed – as does the effectiveness of any psychological therapy as well. The major points that have to be established are, first, whether the person might have improved anyway, even if the drug (or the therapy) had not been administered. Second, it is important to find out whether any beneficial effect from a drug might simply have come from the administration of the drug, no matter what it was, that is, even if it had been a sugar pill. The key point here is that it is important to establish that any effects that a drug might have are due to the drug itself rather than to any *beliefs* that the patient (or the researcher) might have about taking the drug or, perhaps, even due to the attention being given to the patient. Any such effects are known as the placebo effects.

The technique used to establish whether the drug effect is 'real' or a placebo effect is the *double blind*. One group of patients is given the drug and another group of patients is given the placebo, with neither patients nor the researchers knowing which is which – until afterwards. If any effect is greater for the drug group, then the drug is effective. If the two groups are equal, then it is a placebo effect and the drug is useless. Of course, if the placebo group does better than the drug group, then the drug might be said to be worsening the condition!

The interesting thing about placebos is that they are often very effective in their own right, particularly with psychological disorders (of the order of 30–40 per cent). Similarly, placebo effects may account for some psychotherapeutic effectiveness. There is nothing wrong with this. If a placebo helps to improve things for people, then it is useful. And it has been well established that people's attitudes and beliefs are important both to succumbing to a disorder and then to recovery from it. In fact, the placebo effect is what might lie at the basis of genuine cases of faith healing. If a person has faith in whatever the process of healing might be, then this, in and of itself, might bring about an improvement.

▶ Psychological therapies

Psychological therapies use psychological rather than physical means to bring about changes. They deal, then, with thoughts, feelings and behaviours. There are many types of psychological therapy, two of which were characterised briefly in the second example at the start of this chapter. What follows is a description of the main types of therapy, but the list is by no means exhaustive.

Psychoanalytic/psychodynamic therapies

The basis of psychoanalytic or psychodynamic therapies is the need to understand the unconscious, concentrating on its formation from the early relationships in a person's life, particularly with the parents. The aim of the therapy is to bring any underlying conflicts that might be lurking in the unconscious up into awareness. The major techniques used (other than a great deal of conversation) involve free association and analysis of dreams. (Free association is simply listening to what a patient might say in free response to certain key words.)

In this type of therapy a great deal depends on the interaction between patient and therapist. A major aspect of this interaction is *transference*. When transference occurs, the patient makes the therapist into the object of his or her emotional reactions. Normally, such reactions have been to other people or circumstances in the patient's life and now they have been transferred to the therapist. Sometimes, *counter-transference* can also occur in which the therapist makes the patient the object of his or her emotional reactions.

Generally, psychoanalytic or psychodynamic therapy is very lengthy and, hence, very expensive and so it is open only to those with sufficient time and money. Also, it is not useful for people with some conditions, such as extreme anxiety and/or depression.

Behavioural therapies

All behavioural therapies are based squarely on the principles of learning and conditioning that were described in Chapter 12. Also described were many of the types of therapy that have derived from these principles. A core aspect of behaviour therapy is that although insight is useful on the part of the person, it is the behaviour that has to change. Take the example of someone who is anxious about examinations. This could be due to a great variety of reasons that are a mixture of past experiences and present circumstances. Those past experiences cannot be changed, but it is still important to change the person's behaviour when he or she walks into the examination room.

Behaviour therapy, then, is very specific to behaviour that occurs in particular settings and is predicated on very clear aims that are discussed with the patient about exactly what needs to change. For example, what does 'anxious' mean behaviourally for this person in his or her particular circumstances? If a person says that she 'feels inadequate', what exactly does this mean in terms of what she does? If a young man describes himself as scared to join any social group, what does this mean in the exact terms of what he does and does not do on all social occasions? If a couple describe themselves as 'always rowing and bickering', what does 'always' mean and what defines 'rowing and bickering' for them? Once the precise behaviours have been described and once an agreement has been reached about what exactly the person wants to change, then the sorts of behaviour change techniques described in Chapter 12 can be employed.

Cognitive behaviour therapies

Behaviour therapies deal solely with behaviour; this is their defining characteristic. So, they have nothing to do with thoughts and feelings. However, if one believes that thoughts and feelings influence or help to determine behaviour, then it might be useful to work on them as well as directly on the behaviour itself. This is certainly a widespread everyday belief.

The various types of cognitive behaviour therapy (CBT) were developed as a way of achieving this, aimed at dealing with both behaviour and maladaptive beliefs. The simple aim of CBT is to bring about the control of unpleasant emotions and feelings by helping to provide patients with better ways of interpreting their experiences. To take a commonplace example, very anxious or very depressed people distort their thinking in ways that are, naturally enough, dominated by anxiety or depression. The cognitive behaviour therapist helps them to find ways of changing that type of thinking and so alleviate the anxiety or depression.

Behaviour is not forgotten; it becomes relevant at the end of the therapeutic process. New thoughts or new ways of thinking lead to new ways of testing other behaviour and of doing new things. For example, someone who is experiencing large-scale mood changes, particularly in the negative direction, might be encouraged to keep a precise record of any changes of mood that occur at work and at home. Keeping and reviewing such a record might well lead to changes in the person's ideas about 'things that go wrong at work and make me irritable at home'. In this instance of CBT, behaviour (keeping records) has been suggested that, in turn, alters beliefs or ideas or ways of thinking that, in turn, alters feelings about the situation.

Cognitive behaviour therapists help patients replace one type of thought with another. For example, typical thoughts might be: 'Why am I always so useless?', 'Why does nothing go right for me?', 'There I go again, messing up as usual.' Such thoughts only help to drive the person down into greater depths of negative moods and feelings. Alternative thoughts that might be prompted are: 'I'm good at this', 'I can cope with this; I've coped with much worse', 'This is a challenge that I know I can meet.' If this type of thought replacement seems like the 'power of positive thinking', long known in self-help books, then it is because it is. Positive thinking does carry a great deal of power.

Like many therapies, then, CBT is verbally based and deals with changing beliefs in order to change behaviour. Nevertheless, it is important to say that the successful performance of something is more effective for a person than simple changes in beliefs. For example, actually taking an examination successfully or going to a party or giving a speech without breaking down with anxiety is clearly more effective than simply believing that one might be able to without actually trying it. Both changed beliefs and changed behaviours are important, but it is changes in behaviour that lead to greater feelings of self-efficacy. This, then, helps to set up a positive feedback system, a very non-vicious spiral.

Humanistic therapies

One of the two therapeutic approaches briefly characterised in the scene-setting example at the start of the chapter is humanistic. Such types of therapy stress growth and self-actualisation and deal with the whole person rather than with some aspects of the person's behaviour or belief system. The idea is to help patients make some contact with their 'real' selves and find out what their basic goals and desires are. As part of this they are encouraged to bring their underlying emotions and motivations into conscious awareness.

So far this description may suggest that humanistic therapies are similar to psychodynamic therapies. To the extent that they are concerned with underlying forces in the person, this is true. However, the humanistic approach is very much centred on the here and now rather than with past experiences. To this extent, it is rather like a mixture of the psychodynamic and the behavioural types of therapy.

The best known of the many varieties of humanistic therapy is *client-centred therapy*, championed by Carl Rogers (1961). It is based on the understanding that a person, whatever his or her psychological trouble might be, knows himself or herself better than anyone else could. Against this background, the therapist is merely a facilitator rather than someone who probes and questions. The aim is to help the person gently towards self-insight and the main technique is through empathy, frequently in the form of neutral to positive affirmations of whatever the person might be saying, for example, 'Mmm-hmm', etc.

Humanistic therapies, then, again are very verbal techniques, although relying more on talking on the part of the patient than the therapist. Given their nature, they are scarcely effective with any of the more extreme types of disorder. If someone is severely unresponsively depressed, for example, or is out of touch with anything that is going on around them, then any type of therapy that depends on subtly guiding what the person might be saying is unlikely to succeed.

Broad, mixed and group therapies

Only a few of the major types of therapy have been briefly discussed so far. There are many other types of therapy. For example, Gestalt therapy is concerned with uncovering conflicts and blocks and becoming aware of one's present feelings, working through a mixture of psychoanalytic, behavioural and self-actualising techniques, often in a group setting.

Reality therapy is aimed at making a patient's values very clear and seeking realistic goals in life. Rational-emotion therapy aims at replacing irrational ideas (I must always be liked by everyone) by more realistic ones through a quite confrontational psychotherapeutic style. Transactional analysis has the goal of making all communications honest and open often in a group setting with people asked to confront within themselves the 'parent', the 'child' and the 'adult'. In the end, many practising therapists use a mixture of techniques (including drugs), with each therapeutic intervention designed to suit the particular patient, uniquely.

There is, however, one type of therapeutic approach, previously mentioned in passing, that differs from any of the others so far discussed. The majority of therapies take place between a single patient or client and a therapist. Some therapies involve more than one client, sometimes many clients at once. This is traditional group therapy involving a number of people who do not know one another outside the therapeutic situation. Within this group context, all types of therapy have been used.

The significance of the group is that mutual encouragement can develop, with praise and pertinent comments from group members about any contributions that might be made. This provides a system of social support (which normally might well be lacking for the individuals that make up the group) in which successes and failures can be shared, helping to increase the impact of the former and decrease the impact of the latter.

The other type of group therapy is when either couples or families are involved. This type of therapy is based on the view that any problem that might exist does not reside within an individual but rests within the interactions of a couple or of an entire family. This is very much a systems approach in which the behaviour of each individual is seen as, in part, due to the needs and the desires and the behaviours of the other family members. The result is a very complex system. Of course, changing the behaviour and the beliefs and the perceptions of any one member of the system would no doubt make some changes to the system as a whole. However, the foundation of this type of therapy is that the changes would be the better made by working on the system as a whole, that is, by dealing with more than one of its parts at a time.

▶ **Evaluation**

The basic question about therapy is not 'Which is the best therapy?' but rather 'Does therapy work?' How useful are these techniques and do they change people? Do they make people happier and more content with their lives? Does therapy solve people's psychological problems or cure their psychological disorders?

There is a long history of investigations carried out to evaluate the effectiveness of therapy. The general result of these studies and therefore the general answer to the questions just posed is: psychotherapy does help, but not always. It is clear that no one type of therapy is best. It is impossible, from the evidence, to say, for example, that CBT is better than humanistic therapy. The different types of therapy are appropriate for different types of problem or condition.

The crucial factor in all evaluations of therapy turns out to be the therapist. Some therapists are simply better than others no matter what type of therapy they might turn to. The major question then becomes: what are the characteristics of those who are particularly good therapists? They tend to be very highly motivated people who have a natural warmth and empathy for the plight of others. The final question then becomes: can such qualities or characteristics be learned or are they in place (or not) naturally? The answer is almost certainly a mixture of both of these possibilities.

Meanwhile, the placebo effect is always there. On the one hand, it can be seen as something that awkwardly gets in the way of evaluating the efficacy of therapy. On the other hand, if the placebo effect *is*, in fact, an effect and makes a difference to the person, then it is all to the good. The problem is working out just what is affecting what. However, from the viewpoint of the person with the problem, it does not much matter what is proving to be effective as long as it continues to be effective.

▶ Seeking help

From a practical and personal point of view, when should a person seek professional help for a psychological difficulty? It is hard enough attempting to judge when or whether a friend or a family member would benefit from psychotherapy or counselling. It is even more problematic when considering one's own circumstances.

Ultimately, a person is concerned with his or her own emotional well-being. When this goes wrong in some way, when the emotional state is unpleasant or unenjoyable or so extreme as to interfere with day-to-day existence, then help might be needed, be this in the form of drugs or psychotherapy. To begin with, then, what can be done about maintaining one's emotional well-being?

To some extent the answer to this question is about training one's own emotional intelligence. For a start it is important to learn to accept one's own feelings. One way of doing this is to separate oneself from them slightly and simply observe them coming and going rather than being consumed by them. If a feeling of anxiety comes over one, then it is easy to slip into it further and further and let it become overwhelming. It is also reasonably easy to suppress it, to push it under. In neither case is the result useful or pleasant. A better way might be simply to see it coming, to engage with it, think about what might have led to it, and then to quietly observe it and see what happens. What is certain is that it will pass. Nothing, including feelings, is permanent; nothing lasts forever.

Part of accepting, rather than fighting, against one's own feelings is learning to recognise when one is vulnerable. For example, if one has had several sleepless nights or has just had a succession of unpleasant, anxiety-making interactions at work or at home, or if one has just experienced the break-up of a relationship, then one is psychologically and physically vulnerable. This means that one is more prone to make mistakes, from bumping into things to saying what in retrospect seem to be foolish things to other people. One is even more vulnerable to catching a cold or getting influenza. In other words, one's defences, even including one's immune system, are not in place as they usually are. At such times, it is important to recognise the vulnerability and simply to take it easy, not too push at life to hard, even to cosset oneself a little.

On the positive side, it is also important to work out one's strengths and weaknesses and then play to one's strengths. Of course, it might be useful to improve on one's weaknesses, but it is even more important to work out exactly what one's talents might be and learn to develop them. The result is inevitably an increase in self-esteem which, in turn, will also help one to improve across most areas of life. Again, this is about promoting one's own emotional well-being.

Another way in which one can strengthen one's personal state of well-being is through an involvement with other people. It never helps to sit and stew in one's own juices when things go wrong, or, in general, to turn inwards. Having sorted out one's vulnerabilities and become accepting of whatever is going on emotionally, it is then important to think outside of oneself and to be concerned with the welfare of others. Again, this helps to promote one's own emotional well-being.

In the end, even if a person has done all of these things and whatever else he or she can think of to look after themselves and there is still an overwhelming anxiety or depression or swings of mood or tendency to hallucinate or think dark, paranoid thoughts, then it is time to seek help. At the point of thinking about seeking help it is then important to remember that this is not a sign of weakness but rather of strength through the maturity of recognising one's limitations.

In a similar vein it is important to recognise that there is no shame attached to taking prescribed drugs in order to elevate one's mood, for example, or to decrease the level of one's anxiety. Being in a less depressed or less anxious state makes it that much easier for psychotherapeutic interventions to happen. It is very difficult for a therapist to engage in a therapeutic relationship with a patient who is too depressed to respond or too anxious to be able to speak coherently. While drugs might not 'cure' psychological problems, they certainly can provide a lift on the road to a cure.

After this, the only decision is what type of therapy to decide on. This is very much a matter of personal choice and depends on simply what suits the individual.

Irrespective of this, perhaps the most important choice is of therapist rather than of type of therapy. Choose a therapist with whom you feel some natural affinity and the chances are that the therapy will be more effective. At this point, whether it is due to the therapist, the therapy or is a placebo effect won't matter to you.

▶ Summary

- In Western society there has been a long history of cruel treatment of those with serious mental disorders. It is only within the past century that matters have improved.

- There are various types of provider for those with mental disorders, from psychiatrists and clinical psychologists through to psychiatric nurses.

- The ethics of mental health treatment is intricate, including the nature of the relationship between patient and therapist and the question of privacy and disclosure of information.

- There are cultural and sub-cultural (including gender) differences between proneness to particular types of mental disorder.

- Therapy can be divided into biological and psychological types.

- The major types of drugs used in therapy for mental disorder are to reduce anxiety, to reduce psychotic symptoms such as hallucinations and false beliefs, to reduce swings in mood, particularly to reduce depression, and to treat hyperactivity in children.

- Electroconvulsive therapy has been used for more than 50 years in the treatment of extreme depression. Its use is now more subtle than it was in the 1960s.

- In assessing the efficacy of drug therapy (or psychotherapy), it is important to be aware of possible placebo effects. Effectiveness might be due to the person's *beliefs* about effectiveness.

- The major types of psychological therapy are: psychodynamic/psychoanalytic, behavioural, cognitive, behavioural and humanistic; but also include: Gestalt, reality, rational-emotive and transactional analysis.

- Group therapy is undertaken with people who do not know one another outside of the group and uses any of the psychotherapeutic techniques.

- Couple and family therapy is based on the view that it is a system that has in some way gone wrong rather than simply one individual.

- Psychotherapy has been proven to be effective, but not in all cases. The most crucial factor seems to be a warm, empathetic, highly motivated therapist.

- It is possible to enhance one's own emotional well-being by using a number of techniques in life, such as being accepting of one's own feelings. It is only when such self-help is no longer sufficient that it is useful to seek therapeutic help.

▶ Questions and possibilities

- Do you think that the present types of treatment in the Western world of those with significant mental disorders could be improved in any way? How would you go about this?

- Under what circumstances, if any, would it be appropriate for a therapist to form a personal relationship with a patient?

- Are there any circumstances under which a therapist should breach confidentiality?

- Do you think it reasonable that patients should always be asked to give their consent if they are being used in the trial of a new type of therapeutic procedure?

- In your experience, what are the major differences in proneness to psychological problems in men and women? To what extent do you think that these differences are learned?

- Think of the people that you know to have been prescribed drugs to alleviate their psychological problems. Have the drugs been effective? How would you feel about taking such drugs if you were to be prescribed them? If you are uncertain about how acceptable this would be to you, attempt to think about exactly why you would find it problematic.

- To what extent do you subscribe to the view that anyone with a psychological problem could pull themselves together if they tried hard enough? Many people believe that this is so in some cases but not in others. If you have these mixed feelings, list the differences between the two types of disorder. Why do you think that one type is more easily controllable without outside help than the other?

- If you had a psychological difficulty or mental disorder, would you prefer to have drug therapy or psychotherapy or both?

- Have you had any personal experience of the placebo effect? How would you explain the mechanism? In other words, how is it that our attitudes and beliefs can affect our health?

- If you needed psychological help, which of the psychological therapies would you choose. Why would you choose as you have? What is it about the other therapies that appeals less? Would you make the same suggestion to members of your family or your friends or do you think different people might be suited to different styles of therapist?

- Have you known any 'natural' therapists, people that simply seem able to naturally help others with their psychological problems? What characteristics do these people have?

- Think of situations in which you have experienced the power or the effectiveness of a group. Do you think it reasonable that such effects can be used therapeutically?

- Apart from the 'official' evidence, what do you imagine to be the general effectiveness of psychotherapy? To what extent do you imagine that it would be effective? What factors would make it more or less effective?

- In what ways do you work to promote your own emotional well-being and psychological health? Do your friends and members of your family follow the same ways or have they developed their own approaches? What are the differences and why do you think they have come about?

- Do you know yourself well enough to know when you would seek psychological help, if you have not already done so in your life? If you think that you never would seek such help, explore the reasons for this.

CHAPTER NINETEEN

Life in general

▶ Developing personal potential

Although this book is a psychology text and although the material it contains all derives from sound research that is fully accepted by psychological researchers, it is not objectively written. It is written with an openly admitted positive bias, the goal being not only to inform but to provide a useful basis for the reader to develop his or her personal life. This naturally assumes a positive approach on the part of the reader as well as the writer.

The goal of the book has not only been to inform but also to be useful and practical in everyday life. It rests on the conviction that it is possible to take some of the findings of 'objective' psychology and use them to improve one's daily life, to take out the daily hassles, to make one more comfortable with oneself, to improve one's interactions with family and friends and to make one's working and leisure life more enjoyable.

One way to start to achieve this is to work through this book again, taking from each chapter the suggestions and directions described. This should allow any reader to develop a personal armoury of techniques and possibilities to bring about useful changes. As a corollary, it would also be a useful way of revising the material in the book. What follows is a summary of the type of programme it should be possible to develop.

These suggestions are simply a beginning. They all derive from the chapters in this book. It is possible to work out a much fuller system than this that would be aimed at developing your own personal potential in all aspects of life. In studying psychology, it is both useful and rewarding to have this as one of the main goals.

Emotion

Work to improve your skills at emotion recognition, that is, at recognising emotions in others and what they mean. Develop your emotional self-control, learning to better head off unwanted emotions and maintain enjoyable ones. Pay greater attention to your own inner emotional life and to what you can see of the emotional reactions of others. Work out exactly what information your own emotional reactions are providing you with. In other words, aim to improve your emotional intelligence – it can be done.

Motivation

Think about your life in terms of Maslow's hierarchy of motives (see Chapter 5). Are you stuck at a particular level? How can you become unstuck? In what areas of your life are you self-actualised? Set up conditions so that you can aim at self-actualisation throughout all areas of life. Prioritise your goals. Consider the degree to which you are unwittingly driven by the need to achieve or the need to have power or the need to amass money. Think about the occasions when you experience flow-time and work out a programme to increase their frequency. Think about the occasions when you have had peak experiences and decide how you can have more.

Social life

1 Work out ways to improve all of your social relationships, from family to friends to those with whom you work. Consider in detail any intimate relationships you have had or are currently having and list their good and bad qualities. Develop ways in which they could be improved. Think about all the types of love you have experienced and, again, work out ways in which they could be improved by changes in your own behaviour and attitudes.

2 Work out ways to improve your own communication with other people, both verbally and non-verbally. Spend time paying close attention to your body language and compare it with that of other people. Develop ways to improve it. Study effective communicators and work out ways to make your own communication more effective.

3 Think about all of the communication networks of which you are a part and develop ways in which they might be improved. Ask yourself genuine and penetrating questions about whether or not you use stereotypes about other people and whether or not you are ever prejudiced and practise discrimination. Develop a personal programme to ensure that this no longer happens.

4 Consider your own leadership and follower behaviour and work out ways in which they can be more effective. Think about whether you would prefer to be a transactional or a transformational leader, and why. If you very much dislike taking the lead, try to work out why this is and whether or not you are content to continue in this way.

Personality and the self

Make a full description of your own personality and the extent to which it has problems or flaws, then think about ways in which the more negative parts can be changed. Think about how you define your self and whether or not you are happy with that way of doing it. Develop the best definition of your self that you can and think about ways in which your early maladaptive schemas might be changed. Develop a meditative practice and, in so doing, learn to observe yourself in whatever you are doing. Compare your own behaviour if and when you drink alcohol, smoke and/or take any other drugs with your behaviour ordinarily. Work out the reasons why you take such substances (if you do) and whether or not you wish to continue.

Bringing up children

Compare your own upbringing with the upbringing that you are providing for your children, if you have them, or that you would provide in the future. Think about mistakes that might be repeated from one generation to the next and work out a programme for ensuring that they are not. Think about whether or not you would treat girls and boys differently and why. Make a list of those aspects of bringing up a child that you have found to be the most difficult or that you think that you would find to be the most difficult. Develop a scheme to deal with the difficulties.

Ageing

Consider in detail all of the changes that you have observed in yourself as you have grown older. Think about the degree to which your basic personality has changed or might change in the future. Consider ways in which you could improve your treatment of older people. List the advantages that accrue to each different age bracket.

The intellect

In all of those areas of life in which you have to learn things, develop techniques for more efficient learning. Develop your own personal techniques to improve your memory, having first sorted out the areas in which it is weakest. Also develop ways in which you can avoid being unduly influenced or conditioned by your circumstances at home or at work when you do not wish to be. Practise thinking both lineally and laterally. Devise situations in which you are creative and simply practise creativity. Think about the problems in your own life and the lives of those that you know and practise solving them with flexible and original thinking.

Problems and health

Spend some time considering your own mental health and well-being and what disorders you might have experienced (even in part) or might be experiencing currently. Work out what has led to these difficulties and sort out whether or not you are able to control them yourself. If not, seek help. Work out a system for yourself in which you stay in good psychological health rather than succumbing to stress in its various forms. Practise talking and writing about any difficulties that might arise. Think about those situations in which you would not try to struggle onwards but would seek professional help. Find out what professional help is available to you and where it is. Consider the degree to which you wish to be in charge of your own well-being and own destiny and how best you can bring this about.

▶ Some final words

Having read and worked through this book, you will know and appreciate a fair amount of basic psychology, some of which might well have seemed to be simply common sense to you and some of which won't. The difference between these two reactions might well have depended on whether or not you 'knew' something beforehand or not. In other words, if you read something that you had already thought about a great deal or felt that you knew intuitively or had simply often observed, then it might well have seemed that you were reading about something that you already knew and that you might therefore think of as merely being 'common sense'.

Sometimes, reading about something that we have known intuitively or implicitly brings about an 'Aha!' experience. In this book, I have tried to make explicit some ideas that you might already have had and which are, nevertheless, derived from basic research.

My hope is that as a result of having read this book you will be armed with a series of practical techniques and possibilities that you can apply to your own life and your relationships at work and at home. The aim of doing this is, of course, precisely the aim that most people have ordinarily, that is, to make some improvements to their daily experiences and to their lives in general. As was pointed out in the introductory chapter, psychology is about the lives of people; both their inner lives and their interactions with the world around them, particularly the world of other people.

However scientifically respectable and methodologically sound research in psychology becomes, it must stay grounded in everyday life and, therefore, return to it at every opportunity. Psychology might be the scientific study of behaviour and mental processes but it is also essentially practical. Part of being human is to be curious, to seek to understand the world and one's own place within it. On this basis, anything is worth studying simply for its own sake. However, if such study can be directed to improving the world and to developing the lives of those who live in the world, then so much the better. Such a view can reasonably be applied to the study of *anything* at all, but it seems particularly pertinent to psychology where the person doing the study is also the object being studied.

This point also reflects back to the introductory chapter in which some gentle criticism was levelled at the approach taken by academic psychologists in the past 100 years. In short, they have become too 'scientific' for their own good, or, at least, for the good of the subject. The essence of traditional science is objectivity and research psychologists have attempted (sometimes very creatively) to apply the fully 'objective' approach to what they do. Although laudable, this aim is surely doomed to failure. Subjectivity is integral to the human condition, so how can it be possible to be truly objective when the human being is studying the human being? This is a difficult enough task when studying a rock or a chemical or the floor of the ocean or the planets and stars. Bring it to the study of human beings and the subjective and objective inevitably merge. It is, perhaps, important to recognise this and so take it into account.

To make this point a little more fully, science rests on the belief that there *is* an objective reality and that this reality is knowable by the scientist as a trained observer. There are two important points to make here. First, however fully the observer is trained, he or she remains a human being and is essentially subjective, a creature with an inner life of emotions, conflicts, even an unconscious. These facets of what it is to be human cannot simply be ignored. Second, what, for example, would be an objective view of a table? From the left, from the right, from underneath, from on top? From close up? From far away? What about from the inside of the table? And so on. If an objective view of a table is problematic, think about what might be the objective view of a human being.

The attempt to 'be objective' is understandable, particularly given the legacy of Victorian ideas on which contemporary science is based. But many 'scientific' results have begun to call into question the nature of so-called objectivity, not the least of them coming from the apparently ultra-objective area of sub-atomic physics. So, what has happened in psychology is that the subject has been taken a little too far in the objective measurement direction, so much so that some of the richness of the human experience has been lost. Fortunately, that richness is still there in everyday life and if one picks one's way carefully through the scientific thicket of research psychology, then it is possible to find a path that is both interesting and useful. Such has been the aim of this book.

References

Ainsworth, N.D.S. (1979) Infant–mother attachment. *American Psychologist*, **34**(10), 932–937.

American Psychiatric Association (1994) *Diagnostic and Statistical Manual*, 4th edn. Washington, DC: APA.

Asch, S. (1956) Studies of independence and conformity: a minority of one against a unanimous majority. *Psychological Monographs: General and Applied*, **70**, 1–70.

Bowlby, J. (1973) *Attachment and Loss*, vol. 2. *Separation*. New York: Basic Books.

Bowlby, J. (1980) *Attachment and Loss*, vol. 3. *Loss*. New York: Basic Books.

Csikszentmihalyi, M. (1990) *Flow: The Psychology of Optimal Experience*. New York: Harper & Row.

Ekman, P. & Friesen, W.V. (1969) Nonverbal leakage and cues to deception. *Psychiatry*, **32**, 88–106.

Erikson, E.H. (1971) *The Life Cycle Completed*. New York: Norton.

Freud, S. (1933) *New Introductory Lectures on Psychoanalysis*. Trans. 1975, J. Strachey. London: Pelican Books.

Goffman, E. (1967) *Interaction Ritual*. Garden City, NY: Doubleday/Anchor.

Gross, J.J. (1998) The emerging field of emotion regulation: an integrative review. *Review of General Psychology*, **2**(3), 271–299.

James, W. (1884) What is an emotion? *Mind*, **9**, 188–205.

Kohlberg, L. (1984) *The Psychology of Moral Development*. San Francisco: Harper & Row.

Konin, E. (1995) Actors and emotions: a psychological perspective. *Theatre Research International*, **20**(2), 132–140.

Kubler-Ross, E. (1969) *On Death and Dying*. New York: Macmillan.

Larsen, R.J. & Buss, D.M. (2002) *Personality Psychology: Domains of Knowledge about Human Relationships*. New York: McGraw-Hill.

Lazarus, R.S. (1991) *Emotion and Adaptation*. New York: Oxford University Press.

Lazarus, R.S. (1993) From psychological stress to the emotions: a history of changing outlooks. *American Psychologist*, **46**(8), 819–834.

Lazarus, R.S. (1999) *Stress and Emotion*. New York: Springer-Verlag.

Lefton, R. & Buzzotta, V. (2004) *Leadership through People Skills*. New York: McGraw-Hill.

Maslow, A. (1954) *Motivation and Personality*. New York: Harper & Row.

Maslow, A. (1971) *The Further Reaches of Human Nature*. New York: Viking Press.

Melzack, R. & Wall, P. (1983) *The Challenge of Pain*. Harmondsworth: Penguin.

Milgram, S. (1974) *Obedience to Authority*. New York: Harper & Row.

Overton, A. (2005) *Stress Less*. Auckland, NZ: Random House.

Pavlov, I.P. (1927) *Conditioned Reflexes*. Oxford: Oxford University Press.

Pennebaker, J.W. & Segal, J.D. (1999) Forming a story: the health benefits of narrative. *Journal of Clinical Psychology*, **55**(10), 1243–1254.

Pervin, L.A. (1989) *Goal Concepts in Personality and Social Psychology*. Hillsdale, NJ: Laurence Erlbaum.

Piaget, J. (1952) *The Origins of Intelligence in Children*. New York: International Universities Press.

Rogers, C.R. (1961) *On Becoming a Person: A Therapist's View of Psychotherapy*. Boston: Houghton Mifflin.

Schachter, S. (1964) The interaction of cognitive and physiological determinants of emotional state. In L. Berkowitz (ed.) *Mental Social Psychology*, vol. 1. New York: Academic Press, pp. 49–80.

Scherer, K.R., Wallbott, H.G. & Summerfield, A.B. (1986) *Experiencing Emotions*. Cambridge: Cambridge University Press.

Selye, H. (1956) *The Stress of Life*. New York: McGraw-Hill.

Skinner, B.F. (1938) *The Behaviour of Organisms*. New York: Appleton-Century-Crofts.

Solomon, R.C. (1994) *About Love: Reinventing Romance for Our Times*. Lanham, MD: Rowman & Littlefield.

Sternberg, R.J. (1986) A triangular theory of love. *Psychological Review*, **93**, 119–135.

Super, D.E. (1990) A life-span, life-space approach to career development. In D. Brown, L. Brooks and Associates. (eds) *Career Choice and Development*, 2nd edn. San Francisco: Jossey-Bass.

Thase, M.E. & Lang, S.S. (2004) *Beating the Blues*. New York: Oxford University Press.

Index